Building IoT Visualizations using Grafana

Power up your IoT projects and monitor with Prometheus, LibreNMS, and Elasticsearch

Rodrigo Juan Hernández

BIRMINGHAM—MUMBAI

Building IoT Visualizations Using Grafana

Group Product Manager: Rahul Nair
Publishing Product Manager: Meeta Rajani
Senior Editor: Runcil Rebello
Content Development Editor: Yasir Ali Khan
Technical Editor: Shruthi Shetty
Copy Editor: Safis Editing
Project Coordinator: Ajesh Devavaram
Proofreader: Safis Editing
Indexer: Hemangini Bari
Production Designer: Shankar Kalbhor
Senior Marketing Coordinator: Sanjana Gupta
Marketing Coordinator: Nimisha Dua

First published: July 2022

Production reference: 1110722

Published by Packt Publishing Ltd.
Livery Place
35 Livery Street
Birmingham
B3 2PB, UK.

ISBN 978-1-80323-612-4

www.packt.com

To my loved daughter, Ana Paula.

~ Rodrigo Juan Hernández

Contributors

About the author

Rodrigo Juan Hernández is an electronic engineer who was passionate about IoT even before it existed. He has been working on tech for more than 18 years. He has worked for local government, and has been involved in a wide variety of projects and technologies, including IP networks, IP video surveillance, IT services, energy systems, and many others.

For several years, he has been focusing on the IoT ecosystem. He is currently working as an IoT system consultant to clients around the world. He also produces content online about IoT and related subjects. This content is available on his blog, YouTube channel, and social networks – mainly LinkedIn.

He also writes for companies that need good-quality content about their products and services. His main objective nowadays is to help others to understand and implement IoT solutions.

I want to thank Vivi for her support in this project.

About the reviewer

Atif Ali is a mechatronics engineer specializing in automation, robotics, and IIoT, with a focus on electro-mechanical design and software integration for complex physical systems and processes. He is a passionate open-source advocate, focused on the intersection of hardware and software for perceptive physical world observability.

Atif has been heavily involved in both the industry and academia for the past several years, in sectors ranging from clean energy and web3, to cybersecurity and mining, holding positions at ETH-Zürich, UBC-Vancouver, and Grafana, among others. He also serves as a technical advisor for start-ups in the emerging market, and is on the faculty board for the Global Master's in IoT at the Zigurat Global Institute of Technology.

Table of Contents

Part 2: Collecting Data from IoT Devices

3

Connecting IoT Devices

4

Data Sources for Grafana

5

Using Time Series Databases

Part 3: Connecting Data Sources and Building Dashboards

6

Getting Data and Building Dashboards

7
Managing Plugins

8
Organizing and Managing Dashboards

Part 4: Performing Analytics and Notifications

9
Performing Analytics in Grafana

10
Alerting and Notifications in Grafana

Part 5: Integrating Grafana with Other Platforms

11
Using Grafana with Prometheus

12
Using Grafana with OpenSearch

13
Showing Data from LibreNMS in Grafana

14
Integrations for Grafana Cloud

Index

Other Books You May Enjoy

Preface

In this book, you will learn how to implement an IoT system using open source tools.

The main focus of this book is the use of Grafana as an IoT platform. However, we will also cover many technologies involved in the transmission, storage, management, and visualization of data.

These technologies include IoT communication protocols, time-series databases, and Docker containers.

Also, you will learn how to integrate other systems with Grafana, including Prometheus, OpenSearch, LibreNMS, and Fluent Bit.

After finishing this book, you will have a clear idea about IoT systems, communications, and platforms, and you will be able to test and implement your IoT systems using Grafana according to specific requirements.

Who this book is for

People with a background in IT, technology, and systems who want to learn how to get data from sensors and devices and show it using Grafana, IoT developers who want to build visualizations and analytics for their projects and products, technicians from the embedded world who need to learn how to build systems and platforms using open source software, and technology enthusiasts who want to learn about IoT systems will benefit from this book.

What this book covers

Chapter 1, *Getting Started with Grafana*, explains what Grafana is and what it is useful for. You will also learn to install it and make basic configurations.

Chapter 2, *Exploring Grafana*, covers all the sections and capabilities of Grafana. Also, you will learn about user management, including groups, authentication, and permissions.

Chapter 3, *Connecting IoT Devices*, explains how to connect IoT devices and send data to IoT platforms using different protocols and systems.

Chapter 4, Data Sources for Grafana, explores different types of data sources. These data sources will be used in later chapters to feed data to Grafana.

Chapter 5, Using Time Series Databases, explains how to store data in time-series databases.

Chapter 6, Getting Data and Building Dashboards, discusses how to connect data sources and build visualization dashboards.

Chapter 7, Managing Plugins, covers the installation and management of Grafana plugins.

Chapter 8, Organizing and Managing Dashboards, explains how to manage dashboards, variables, annotations, links, and permissions. You will also learn how to export and share dashboards.

Chapter 9, Performing Analytics in Grafana, covers analytics using data source capabilities and plugins.

Chapter 10, Alerting and Notifications in Grafana, explains how to configure and use alerts and notifications in Grafana.

Chapter 11, Using Grafana with Prometheus, discusses getting data from Prometheus and displaying it in Grafana dashboards.

Chapter 12, Using Grafana with OpenSearch, covers integrating OpenSearch and Grafana.

Chapter 13, Showing Data from LibreNMS in Grafana, explains how to connect LibreNMS and Grafana, use data from LibreNMS, and display it with Grafana.

Chapter 14, Integrations for Grafana Cloud, discusses monitoring Home Assistant, RabbitMQ, and Linux nodes using the Grafana Cloud integrations.

To get the most out of this book

You will need at least basic knowledge of Linux use and administration. You will need access to a Linux server, local or in the cloud. You will get more from this book if you have a Raspberry Pi computer. You will need to have a Docker instance. You will need accounts in cloud services, such as Grafana, InfluxDB, and MQTT brokers.

Software/hardware covered in the book	Operating system requirements
Raspberry Pi	Raspberry Pi OS
Docker	Ubuntu
Time-series databases	
Grafana	
Prometheus, OpenSearch, LibreNMS	
IoT protocols	

All the software used in this book is free and open source.

If you are using the digital version of this book, we advise you to type the code yourself or access the code from the book's GitHub repository (a link is available in the next section). Doing so will help you avoid any potential errors related to the copying and pasting of code.

After reading this book, you will be able to implement your own IoT system using Grafana and many of the tools used in this book.

Download the color images

We also provide a PDF file that has color images of the screenshots and diagrams used in this book. You can download it here: `https://packt.link/r9a1L`.

Conventions used

There are a number of text conventions used throughout this book.

`Code in text`: Indicates code words in text, database table names, folder names, filenames, file extensions, pathnames, dummy URLs, user input, and Twitter handles. Here is an example: "The `app_mode` variable accepts two options: development and production."

A block of code is set as follows:

```
{ "sensorType": "Thermometer",
"sensorModel": "AM2302",
"temp": 25,
"hum": 40}
```

When we wish to draw your attention to a particular part of a code block, the relevant lines or items are set in bold:

```
[default]
exten => s,1,Dial(Zap/1|30)
exten => s,2,Voicemail(u100)
exten => s,102,Voicemail(b100)
exten => i,1,Voicemail(s0)
```

Any command-line input or output is written as follows:

```
$ mkdir css
$ cd css
```

Bold: Indicates a new term, an important word, or words that you see onscreen. For instance, words in menus or dialog boxes appear in **bold**. Here is an example: "Select **System info** from the **Administration** panel."

> **Tips or important notes**
> Appear like this.

Get in touch

Feedback from our readers is always welcome.

General feedback: If you have questions about any aspect of this book, email us at customercare@packtpub.com and mention the book title in the subject of your message.

Errata: Although we have taken every care to ensure the accuracy of our content, mistakes do happen. If you have found a mistake in this book, we would be grateful if you would report this to us. Please visit www.packtpub.com/support/errata and fill in the form.

Piracy: If you come across any illegal copies of our works in any form on the internet, we would be grateful if you would provide us with the location address or website name. Please contact us at copyright@packt.com with a link to the material.

If you are interested in becoming an author: If there is a topic that you have expertise in and you are interested in either writing or contributing to a book, please visit authors.packtpub.com.

Share Your Thoughts

Once you've read *Building IoT Visualizations using Grafana*, we'd love to hear your thoughts! Scan the QR code below to go straight to the Amazon review page for this book and share your feedback.

https://packt.link/r/1-803-23612-4

Your review is important to us and the tech community and will help us make sure we're delivering excellent quality content.

Part 1: Meeting Grafana

In this part, you will learn what Grafana is and what it is used for. You will learn how to install it and make basic configurations.

This part contains the following chapters:

- *Chapter 1, Getting Started with Grafana*
- *Chapter 2, Exploring Grafana*

1

Getting Started with Grafana

In this chapter, you will learn what is Grafana and why it is an excellent option for building IoT solutions. Throughout this chapter, you will learn to install Grafana in different scenarios.

Also, you will be able to perform a basic configuration and make it run at boot.

Finally, we will explore the Grafana Cloud service, which you can use instead of installing and maintaining a Grafana instance.

In this chapter, we're going to cover the following main topics:

- Installing Grafana on a Raspberry Pi
- Installing Grafana on Ubuntu Server
- Installing Grafana with Docker
- Initial configuration of Grafana
- Maybe you prefer the cloud option

Let's explore some of these functionalities.

Technical requirements

Depending on the type of implementation that you want to use, you will need some of the following requirements:

- A Raspberry Pi: version 2, 3, or 4 will work. However, depending on the size of your solution, you will have to size your hardware according to it.

- If you prefer to use an Ubuntu Server or a Docker implementation, then you will need a virtual machine, either local or in the cloud. The resources of the virtual machine will have to adapt to your system needs.

Managing data

Grafana allows to capture and manage data from many different sources, such as relational databases, time-series databases, NoSQL databases, Excel or CSV files, logs, and many others.

In this way, Grafana can be connected to different data sources, isolating the visualization and analytics app from the databases. All databases are independent and can be managed by the corresponding applications.

So, even if the database is managed by another department, read-only access can be granted to Grafana to perform analytics on that data.

With the release of Grafana 8.x, it is possible to feed live events into Grafana using MQTT, HTTP, or other streaming data sources. This is a great new feature for IoT systems.

Performing visualizations

Grafana allows you to build a broad range of dashboards, from the typical time-series plot to advanced visualizations.

The dashboards are made up of panels, which provide different types of visualizations.

Some of the possible visualization panels are as follows:

- Time-series plots
- Statistical graphs
- Categorical or boolean panels
- Text and logs
- Topological views
- Geographical or georeferenced data

Every dashboard can be easily modified through drag and drop and resize operations.

Dashboards can be shared with specific users or teams, allowing the data to be used in a cooperative way. Also, dashboards can be published on a website to make information available to the public.

Transformations, alerts, and annotations

With Grafana, you can perform transformations directly on the visualization panels. For instance, you can summarize, combine, rename, and make calculations just with a few clicks.

With Grafana, you can create, modify, and silence all the alert conditions in a centralized way. This functionality simplifies the management of alerts.

Finally, with annotations, you can make comments on data directly on the visualization panels. You can include descriptions and tags for every event of interest.

Now that you have learned about the capabilities of Grafana and the reasons that lead to its use in IoT systems, in the following sections, you will learn how to install Grafana on Raspberry Pi, Ubuntu Server, and Docker.

Installing Grafana on a Raspberry Pi

The **Single Board Computer** (**SBC**) Raspberry Pi has been widely adopted for many uses, including IoT. So, it is quite natural to try to use Grafana on it.

In this section, we will see how to install and configure Grafana on a Raspberry Pi. To achieve good performance, we will use a Raspberry Pi version 2 or later.

Installation instructions

All the following instructions assume that you are using Raspberry Pi OS as the operating system.

Let's start:

1. First, it is always recommended to start with an update.

    So, we run the following:

    ```
    $ sudo apt-get update
    $ sudo apt-get upgrade
    ```

2. After that, we need to download the binary files for the installation:

```
$ wget https://dl.grafana.com/oss/release/grafana-
rpi_8.0.6_armhf.deb
$ sudo dpkg -i grafana-rpi_8.0.6_armhf.deb
```

> **Note about Versions**
>
> Change the package version to the most recent stable version available. You can find all the available options at https://grafana.com/grafana/download?edition=oss.

3. The next step is to make Grafana start at boot. To do this, we can use the systemd service file, included in Grafana packages.

    So, we enable it by running the following:

    ```
    $ sudo systemctl enable grafana-server
    ```

    And that's it. Grafana will start at every boot.

4. Now, to start Grafana manually, we can use the following:

    ```
    $ sudo systemctl start grafana-server
    ```

Now that you know how to install Grafana on a Raspberry Pi, let's dive into how you can access Grafana for the first time.

Accessing Grafana for the first time

Now that you have Grafana running in your Raspberry Pi, you can access it through any web browser, pointing it to http://your-raspberry-ip-address:3000.

You can use your Raspberry Pi IP address, as well as its DNS name. Or, if you are accessing Grafana from the Raspberry Pi itself, you can use localhost or 127.0.0.1 in the URL.

After you access the web interface, you will have to enter the username and password to enter the platform.

The default credentials are user = `admin` and password = `admin`.

Figure 1.1 – Grafana login page

In this section, you have learned to install Grafana on a Raspberry Pi. In the next section, you will see how to do it on Ubuntu Server.

Installing Grafana on Ubuntu Server

Ubuntu is one of the most popular operating systems for servers, so we will learn how to install Grafana on it.

Installing Grafana on Ubuntu is a very straightforward procedure because there are Ubuntu packages.

Installation instructions

Let's look at what we need to do here:

1. As before, we first run updates:

    ```
    $ sudo apt-get update
    $ sudo apt-get upgrade
    ```

2. Next, if you do not have wget installed on your server, you can install it as follows:

    ```
    $ sudo apt-get install apt-transport-https
    $ sudo apt-get install software-properties-common wget
    ```

3. Then you can use wget to download the GPG key and add it to the APT keys. In this way, you authorize Grafana packages to be installed on the system:

    ```
    $ wget -q -O - https://packages.grafana.com/gpg.key |
    sudo apt-key add -
    ```

4. After that, you can add the Grafana repository (stable release) to the APT source list:

    ```
    $ echo "deb https://packages.grafana.com/oss/deb stable
    main" | sudo tee -a /etc/apt/sources.list.d/grafana.list
    ```

5. Finally, run the following commands:

    ```
    $ sudo apt-get update
    $ sudo apt-get install grafana
    ```

Now that you have installed Grafana on Ubuntu Server, let's see how to run it.

Running Grafana on Ubuntu Server

There are two ways of running Grafana as a service. Let's have a look at them.

Running Grafana using systemd

Grafana services can be managed by systemd.

To start Grafana, simply execute the following:

```
$ sudo systemctl start grafana-server
```

To see the Grafana service status, run this command:

```
$ sudo systemctl status grafana-server
```

To stop the service, use this command:

```
$ sudo systemctl stop grafana-server
```

And to enable start at boot, use this command:

```
$ sudo systemctl enable grafana-server.service
```

Now that you know how to do it with systemd, let's see how to do it with initd.

Running Grafana with initd

You can run Grafana as follows:

```
$ sudo service grafana-server start
```

To stop Grafana, use this command:

```
$ sudo service grafana-server stop
```

To get the service status, run this command:

```
$ sudo service grafana-server status
```

To configure it to start at boot, use the following command:

```
$ sudo update-rc.d grafana-server defaults
```

You have now installed and executed Grafana on Ubuntu Server. You also configured it to start on boot. Now let's see how to access Grafana from a browser.

Accessing Grafana

Before trying to access Grafana, make sure that the service is running. You can check it using the preceding commands. If it is stopped, you must start it as shown earlier.

As soon as you have Grafana installed and running, you can access it by pointing the browser to http://your-server-ip-or-name:3000.

The default credentials are admin/admin.

Now that you have learned how to install and run Grafana on Ubuntu Server as well as how to manage start-up at boot using two different methods, let's move on to the next section, where you will learn how to deploy Grafana using Docker.

Installing Grafana with Docker

Docker is a great option to deploy Grafana quickly and easily.

With Docker, you can manage multiple applications on the same server, avoiding conflicts between them. Each application can depend on different versions of libraries and software packages, but their files are completely isolated from each other.

Docker also allows us to start, stop, remove, and update applications in a few seconds. In a more advanced implementation, you can create a cluster with multiple hosts and containers. This cluster can be managed by Swarm or Kubernetes. However, this is beyond the scope of this book.

In this section, you will learn how to deploy Grafana using Docker.

You will be able to use two different methods: the Docker CLI and Docker Compose.

Deploying Grafana with Docker CLI

There are many ways to deploy Grafana with Docker.

One of these options is the operating system selection of the container. You can choose between Alpine and Ubuntu.

The most recent version of Grafana uses Alpine by default, which is a very light operating system based on **musl libc** and **BusyBox**. This is the option recommended by GrafanaLabs.

> **Important note**
>
> Please, do not run Docker on Windows. Docker is designed to run in a Linux host. If you run Docker on Windows, it will create a virtual machine running Linux (you need Windows Professional and Hyper V installed). It is more natural and easier to run Docker directly in a Linux host. So, I recommend you do this.

Now, let's see how to deploy Grafana with Docker.

Running Grafana with Docker

To run Grafana from Docker with the default options, simply execute the following:

```
$ sudo docker run -d -p 3000:3000 grafana/grafana
```

The command options are as follows:

- -d: Detached mode, which means to execute the container in the background.
- -p 3000:3000: Container port and published port are set to 3000. You can change it at your convenience.

The grafana/grafana image comes with the Alpine operating system and the latest stable version of Grafana.

The deployment of Grafana can be modified through options and environment variables. Let's see some examples:

```
$ sudo docker run -d \
  -p 3000:3000 \
  --name=grafana \
  -e "GF_INSTALL_PLUGINS= grafana-piechart-panel, agenty-
flowcharting-panel " \
  grafana/grafana
```

The name option is used to give a specific name to the container and e to open the environment section.

In this particular example, the grafana-piechart-panel and agenty-flowcharting-panel plugins are installed when the container is created.

Using persisting storage

Every time a container is created, new files are generated by being copied from the image file, which contains all the necessary code, libraries, and dependencies to run the application.

In the same way, each time a container is deleted, all these files are removed and lost. So, if you want to have persistent data, such as configuration or data files, you will have to attach some storage located in the host (outside of the container).

There are two ways of doing this:

- Using bind mounts
- Using Docker volumes

Let's explore these options.

Bind mounts

With bind mounts, you can mount a host directory in the container. This is typically used with configuration files, although it can be used either with databases or other data.

In this way, you keep a configuration file in the host (outside the container) that persists even if the container is deleted. Then, to create a new container with the previous configuration, you only have to bind the corresponding directory or file.

Let's see how to do it with the command line:

```
$ sudo docker run -d --name grafana -v "$PWD/config/grafana.
ini:/etc/grafana/grafana.ini" -p 3000:3000 grafana/grafana
```

In this example, the `config` directory is mounted in the container and the `grafana.ini` file is accessible from the container. If you want to modify the configuration of Grafana, you can simply edit the `grafana.ini` file in the host and run the container again.

> **Important Note**
>
> `$PWD/config/grafana.ini` is where you have the `ini` file. It can be anywhere as long the directory has the appropriate read permissions.

Moreover, editing a file in the host is easier than editing it in the container.

Volumes

If you need to keep data stored even if you delete a container, you will have to use volumes. This will allow you to have persistent data into a host directory that can be read and write from the container.

Bind mounts are dependent on the directory structure and operating system of the host. In contrast, volumes are fully managed by Docker.

Volumes have some advantages with respect to bind mounts:

- They are easier to move or back up.
- You can manage them with the Docker CLI.
- They can be shared safely among containers.
- They can be created in remote hosts and accessed from any container.

Let's see how to use Docker volumes:

```
$sudo docker run -d --name grafana -v grafanavol:/var/lib/
grafana -p 3000:3000 grafana/grafana
```

In this command, we are creating a volume named `grafanavol` and mapping it to the directory `/var/lib/grafana`. This directory corresponds to Grafana data files.

You will learn about Grafana configuration and files in the next section.

By combining bind mounts and volumes, you can have the best of both worlds, as shown in the next command:

```
$ sudo docker run -d -v "$PWD/config/grafana.ini:/etc/grafana/
grafana.ini" -v grafanavol:/var/lib/grafana -p 3000:3000
grafana/grafana
```

In this case, we can configure Grafana by modifying the `grafana.ini` file in the host while storing persistent data in the `grafanavol` volume.

Using environmental variables

You can customize the building process of the container with environmental variables.

You can find the complete list of environmental variables here: `https://grafana.com/docs/grafana/latest/administration/configuration/#configure-with-environment-variables`.

The environmental variables allow you to specify all the parameters included in the configuration file. In fact, you can use the environment variable instead of editing the configuration file.

Any environment variable specified when launching the container will override the corresponding configuration in the configuration file.

Let´s see how you can use environment variables.

Suppose you want to set admin user and password. You can specify the following environment variables:

- `GF_SECURITY_ADMIN_USER=youradminuser`
- `GF_SECURITY_ADMIN_PASSWORD=youradminpassword`

Let's see how to include them in a docker command.

```
$ sudo docker run -d \
-p 3000:3000 \
--name=grafana \
-e "GF_SECURITY_ADMIN_USER=youradminuser" \
-e "GF_SECURITY_ADMIN_PASSWORD=youradminpassword" \
grafana/grafana
```

You have seen how to use environment variables with the Docker CLI. Now you will learn how to use Docker Compose.

Using Docker Compose

Docker Compose is a very useful tool for managing and running Docker containers. It uses a YAML file to configure all the services of the applications. With Docker Compose, you can launch all the applications and services that you need in a single command.

> **Important Note**
>
> Docker Compose is not installed by default, so you may need to do it. To install it, follow the instructions at https://docs.docker.com/compose/install/.

Besides practicality, using a YAML file allows you to have a clear picture of your deployment. When using the Docker CLI, things can get messy if you need to pass a lot of parameters and environment variables. In these cases, Docker Compose offers a structured and clean solution.

Also, if you need to deploy more than one application or container, you can use Docker Compose to do it in a single command. With the Docker CLI, you would have to run it for every application/container.

Let's see an example of YAML file. Take into consideration that you have to name the file docker-compose.yml:

```
version: '2'
services:
    grafana:
        image: grafana/grafana:latest
        container_name: grafana
        ports:
```

```
          - 3000:3000
        environment:
          - GF_SECURITY_ADMIN_USER=youradminuser
          - GF_SECURITY_ADMIN_PASSWORD=youradminpassword
        volumes:
          - grafanavol:/var/lib/grafana
  volumes:
    grafanavol:
```

Building and running the container is as easy as executing this:

```
$sudo docker-compose up
```

You must run the command from the same directory where the docker-compose.yaml file is.

Further considerations

When installing Grafana with Docker, you will have to consider a variety of factors, such as security, networking, and storage.

All these factors will affect the installation and configuration needs.

In this section, you have all the information you need to start using Grafana with Docker. However, more complex use of Docker is far beyond the scope of this book.

Now, let's look at the initial configuration of Grafana.

Initial configuration of Grafana

You can configure Grafana whether editing the grafana.ini file or by specifying environment variables.

In this section, you will learn how to do it both ways.

Configuration files

Grafana comes with a default configuration file that you should not edit: defaults.ini.

To override the settings in this file, you must edit grafana.ini. This file is located – in Linux systems – in the /etc/grafana/grafana.ini directory.

You can find the locations for different operating systems at `https://grafana.com/docs/grafana/latest/administration/configuration/#config-file-locations`.

All configuration options are shown here: `https://grafana.com/docs/grafana/latest/administration/configuration/`.

We will explore some basic options to start using Grafana. In later chapters, you will learn about some other specific configuration settings.

The `app_mode` variable accepts two options: development and production. The default option is `production` and you must keep it unless you are planning to do some development:

```
app_mode   production
```

In the `date_formats` section, you can set date and time formats used in graphs and date-time boxes. In this section, you will find several options.

`full_date` is used to show a full date format where it is applicable.

Here's an example:

```
full_date YYYY-MM-DD HH:mm:s
```

`interval` options are used in the graph to show partial dates or times.

The default options are as follows:

```
interval_second = HH:mm:ss
interval_minute = HH:mm
interval_hour = MM/DD HH:mm
interval_day = MM/DD
interval_month = YYYY-MM
interval_year = YYYY
```

`use_browser_locale` allows us to use date formats derived from the browser location. It is set to `false` by default.

With `default_timezone`, you can set your own time zone, or set it to use the browser location. The default option is the browser.

In the `security` section, you can set the administration user and security-related options. Some of these options, such as admin username and password, can be edited from the web interface.

In the `paths` section, you can see the paths that Grafana is using in your system.

In a Linux system, these paths are as follows:

```
data          /var/lib/grafana
logs          /var/log/grafana
plugins          /var/lib/grafana/plugins
provisioning      /etc/grafana/provisioning
```

> **Important Note**
> If you are using Docker to deploy Grafana, these paths cannot be modified in the configuration file. Instead, you will have to use environment variables.

You have now learned to use the configuration file to modify the behavior of Grafana. You also have seen the paths to important Grafana files.

In the next section, you will learn how to configure Grafana using environment variables.

Environment variables

In the previous section, you learned how to use environment variables with Docker. Now, you will see how to do this in the Linux host.

You can override any option in the configuration file using environment variables.

The syntax is as follows:

```
GF_<SectionName>_<KeyName>
```

So, if you want to change the admin user, you must type the following in the console:

```
export GF_SECURITY_ADMIN_USER=newadminuser
```

The same applies to every other option.

> **Note**
> You will have to restart Grafana for any configuration change to take effect.

Until here, you have learned how to install Grafana on-premises using different deployment options.

In the next section, you will learn how to use the **Grafana Cloud** service to avoid the installation and management process.

Maybe you prefer the cloud option

If you want to avoid all the work related to the installation and configuration of Grafana, maybe you can try using the Grafana Cloud service.

It takes a matter of minutes to create an account on Grafana Cloud and start using the platform. In the next screenshot, you can see the registration page:

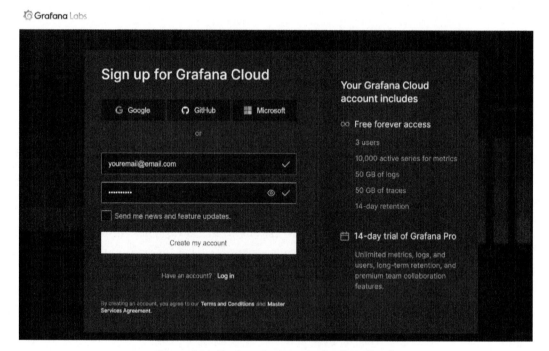

Figure 1.2 – Registration page in Grafana Cloud

After you enter your email and password, you will receive an email to confirm the registration.

You will then access a 14-day trial of Grafana Pro. After those 14 days, you can subscribe or continue using the free version.

You can see the plans at `https://grafana.com/products/cloud/pricing/`.

Following the registration process, you will be able to access the Grafana Cloud services.

The first step when configuring your stack of Grafana is to select a name. In the free or trial versions, you have to use a domain ending with `grafana.net`, as shown in *Figure 1.3*. In the paid options, you can choose your domain.

Figure 1.3 – Naming your Grafana stack

After you name your stack, you will access the integration page.

Figure 1.4 – First screen accessing Grafana

Now you have a running instance of Grafana Cloud and can start using it.

Summary

In this chapter, you have learned how to install, configure, and run Grafana in three different scenarios. We first installed it on a Raspberry Pi, then on Ubuntu Server, and finally using Docker. Then you learned how to configure Grafana using the `grafana.ini` file and environment variables. Finally, you met the Grafana Cloud service, registered a new user, and set a stack name. Now you will be able to implement and run your own Grafana instance.

In the next chapter, you will explore the entire Grafana platform, learning about dashboards, plugins, data sources, users, and other things.

Invitation to join us on Discord

Read this book alongside other Grafana users and the author Rodrigo Juan Hernández.

Ask questions, provide solutions to other readers, chat with the author via Ask Me Anything sessions and much more.

SCAN the QR code or visit the link to join the community.

https://packt.link/iotgrafana

2

Exploring Grafana

In this chapter, you will learn about all the features included in Grafana. You will start to get familiar with the platform, understanding every aspect of it. First, you will discover all the menu options in the main interface. Then, you will learn about the graphical organization of Grafana, with organizations, dashboards, and panels. After that, you will learn how to ingest data into Grafana with data sources and find out about the different types.

Then, you will be introduced to plugins, which are pieces of software that make Grafana very easy to use. After that, you will learn about user management, through the topics of organizations, teams, and users. Finally, you will see some authentication methods that you can use with Grafana.

In this chapter, we'll cover the following topics:

- Exploring the Grafana interface
- Organizations, dashboards, and panels
- How to get data into Grafana
- Making integrations easy with plugins
- Organizations, teams, users, and permissions
- Authentication methods

Technical requirements

To get the most out of this chapter, you will need a running instance of Grafana. It can be running either on your server or in a Grafana Cloud service instance.

Exploring the Grafana interface

The user interface of Grafana is quite easy to navigate and use. In this section, you will explore all the options available on it.

Let's start with the main screen.

The main menu

On the left side of the screen, you will find a menu, represented by some icons. Now, we will explore each of these options.

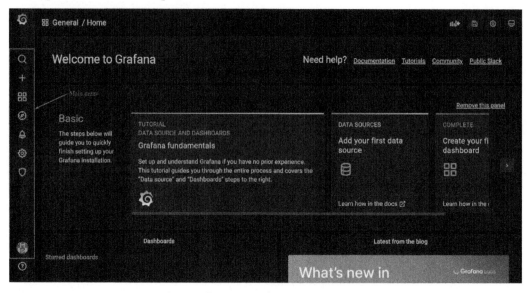

Figure 2.1 – Main menu

As you can see, Grafana offers a clean and easy-to-use user interface.

Search tool

Starting from the top, you can see a magnifying glass, which represents a search element. Using this tool, you can search for dashboards.

According to the user permissions, every user will find the dashboards that they are allowed to see and manage.

Create menu

Then, you will find a plus symbol, which opens up some options when you put your mouse over it.

The options available are as follows:

- **Dashboard**
- **Folder**
- **Import**
- **Alerting**

Each of these options is quite self-explanatory, but let's see a little more about each of them.

Dashboard

This allows you to create a new dashboard, where you can add panels to show and analyze data. We will learn more about dashboards later.

Folder

By clicking on this option, you can create a folder. You can use folders to organize your dashboards, keeping them in different folders according to application and user needs.

Import

With this option, you can easily import dashboards into the running instance of Grafana.

There are three different methods by which you can do this:

- Uploading a JSON file
- Via the Grafana URL or ID
- Importing via panel JSON

Every dashboard can be exported using a JSON file, as we will see later on in this chapter. So, importing only requires uploading the corresponding file.

The second method is useful if you have a dashboard running in an instance of the Grafana Cloud service and you want to import it into another.

Finally, the third method is basically the same as the first one, but in this case, you use copy/paste instead of uploading a file.

Alert rule

This option lets you create alerts based on conditions. We will learn about alerts in *Chapter 10, Alerting and Notifications in Grafana*.

Dashboard menu

Below the create menu, you can find the dashboard menu. This menu offers several options to manage dashboards. Let's see all of them.

Home

This option leads you to the home page of Grafana. On this page, you will find some panels, depending on the version that you are running (Community or Enterprise).

The main panels are as follows:

- **Welcome to Grafana**: Here, there are links to online documentation, tutorials, the community, and the Slack channel.
- **Dashboards**: Here, you will find links to your favorite or recently opened dashboards.
- **Articles from the blog**: Here, the latest articles published on the blog of Grafana Labs are listed.
- **Getting Started**: This option leads you to valuable information to help you start using Grafana.

Dashboards

As its name suggests, this option lets you manage all the dashboards defined in the instance.

When you click on **Dashboards**, you land on **Dashboards**, but also see another three tabs: **Playlists**, **Snapshots**, and **Library panels**. You can go directly to any of these tabs just by clicking on the corresponding option in the menu. We will see all these features later in this chapter.

Explore

This menu gives you direct access to an explorer, where you can run a rapid query on any data source available and see the results on a visualization panel.

Alerting

By clicking on this menu, you will access the alerting and notification tabs, where you can manage both. You will learn how to create and manage alerting rules and notifications in *Chapter 10, Alerting and Notifications in Grafana*.

Configuration

In the **Configuration** section, you will be able to manage the following items:

- **Data sources**
- **Users**
- **Teams**
- **Plugins**
- **Preferences**
- **API keys**

All these menu elements will bring you access to most of the configuration options for Grafana.

Server Admin

Finally, the **Server Admin** menu allows you to manage the following:

- Users
- Organizations
- Settings
- Plugins
- Stats and license

This menu allows you to set high-level configurations, such as users and organizations.

Account

Almost at the bottom of the left bar, you will find a menu to manage your account.

This includes the following:

- Preferences
- Changing password
- Signing out

In this section, we explored all the menu options that Grafana provides us with. In the following section, you will learn how to manage organizations, dashboards, and panels.

Organizations, dashboards, and panels

The user interface of Grafana is organized using a hierarchical structure.

From a high level to low, the structure is **organizations**, **dashboards**, and **panels**. Let's understand these three entities.

Organizations

In Grafana, you can build multiple organizations to organize dashboards. Imagine you have several departments in an enterprise, and each of them is interested in different metrics.

You can create different organizations and assign the users of each department to the corresponding organization. In this way, each user only accesses the information that is relevant to them.

So, with a single instance of Grafana, you can manage information across all organizations without messing them up.

You can also assign a user to one or many organizations. Imagine a general manager that wants to see relevant information on the departments that depend on them. Each of these areas can have its organizational entities with dashboards, and the general manager would be able to see all of them.

To sum up, organizations are the highest level of the hierarchy for managing dashboards and users. Let's now see what dashboards are.

Dashboards

A dashboard is a graphical entity where you can group multiple panels. In Grafana, you can move, resize, and customize the panels just with some click-and-drag operations.

In an organization, you can arrange the dashboards, deploying them in different folders. So, you can create as many folders as you need to keep a clean visualization experience. Furthermore, you can use **tags** to further refine the purpose of a specific dashboard. Other properties of a dashboard are time zone, auto-refresh period, and delay.

You can find all this in the dashboard settings section, as you can see in *Figure 2.2*.

On each dashboard, you can create annotations and variables. Also, you can add links to other dashboards or external sites.

You have either a log to see all the versions of the dashboard along the time.

You can also manage the user's permissions to the dashboard.

Finally, you can view a JSON model of the dashboard and copy it to deploy it in another dashboard.

We will cover all these subjects in later chapters.

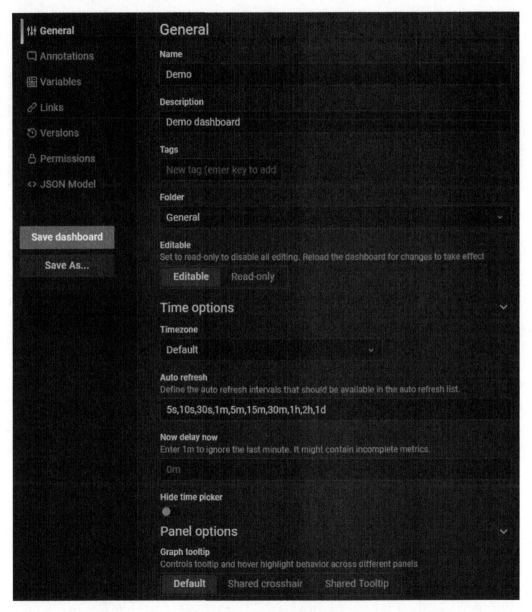

Figure 2.2 – Dashboard properties

Let's now explore the panels.

Panels

The panels are where the fun happens.

When you create a dashboard, it doesn't contain anything. You have to add panels to visualize data.

In a single dashboard, you can deploy different types of panels: time series, bars, gauges, tables, text, logs, and so on. You can see some of them in the following screenshot:

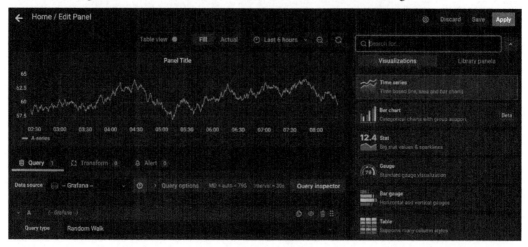

Figure 2.3 – Grafana panels

In this section, you have learned about the hierarchical organization of Grafana. You learned about organizations, dashboards, and panels.

In the next section, you will learn about the options to feed data into Grafana.

How to get data into Grafana

In this section, we will learn about the different data sources that you can use to get data into Grafana.

In this chapter, you will not learn how to configure and use these data sources. Instead, you will acquire a clear picture of data sources, and in *Chapter 4*, *Data Source for Grafana*, you will learn how to use them.

Data sources

Data sources are the data backends that bring different types of data into Grafana. In this book, you will mostly see how to work with **time series** data.

Typically, you will feed data coming from databases, files, and APIs into the panels. However, Grafana has recently added other data sources, such as live data from **WebSocket**. We will cover all of these subjects in later chapters.

Among others, some possible data sources are as follows:

- InfluxDB
- Graphite
- MySQL
- Prometheus
- OpenTSDB
- Elasticsearch

Getting data into Grafana is as simple as follows:

1. Configure Grafana to establish a connection with the data source using an API. To make this easy, Grafana offers a variety of plugins that you can install.
2. Create a dashboard.
3. Create a visualization panel within the new dashboard.
4. Select the desired data source and create a query to get the values you need.
5. Save the dashboard.
6. The data shown on the dashboard will be updated accordingly to the refreshing period.

In this book, you will see how to use several data sources. You will learn the specific details in the appropriate chapters.

In the next sections, you will learn what plugins are in Grafana.

Making integrations easy with plugins

Without a doubt, **plugins** are a powerful tool in Grafana.

Grafana comes, by default, with a wide range of data sources and panels. As soon as you have Grafana running, you have all of them ready to use.

However, there are endless possibilities for using Grafana. Here is where plugins come to the rescue.

There are three types of plugins:

- Panel plugins

- Data source plugins

- App plugins

Besides the plugins developed by Grafana Labs, you can use a lot of community plugins made by independent developers.

Let's see what each of them can be used for.

Data source plugins

You can use data source plugins to access new types of databases. These plugins establish communication with databases and present the information in a way that Grafana understands.

So, connecting a new database is as easy as installing a data source plugin and configuring it.

You will use data source plugins to add access to databases that are not included in the basic installation of Grafana.

Panel plugins

With Grafana, you can build endless panel types. While in the basic installation, you will find a good number of options to display your data, with additional plugins, you will be able to make very specialized graphs.

In the basic installation, you will find panels such as **Time Series, Text, Table, Gauge**, and **Bar chart**, among others.

On the other hand, you can install plugins to add panels such as **Clock, FlowCharting, Worldmap Panel**, or **Pie Chart**, to name a few.

You can use panel plugins to do the following:

- Visualize data.

- Navigate between dashboards.

- Send commands to remote systems and devices.

In this section, you have learned about the three types of plugins available in Grafana. You have seen what you can do with each of them. In the end, the plugins are there to make things easy.

In the next section, you will learn about users, permissions, organizations, and teams.

Users and permissions

In Grafana, you can manage users at different levels. Each of these levels determines the tasks and permissions that a user can have.

You can assign different roles to users, allowing them to access the required resources.

There are four levels of permission management. Let's see what they are.

Server level

The server level is the widest. It includes all the users that belong to the current instance of Grafana.

Users that have the Grafana **Admin** option set to Yes can manage all the organizations and user accounts in the server.

Organization level

Organizations are groups of users on a specific server.

You can create as many organizations as you need and assign users to one or more of them.

Besides users, within an organization, you can use data sources, plugins, and dashboards that are specific to that organization. So, you can have an organization with an InfluxDB database and another with a SQL database. None of these organizations can see the other organization's database.

The members of an organization have permissions based on their roles. We will look at roles and permissions later in this chapter.

The admins in an organization can manage users and teams within the organization.

Teams

You can group users in an organization using teams. When you create a team, you can assign the same permissions to all the users that belong to the team.

Typically, teams are managed by organization admins.

You can, for instance, create teams for the following:

- Granting access to some dashboards to a group of users
- Allowing read-only access
- Allowing edition access
- Creating a group of admins

So, you can use teams mainly to organize users within an organization.

Users

Finally, we have the users. To create a user, you have to specify a username, a password, and an email.

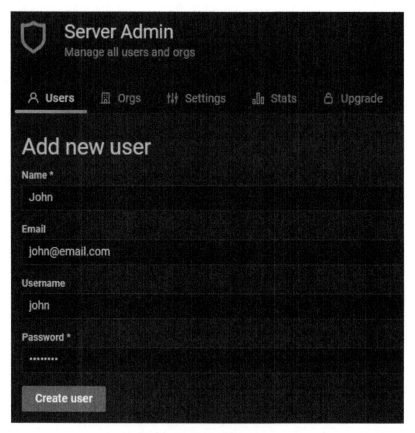

Figure 2.4 – Creating a user

After you have created the user, you can assign them to one or more organizations and teams. Users can manage their account, including changing their password, changing their email address, and switching between organizations if they belong to more than one.

Every time you create a user, you have to assign roles. Let's learn about user roles.

User roles

There are three types of roles:

- Admin
- Editor
- Viewer

You can define different roles for the same users across many organizations. So, a user can be an admin in organization A and a viewer in organization B.

The following is a table that compares the user roles:

	Admin	Editor	Viewer
View dashboards	x	x	x
Add, edit, and delete dashboards	x	x	
Add, edit, and delete folders	x	x	
View playlists	x	x	x
Create, update, and delete playlists	x	x	
Access Explore	x	x	
Add, edit, and delete data sources	x		
Add and edit users	x		
Add and edit teams	x		
Change organization settings	x		
Change team settings	x		
Configure app plugins	x		

Figure 2.5 – Comparison of user permissions

To change the role of a user, you have to click on the user account.

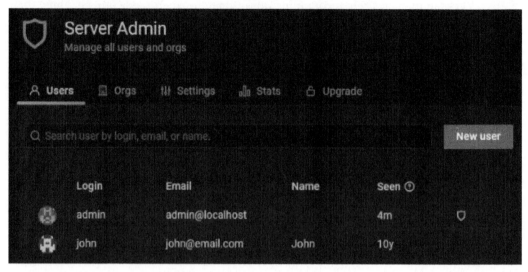

Figure 2.6 – Managing user accounts

Once there, you can do the following:

- Enable admin permission.
- Change the role.
- Add the user to an organization.
- Remove the user from the current organization.

Figure 2.7 – Assigning roles and permissions

Let's see how you can manage dashboard permissions for users and teams.

Dashboard permissions

Let's see how you can customize permissions and user roles for a dashboard.

To configure the permissions for a dashboard, you have to go to the **Settings** section of the dashboard.

You will see by default the admin user and the roles of editor and viewer. That means that any user with the editor role can edit the dashboard and that any user with the viewer role can view it. These are dashboard permissions because they apply to any user in the organization.

Figure 2.8 – Dashboard permissions

Let's see how you can customize permissions and user roles for a specific dashboard.

If you want to have fine-grained access control to the dashboard, you can remove **Editor** and **Viewer** roles from there.

Then, you can add teams or users and assign them the roles for that specific dashboard.

Note that even if a user on a team has a role in their profile, you can apply a different role for this dashboard.

In this section, you have learned about the four levels of permission management: server, organization, team, and user. You also learned how to create, edit, and assign roles to a user.

We have seen how to perform fine-grained access control to dashboards, and manage permissions in the dashboard settings.

In the next section, you will learn about the authentication techniques that you can use in Grafana.

Authentication methods

In this section, you will see all the authentication methods that you can use in Grafana. There are many possibilities, from basic authentication to integrated services.

First, let's see a list of the authentication methods:

- Grafana built-in user authentication
- Auth proxy
- Azure Active Directory OAuth
- Generic OAuth
- GitHub OAuth
- GitLab OAuth
- Google OAuth
- **JSON Web Token (JWT)**
- LDAP
- Okta OAuth
- SAML (Enterprise Edition only)

In the following sections, we will see some authentication methods.

Grafana authentication

In this section, you will explore some authentication methods that you can use with Grafana. However, due to the extensive configuration that these methods require, we will just see introductory information on each one.

The simplest method that you can use to authenticate users is the built-in user authentication system. This method is enabled by default, and you can use it as soon as you install Grafana, as we saw in *Chapter 1, Getting Started with Grafana*.

Short-lived tokens

Short-lived tokens allow active users to stay logged in. These short-lived tokens are rotated after a time equal to the specified by the `token_rotation_interval_minutes` configuration setting.

If the token or an active user is rotated, then `login_maximum_inactive_lifetime_duration` will be extended. So, the user can be inactive or even close the browser for a maximum time of timestamp of rotated token + `login_maximum_inactive_lifetime_duration`.

Besides these intervals, the user will stay logged in whenever the time from user login is less than `login_maximum_lifetime_duration`.

Let's see the environment variables that you can set to modify the user login intervals:

```
[auth]


# Login cookie name
login_cookie_name = grafana_session


# The lifetime (days, minutes, seconds, etc) an authenticated
user can be inactive before being required to login at next
visit. Default is 7 days.
login_maximum_inactive_lifetime_duration = 7d


# The maximum lifetime (days, minutes, seconds, etc) an
authenticated user can be logged in since login time before
being required to login. Default is 30 days.
login_maximum_lifetime_duration = 30d


# How often should auth tokens be rotated for authenticated
users when being active. The default is each 10 minutes.
token_rotation_interval_minutes = 10


# The maximum lifetime (seconds) an api key can be used. If it
is set all the api keys should have limited lifetime that is
lower than this value.
api_key_max_seconds_to_live = -1
```

Let's see now how to use anonymous authentication.

Anonymous authentication

You can enable anonymous authentication if necessary. However, you have to consider some concerns:

- Anyone that knows the URL can access the dashboard.
- Anyone can invoke the API and list all folders, dashboards, and data sources.
- Anyone can make queries to any data source of the Grafana instance.

Let's see how you can configure Grafana to enable anonymous authentication:

```
[auth.anonymous]
enabled = true


# Organization name that should be used for unauthenticated
users
org_name = Main Org.


# Role for unauthenticated users, other valid values are
'Editor' and 'Admin'
org_role = Viewer


# Hide the Grafana version text from the footer and help
tooltip for unauthenticated users (default: false)
hide_version = true
```

Let's see how you can manage the basic authentication options.

Authentication options

You can enable or disable basic authentication in Grafana. Basic authentication is used with the built-in Grafana authentication system and with LDAP integration.

To enable or disable authentication, just set the following variable:

```
[auth.basic]
enabled = false
```

You can also hide the Grafana login form by setting the following variable:

```
[auth]
disable_login_form = true
```

You can configure automatic OAuth login, bypassing the login screen. We will look at OAuth later, but for now, let's see how you can set this option:

```
[auth]
oauth_auto_login = true
```

Another available feature is to hide the logout menu. This can be useful if you use an authentication proxy or JWT:

```
[auth]
disable_signout_menu = true
```

Finally, you can configure a redirection after the user logout:

```
[auth]
signout_redirect_url = your url here
```

Up until now, we have explored several basic authentication configuration options.

In the next subsection, you will learn how to implement proxy authentication.

> **Important Note**
> To keep secure the data exchanged with the server, you will have to implement encryption using TLS with HTTPS. You will have to create certificates and keys and configure the web server.

So far, we have explored the basic authentication included in Grafana. Over the following sections, you will learn how to implement other authentication techniques.

Proxy authentication

You can use a reverse proxy to drive authentication in Grafana. Two popular web servers that you can use to do this are Apache and NGINX.

The following environment variables control the behavior of proxy authentication:

```
[auth.proxy]
# Defaults to false, but set to true to enable this feature
enabled = true
# HTTP Header name that will contain the username or email
header_name = X-WEBAUTH-USER
# HTTP Header property, defaults to 'username' but can also be
'email'
header_property = username
# Set to 'true' to enable auto sign up of users who do not
exist in Grafana DB. Defaults to 'true'.
auto_sign_up = true
```

```
# Define cache time to live in minutes
# If combined with Grafana LDAP integration it is also the sync
interval
sync_ttl = 60
# Limit where auth proxy requests come from by configuring a
list of IP addresses.
# This can be used to prevent users spoofing the X-WEBAUTH-USER
header.
# Example 'whitelist = 192.168.1.1, 192.168.1.0/24, 2001::23,
2001::0/120'
whitelist =
# Optionally define more headers to sync other user attributes
# Example 'headers = Name:X-WEBAUTH-NAME Role:X-WEBAUTH-ROLE
Email:X-WEBAUTH-EMAIL Groups:X-WEBAUTH-GROUPS'
headers =
# Check out docs on this for more details on the below setting
enable_login_token = false
```

Naturally, you will have to configure your web service to handle the requests.

JWT authentication

Another authentication method that you can use with Grafana is JWTs.

There are three ways of verifying the token:

- With a PEM-encoded key file
- With the **JSON Web Key Set (JWKS)** in a local file
- With the JWKS provided by the configured JWKS endpoint

To use a JWT, you will have to enable it in the config file and specify the HTTP header, as follows:

```
[auth.jwt]
# By default, auth.jwt is disabled.
enabled = true


# HTTP header to look into to get a JWT token.
header_name = X-JWT-Assertion
```

JWTs use fields named claims to identify the information included in the token. You can use a username as well as an email address to specify a claim for the JWT.

In the configuration file, you can set the following:

```
# [auth.jwt]
# ...


# Specify a claim to use as a username to sign in.
username_claim = sub


# Specify a claim to use as an email to sign in.
email_claim = sub
```

You now know about JWT authentication in Grafana. In the next subsection, you will learn about LDAP integration with Grafana.

LDAP authentication

You can authenticate your Grafana users using LDAP credentials. This can be useful in enterprise or government environments.

Grafana supports LDAP v3, so you can use OpenLDAP or Active Directory, among others.

To enable LDAP authentication, you have to edit the configuration file in the corresponding section, as follows:

```
[auth.ldap]
# Set to 'true' to enable LDAP integration (default: 'false')
enabled = true


# Path to the LDAP specific configuration file (default: '/etc/
grafana/ldap.toml')
config_file = /etc/grafana/ldap.toml


# Allow sign up should almost always be true (default) to allow
new Grafana users to be created (if LDAP authentication is ok).
If set to
# false only pre-existing Grafana users will be able to login
(if LDAP authentication is ok).
allow_sign_up = true
```

Grafana allows debugging LDAP connections and users using the web interface. In the following screenshot, you can see the debug view:

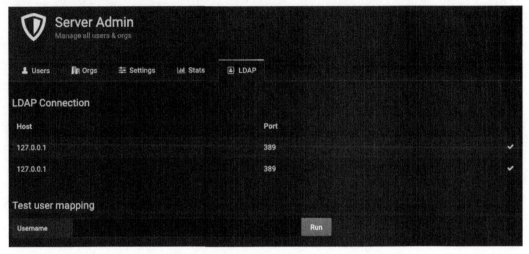

Figure 2.9 – LDAP connections

If you want to use the debug view, you must enter a username in the dialog box and press **Run**. If the user is found in the LDAP, their information will be displayed.

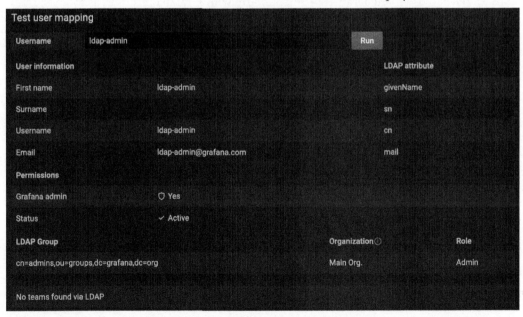

Figure 2.10 – Showing LDAP user information

You have now had an introduction to LDAP authentication with Grafana.

In the next subsection, you will learn about GitHub OAuth integration in Grafana.

GitHub OAuth2 authentication

To use GitHub OAuth2 authentication, you have to register your Grafana instance with GitHub. After that, you will obtain a client ID and a secret key that you can use in your Grafana instance.

On the settings page of GitHub, you have to create a GitHub OAuth application. To do this, you have to specify a callback URL, as follows:

```
http://<my_grafana_server_name_or_ip>:<grafana_server_port>/
login/github
```

Take into consideration that this URL must match the full address that you use to access your Grafana instance. At the end of the URL, you have to add the /login/github path.

After you create this GitHub OAuth application, you will obtain a client ID and a client secret.

You will have to use these parameters to configure your Grafana instance, as follows:

```
[auth.github]
enabled = true
allow_sign_up = true
client_id = YOUR_GITHUB_APP_CLIENT_ID
client_secret = YOUR_GITHUB_APP_CLIENT_SECRET
scopes = user:email,read:org
auth_url = https://github.com/login/oauth/authorize
token_url = https://github.com/login/oauth/access_token
api_url = https://api.github.com/user
team_ids =
allowed_organizations =
```

As you can see from the configuration section shown precedingly, you can also specify teams and organizations from GitHub to allow or restrict access to Grafana.

> **Important Note**
>
> If you are serving Grafana behind a proxy, you will have to set the `root_url` option of `[server]` to the callback URL.

You may want to allow users to sign up using GitHub. To enable this feature, you have to set the `allow_sign_up` option to `true`.

After you have configured Grafana, restart the Grafana service for the changes to take effect.

Summary

In this chapter, you have familiarized yourself with the Grafana interface. Also, you have learned the basics of dashboards, panels, plugins, and data sources.

Furthermore, you learned how to manage users, teams, and organizations. These are important subjects for building a coherent hierarchy in Grafana.

Finally, you have seen several authentication methods that you can use in Grafana, including basic, proxy, JWT, LDAP, and GitHub.

Now that you have learned about the user interface of Grafana and the management of users, you can advance in your use of Grafana.

In the next chapter, you will learn how to send data to Grafana from IoT systems and devices.

Part 2: Collecting Data from IoT Devices

In this part, you will learn how to obtain data from IoT devices using different techniques and protocols. Also, you will learn how to use different types of databases to store and query data.

This part contains the following chapters:

3
Connecting IoT Devices

In this chapter, you will see several methods to get data from IoT devices.

You will learn how to use protocols such as MQTT, HTTP, CoAP, and WebSocket to send data from devices to IoT platforms.

You will learn how to implement your MQTT broker. Also, you will see how to use some cloud platforms to manage data from your devices.

In this chapter, we'll cover the following topics:

- Sending data from IoT devices
- Using an online MQTT broker
- Running your MQTT broker
- Sending data through HTTP
- What is CoAP?
- What about WebSocket?
- How to select the right IoT protocol

Technical requirements

To follow some parts of the chapter, you will need access to cloud MQTT services, virtual Linux servers, or local Linux machines.

Sending data from IoT devices

There are many communication protocols that you can use to send data from your IoT devices. At the end of this chapter, you will learn how to select the most appropriate protocol for your application.

In any case, the general architecture of an IoT solution is as follows.

First, you have the IoT devices. These devices send data to the cloud using different types of communication technologies. Some of these technologies are IP native, such as Ethernet or Wi-Fi, while others are not, such as BLE or LoRa.

If you are using IP native technologies, you can send the data directly to the internet. However, in some cases, it can be a good idea to use a gateway. In this case, the gateway will manage the data sent by the local devices. Then, the gateway will send just the relevant information to the cloud.

On the other hand, if you are using non-IP native technologies, using a gateway is mandatory. For instance, you need a gateway for LoRaWAN devices to communicate with the cloud. The gateway will forward all the frames received from LoRaWAN nodes to the network server. Then, the network server will process the packets, routing or discarding them.

The last step of the IoT data path is the IoT platform. There are different types of IoT platforms, according to their functionalities. Some IoT platforms offer communication and device management, while others use data collected to perform analytics. Also, an IoT platform can deliver the full stack of services. Let's see all the features that an IoT platform can bring forth. An IoT platform can do the following:

- Establish communication with IoT devices.
- Manage devices (deploying, controlling, monitoring, and updating).
- Manage and store data.
- Manage users.
- Showing dashboards.
- Connecting client apps.
- Perform analytics and run ML models.

Commonly, all these functionalities are performed by different platforms that exchange information between them.

In our case, we will use Grafana to manage users, show dashboards, connect clients, and perform analytics.

Over the following sections, you will explore several protocols to send data from IoT devices and gateways. These protocols are MQTT, HTTP, CoAP, and WebSocket.

What is MQTT and what is it used for?

Message Queuing Telemetry Transport (MQTT) is a pure IoT protocol. It was designed in 1999 by *Andy Stanford-Clark (IBM)* and *Arlen Nipper (Arcom, now Cirrus Link)* specifically to address communication between machines - **Machine to Machine (M2M)**.

You can find MQTT in a wide range of applications, such as industrial, health, logistics, mobile, connected cars, smart buildings, and smart cities.

MQTT is based on short messages with a publish-subscribe mechanism.

Let's see some characteristics of MQTT:

- Lightweight and bandwidth-efficient
- Design adapted to constrained devices
- Low power consumption
- Data agnostic
- Management of sessions
- **Quality of Service (QoS)** implementation
- SSL/TLS encryption
- User and client ID management

The basic idea of MQTT is to exchange data between clients. Each client connects to a server running an MQTT service (**broker**).

A client can send data to the broker (**publish**) or receive from it (**subscribe**).

In this architecture, clients are independent entities. All the information is exchanged between clients and the broker.

From a functionality point of view, it's the same with email clients and servers.

Each client has access to certain information through the use of **topics**. These topics are specific fields in the data structure of the MQTT broker.

You can see an example of the MQTT architecture in the following figure:

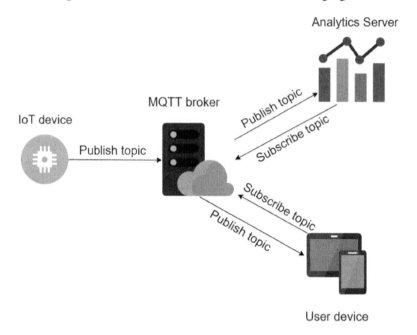

Figure 3.1 – MQTT architecture

Now that we have seen the basic operation of MQTT, let's deep dive into **topics**.

Topics in MQTT

A topic can refer to a single value (string, number, and so on) or an object.

The general approach is using JSON objects to package information in a single topic, as shown in the following example:

```
{ "sensorType": "Thermometer",
"sensorModel": "AM2302",
"temp": 25,
"hum": 40}
```

To organize the information in a structured form, you will need to build your topics in a hierarchical way.

Suppose that you have offices distributed in several cities and you want to monitor their temperature. You can build the topic structure as follows:

```
/city/building/office/tempsensor
```

Besides topics, another important feature of MQTT is QoS. Let's see how MQTT applies QoS.

QoS in MQTT

MQTT offers a QoS implementation. There are three levels of QoS, as follows:

- At most once (level 0)
- At least once (level 1)
- Exactly once (level 2)

To analyze QoS, you have to consider two directions of MQTT communication: from the client to the broker and vice versa.

QoS 0

At this level, the sender transmits the message and doesn't expect any acknowledgment. It is a best-effort delivery service.

We can compare this level of QoS with applications that use the UDP protocol, where there are no ACK messages.

If the communication link is reliable, this type of QoS may be useful to save processing and energy in the IoT device.

QoS 1

In level 1, the message is delivered at least once. To accomplish this, the sender stores the message until receiving a PUBACK packet from the broker.

To send the same message multiple times, the sender uses a packet identifier. So, after every message is delivered, the sender can match the PUBACK packet to the corresponding packet ID.

QoS 2

At this level, every receiver gets a message exactly once. Level 2 is the safest but also the slowest level of QoS in MQTT.

Both the sender and the receiver use the packet ID to match messages.

The process is as follows:

1. The sender sends a PUBLISH packet.
2. The receiver processes the message and responds with a PUBREC packet to the sender.
3. If the sender doesn't receive the PUBREC packet, it sends a new PUBLISH packet with a DUP (duplicate) flag. The sender repeats the operation until it gets an acknowledgment.
4. Whenever the sender receives the PUBREC packet, it discards the PUBLISH packet.
5. Then, the sender saves the PUBREC packet and emits a PUBREL packet.
6. When the receiver finally gets the PUBREL packet, it deletes states and responds with the PUBCOMP packet. The receiver store the packet ID of the original PUBLISH packet until this stage. In this way, it avoids processing duplicate packets.

There are two major versions of MQTT that you can use today: version 3.1.1 and version 5. Let's explore the features of each one.

MQTT 3.1.1

You can find the standard specification of MQTT 3.1.1 at this link:

`http://docs.oasis-open.org/mqtt/mqtt/v3.1.1/mqtt-v3.1.1.html`

The following text is an exact transcription of the abstract of the standard.

Version 3.1.1 was an improvement of version 3.1 that incorporated some new features. Let's see some of them:

- The new specification included MQTT over WebSocket.
- Client IDs were expanded from 23 bytes per client to 65,535 bytes.
- There is no need to wait for a CONNACK response from the broker. With this change, constrained devices can connect, publish, and disconnect.
- The client ID can be set to 0-byte length. This is used in anonymous client implementations.

- A new error in the MQTT SUBACK was added to notify clients about forbidden subscriptions.

- When a client connects to a broker with a persistent session, a flag is set in the CONNACK message to inform to the client that the broker already has information about it. This leads to more efficient communication.

Up till now, we have seen the main characteristics of MQTT 3.1.1. Let's now see what improvements are offered with MQTT 5.

MQTT 5

The main improvements that come with MQTT 5 are as follows:

- Better scalability support

- Improved error reporting

- More efficiency in small clients

- The adding of user properties

Let's look at these improvements in detail.

Header properties

One new feature in MQTT 5 is the properties in the MQTT header. You can assign **custom headers** for transporting metadata.

Reason codes

Another functionality added to MQTT is the **reason codes**. These codes help to determine the type of error that occurs in an MQTT communication.

Return codes

This new version also offers **return codes**. With these codes, the broker can inform clients what specific features it supports.

AUTH packet

MQTT 5 introduced the **AUTH packet**. This packet offers advanced authentication techniques, including **OAuth**. You can even re-authenticate a client without closing the current connection.

Connection termination

In MQTT 5, either the client or the broker can terminate the connection. In version 3.1.1, only the client could finish the communication.

QoS in MQTT 5

If you are working with reliable communication links, it's a good idea to omit the redelivery of MQTT messages. In MQTT 5, either the brokers or the clients don't send retransmissions unless TCP errors occur. This allows better use of QoS.

Payload format

Another interesting feature of MQTT 5 is the **payload format indicator**, which determines whether the payload is binary or text.

We have now explored the main innovations that MQTT 5 offers us. In the next section, you will learn how to use a cloud MQTT service.

MQTT clients

There are several free MQTT clients that you can use. Let's see three of them.

Mosquitto client

You can just use the MQTT client that comes with the Mosquitto broker. Whenever you install the Mosquitto broker, you also install the MQTT client.

For the full documentation, go to `https://mosquitto.org/documentation/`.

To run this client, you must run the `mosquitto_pub` or `mosquitto_sub` commands in the console.

In the following example, you can see how to publish and subscribe to a certain topic:

```
$ mosquitto_sub -h <ip address> -i <client-id-1> -u <user> -P
'<password>' -t topic
$ mosquitto_pub -h <ip address> -i <client-id-2> -u <user> -P
'<password>' -t topic -m "hello world"
```

In the first line, a client subscribes to a topic, using the IP address, default port (not specified), `user`, `password`, and `client-id`.

In the second line, a new client publishes the same topic. As soon as you publish a message, the client that is subscribed to the topic will receive the message.

MQTT Explorer

MQTT Explorer is a cool open source software developed by *Thomas Nordquist*. You can find it here: `http://mqtt-explorer.com`.

MQTT Explorer offers a graphical interface that makes it easy to configure connections and subscribe and publish to topics.

Among the features of this software, you can find the following:

- Visualize topics and activity.
- Delete retained topics.
- Publish topics.
- Plot numeric topics.
- View history of values.

You can see a screenshot of the client in the following figure:

Figure 3.2 – MQTT Explorer graphical interface

Let's see an MQTT client that you can run from your web browser.

MQTTLens

The third option is a Chrome extension. Due to that, you can run this client from your web browser, and it can be practical in many cases.

In the following screenshot, you can see the user interface of the application. One thing that makes it convenient is that you can connect simultaneously to different brokers and send and receive messages from all of them in the same interface:

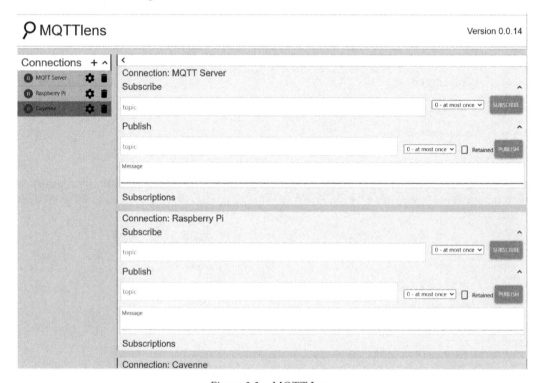

Figure 3.3 – MQTT Lens

In this section, you learned about the MQTT protocol, its different versions, and its capabilities. You also learned about MQTT clients and how to use them.

In the next section, you will learn how to use two online MQTT brokers.

Using an online MQTT broker

There are many online MQTT brokers available out there. We will see two options: **Mosquitto** and **HiveMQ**.

These two MQTT services offer a free layer to make tests and proofs of concept. Let's see each of them.

Mosquitto

As you can guess, this MQTT broker is based on the Eclipse Mosquitto MQTT server/broker. You can find information about this broker here: `https://test.mosquitto.org`.

This MQTT broker should be used just for testing purposes. It is offered as a service for the community and sometimes can run experimental code. In this way, either the testers or the developers can benefit from its use.

The server listens on the following ports:

- `1883`: MQTT, unencrypted, unauthenticated
- `1884`: MQTT, unencrypted, authenticated
- `8883`: MQTT, encrypted, unauthenticated
- `8884`: MQTT, encrypted, client certificate required
- `8885`: MQTT, encrypted, authenticated
- `8886`: MQTT, encrypted, unauthenticated
- `8887`: MQTT, encrypted, server certificate deliberately expired
- `8080`: MQTT over WebSocket, unencrypted, unauthenticated
- `8081`: MQTT over WebSocket, encrypted, unauthenticated
- `8090`: MQTT over WebSocket, unencrypted, authenticated
- `8091`: MQTT over WebSocket, encrypted, authenticated

You can use encrypted communications with TLS v1.3, v1.2, or v1.1. If you use ports `8883` or `8884`, you will have to use the certificate provided on the website.

In ports `8081` and `8086`, there is a *Let's Encrypt* certificate that you can use with your system CA certificates.

Port `8884` requires a client certificate, which you can generate here: `https://test.mosquitto.org/ssl`.

As regards authentication, you will have to use the following credentials:

- Username: `rw`/password: `readwrite`: Read/write access to the # topic hierarchy
- Username: `ro`/password: `readonly`: Read-only access to the # topic hierarchy
- Username: `wo`/password: `writeonly`: Write-only access to the # topic hierarchy

HiveMQ

HiveMQ is a well-known MQTT service provider. It has a free tier that you can use for unlimited time.

This free layer offers up to 100 MQTT devices and 10 GB of data transfer per month. These quantities are enough for most IoT applications.

Unlike the community Mosquitto broker of the previous section, you can use this service in production environments.

In other words, you can have your IoT system with up to 100 devices running in the HiveMQ cloud. Not bad!

To find out the details about the services and plans, please visit `https://www.hivemq.com/mqtt-cloud-broker`.

Once you register, you will have to choose a service option (see the following figure):

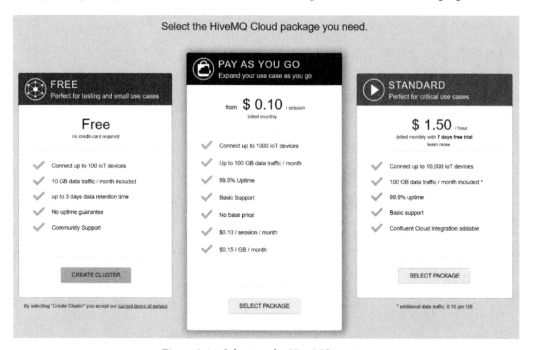

Figure 3.4 – Selecting the HiveMQ service

To create the cluster, you will have to choose what cloud service you want to use. There are two options: AWS and Azure.

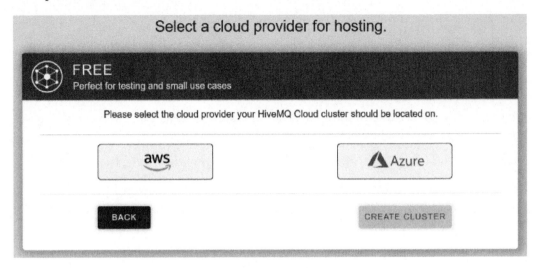

Figure 3.5 – Choosing the cloud

Whenever you create the cluster, you will be able to manage it as follows:

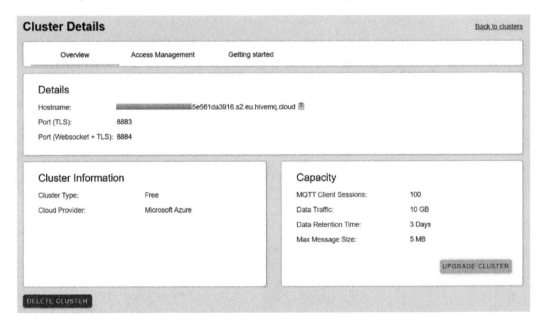

Figure 3.6 – Cluster details

On the **Cluster Details** page, you can see some information about your cluster.

The first line shows the hostname – that is, the address of your MQTT broker instance. It is the address that you will have to point to your MQTT client.

The second line shows the TCP (TLS) port, in this case, 8883. This is the TCP port that you will have to enter in your MQTT client.

The third line shows the TCP port if you are using WebSocket to connect to the broker.

Then, you have some cluster information. In this case, the cluster type is **Free**, because we are using a free service. The cloud provider is Microsoft Azure.

Finally, you have some details about the resources of your cluster in the **Capacity** box.

Then, you will have to create user credentials, as shown in the following figure:

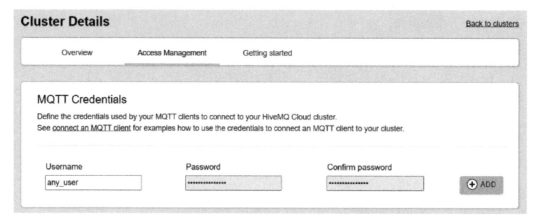

Figure 3.7 – Creating user credentials

Finally, you will be able to connect to the MQTT service using a client. In the following screenshot, you can see the MQTT Explorer example:

Figure 3.8 – Testing connection with MQTT Explorer

You have learned how to use cloud MQTT services. In the next section, you will install your MQTT broker on an Ubuntu server.

Running your MQTT broker

In this section, you will learn how to install Mosquitto in Debian systems such as Ubuntu or Raspberry Pi.

As usual, you should update the packages, as follows:

```
$ sudo apt-get update && sudo apt-get upgrade -y
```

After that, you can install the Mosquitto broker and client from the packages:

```
$ sudo apt-get install mosquitto mosquitto-clients
```

Once you have installed Mosquitto, you can configure it according to your needs.

The main configuration file of Mosquitto is in the /etc/mosquitto/ and /etc/mosquitto/conf.d directories.

Looking into `mosquitto.conf`, you will see something like this:

```
# Place your local configuration in /etc/mosquitto/conf.d/
#
# A full description of the configuration file is at
# /usr/share/doc/mosquitto/examples/mosquitto.conf.example
pid_file /var/run/mosquitto.pid
persistence true
persistence_location /var/lib/mosquitto/
log_dest file /var/log/mosquitto/mosquitto.log
include_dir /etc/mosquitto/conf.d
```

Any option not specified in the configuration file takes its default value.

You can find an example configuration file in the `/usr/share/doc/mosquitto/examples/` directory.

In Raspberry Pi OS, the configuration sample file is in a compressed file (`mosquitto.conf.gz`). You can unzip it with the following:

```
$ gunzip mosquitto.conf.gz
```

Once you decompress it, you will find four files. The one you are looking for is `mosquitto.conf`.

In Ubuntu systems, the file is not compressed.

You can explore the file with any text editor.

One of the configuration options is the TCP port. By default, it is `1883`.

Another basic option is the interface listener. By default, the broker listens in all interfaces, but you can configure a specific one (for example, `192.168.0.1`).

You can explore all the configuration options and set them according to your needs.

To add a basic security functionality, you can set a username and a password with the following command:

```
$ sudo mosquitto_passwd -c /etc/mosquitto/pwfile your_user
```

Here, `your_user` is the username.

After you execute this command, a prompt will ask you to ingress the password twice.

Now, you can test your MQTT broker with any client, as we have seen in previous sections.

In this section, you learned how to install and perform a basic configuration of an MQTT broker in a Debian system. In the next section, you will see how to send data through HTTP.

Sending data through HTTP

HyperText Transfer Protocol (**HTTP**) is one of the foundation protocols of the internet. It has delivered us the World Wide Web since its creation.

Naturally, now it is one of the protocols used to communicate with IoT platforms.

HTTP works in a client-server architecture over TCP connections. By default, HTTP uses port 80 for listening to requests, but you can configure other TCP ports to run your web server.

The three main characteristics of HTTP are as follows:

- **Connectionless**: When a browser starts an HTTP request, wait for a response from the HTTP server. After the server processes the request, send a response to the client. Then, the connection ends, and all session data vanishes. The next time the client and server connect, they will start again from 0.

- **Media independent**: Different types of data can be transferred between the client and server, from text to media, or even binary files.

- **Stateless**: This is related to the connectionless feature. After the end of a connection, the server and the client discard all the associated data. So, none of them keep information from previous connections.

Now, let's take a look at HTTP methods.

HTTP methods

The methods implemented in HTTP are the following:

- **GET**: Asks to get a resource from a specified **Unified Resource Identifier** (**URI**).
- **POST**: Sends the body data to the server. It can be text, file, and so on.
- **HEAD**: This is the same as GET, but only transfers the header section and the status.
- **PUT**: This method replaces the data in the server (at the specific URI) with the data sent in the body.

- **DELETE**: Removes all the current data in the resource given by the URI.
- **CONNECT**: Establishes a connection with the server for a specific URI.
- **OPTIONS**: Describes the connection options for the URI.
- **TRACE**: Asks for the loopback of the request, for testing.

Now, let's take a look at HTTPS.

HTTPS

HyperText Transfer Protocol Secure (HTTPS) adds a layer of security to HTTP. It uses **Transport Layer Security (TLS**, previously **Secure Sockets Layer (SSL)**) to encrypt the data.

HTTPS delivers **authentication**, **privacy**, and **integrity**, the three aspects of communications security.

By default, HTTPS uses TCP port 443, although you can specify another port in your web server.

The security of HTTPS depends entirely on TLS, which uses public and private keys for generating short-term session keys. It also uses certificates that can authenticate both the server and the client (in this case, the IoT device).

The keys and certificates should be different for each IoT device to obtain a good level of security. It is hard work, but it prevents hackers from using the credentials from compromised devices.

HTTP use case

There are endless IoT platforms where you can use HTTP requests for communicating with your IoT devices.

But in this book, you will learn about one that is very easy to use. It is `https://dweet.io`.

One interesting thing about **dweet** is that you don't even need an IoT device to test it. Instead, you can just point your web browser to a URI.

You can, for example, send IoT data, as follows:

```
https://dweet.io/dweet/for/your_sensor_
name?temperature=25&humidity=40
```

Then, to get the data published, you only have to point to the following:

```
https://dweet.io/get/latest/dweet/for/your_sensor_name
```

You will get the following:

```
{"this":"succeeded","by":"getting","the":"dweets","with":
[{"thing":"your_sensor_name","created":"2021-09-14T20:43:32.
752Z","content":{"temperature":25,"humidity":40}}]}
```

Nice! This is a very simple use of HTTP requests. You can add data retention, authentication, and other functionalities as well.

In this section, you learned about HTTP protocol and how it can be used to communicate with IoT devices. In the next section, you will learn about CoAP, a very specific protocol for IoT.

What is CoAP?

Constrained Application Protocol (**CoAP**), as its name implies, is tailored to run in constrained devices, such as microcontrollers.

Let's see some characteristics:

- It runs on UDP.
- It has low header overhead and parsing complexity.
- Its packets are much smaller than HTTP.
- It has asynchronous message exchanges.
- It allows UPD broadcast and multicast.
- It has UIR and content-type support.
- It uses methods like HTTP: GET, PUT, POST, and DELETE.
- CoAP can interact with HTTP using proxies.
- It has low resource and power consumption.

Although CoAP uses UDP, it allows requesting confirmation packets. Any request or response message can be tagged as confirmable or nonconfirmable. If the receiver gets a message tagged as confirmable, it will send an ack to the sender. On the other hand, if the message is tagged as nonconfirmable, it will not send any ACK message. CoAP packets are transported over UDP, so you can't use SSL/TLS to provide security. However, it accepts **Datagram Transport Layer Security** (**DTLS**), which provides the same functionality as TLS.

This protocol is generally even more efficient than MQTT from an energy consumption point of view. This is because CoAP uses UDP packets and avoids the TCP handshake, which requires a longer connection.

In this section, you met CoAP, a protocol designed to be very efficient. In the next section, you will learn about WebSocket.

What about WebSocket?

WebSocket takes the best of both worlds: HTTP and persistent connections.

It uses a handshake to establish communication.

The connection starts with an HTTP GET from the client. In the request, the client specifies an upgrade to WebSocket. You can see this in the following example:

```
GET /chat HTTP/1.1
Host: server.example.com
Upgrade: websocket
Connection: Upgrade
Sec-WebSocket-Key: dGhlIHNhbXBsZSBub25jZQ==
Origin: http://example.com
Sec-WebSocket-Protocol: chat, superchat
Sec-WebSocket-Version: 13
```

After the request from the client, the server can accept it, as follows:

```
HTTP/1.1 101 Switching Protocols
Upgrade: websocket
Connection: Upgrade
Sec-WebSocket-Accept: s3pPLMBiTxaQ9kYGzzhZRbK+xOo=
Sec-WebSocket-Protocol: chat
```

Then, the client and the server can start to exchange data until one of them decides to close the connection.

As you can see, unlike HTTP, WebSocket allows exchanging data without the need to open and close the connection for each transfer (see *Figure 3.9*). This reduces the overhead produced by the protocol:

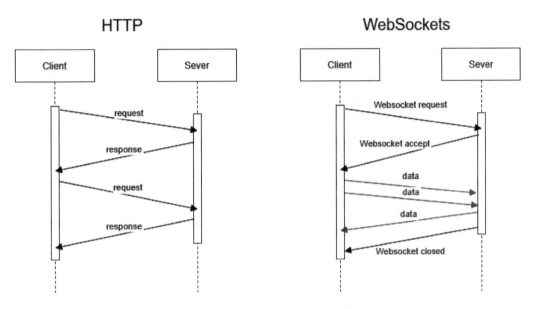

Figure 3.9 – Comparison of HTTP and WebSocket

WebSocket is useful in combination with other protocols. HiveMQ, for example, uses it to encapsulate MQTT sessions. So, any web browser can act as an MQTT client.

In this section, you learned the concepts behind WebSocket and why it can help to transfer data from IoT devices. In the next section, we will evaluate some aspects of choosing the right protocol for an IoT device.

How to select the right IoT protocol

The selection of the right protocol for your IoT device depends on several factors, as follows:

- **Type of communication technology**: Ethernet, cellular, Wi-Fi, BLE, and so on
- **Type of electrical power supply**: Mains, battery, energy harvesting, or any combination of them
- **Electrical consumption**

- **Type of data transferred**: Sensor values, images, sound, video, and so on
- Latency expected
- **Type of application**: Remote sensing, real time, smart building, industrial, and so on

Let's explore some examples.

If you have a wired connection, power usage is generally not a problem. Maybe you are using **Power over Ethernet** (**PoE**) to feed your IoT device, or you feed it directly from the mains.

In this case, you have high power and high bandwidth available. This type of device can be, for example, a network camera, a smart **Power Distribution Unit** (**PDU**), or a wired sensor, to name a few.

In this case, you can use HTTP or WebSocket to transfer data in a reliable and secure way.

Now imagine a wireless sensor and feed it from a little battery. You will try to extend the battery life as long as you can. In this case, you should choose light protocols, such as MQTT or CoAP.

So, to choose the right protocol for your IoT device, you will have to address the specific requirements of your application.

In this section, you explored some conditions to choose the most convenient IoT protocol.

It is a two-way road: applications define protocols and protocols define applications. MQTT is not a good protocol for sending images, but it is better than HTTP for sending sensor values.

Summary

In this chapter, we have seen how IoT devices can send the data that they collect.

We explored the main protocols used to communicate with IoT devices: MQTT, HTTP, CoAP, and WebSocket. You learned about their characteristics, advantages, and challenges. Also, you saw how you can implement them using libraries and software.

Finally, we analyzed the factors that can lead to selecting one protocol or another.

With what you have learned in this chapter, you will be able to select the right protocol for your device and implement it in your IoT system.

In the next chapter, you will learn about different types of data sources that you can use in Grafana.

4

Data Sources for Grafana

In this chapter, you will learn about the various data sources that you can use in Grafana. You will also learn about data concepts that are used in these data sources.

Grafana accepts different types of data sources, but we will focus mainly on **NoSQL databases** and, specifically, on **time series databases** (**TSDBs**). Also, you will learn how to feed Grafana with Excel, CSV files, and live data.

The main topics of this chapter are as follows:

- What is a data source?
- SQL versus NoSQL databases.
- What are TSDBs?
- Google Sheets and CSV files.
- How to use live data.

Data is the cornerstone of any **Internet of Things** (**IoT**) platform. A data source, as its name implies, is the origin of all the data that Grafana uses. So, this is a very important subject for understanding the upcoming chapters.

Let's see the meaning of data sources in the context of Grafana.

What is a data source?

A data source is just a resource that Grafana uses to obtain the data.

Then, Grafana uses this data to perform visualizations, transformations, and analytics. You can control every aspect of this process from the web interface of Grafana.

So, data sources are data repositories that Grafana can access through its API.

There are different types of data sources, and the list is always growing. To connect to the data sources, Grafana uses plugins (we will see how to connect to data sources in *Part 3*).

Let's see some data sources available to use with Grafana:

- **MySQL**
- **MongoDB**
- **Graphite**
- **InfluxDB**
- **OpenTSDB**
- **PostgreSQL**
- **Elasticsearch**
- **Azure Monitor**
- **Prometheus**
- **Loki**
- **Test data**
- **CSV files** and **Excel files**

This is just a short list of data sources. You can find all the available data sources at `https://grafana.com/grafana/plugins/?type=datasource`.

To navigate and explore the data source plugins installed on your Grafana instance, you can go to **Configuration | Data source** in the left menu and click on **Add data source**. You can see an example in the following figure:

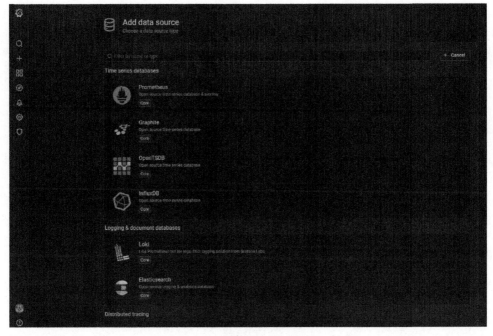

Figure 4.1 – Adding a data source

In the next section, you will learn about **Standard Query Language** (**SQL**) and NoSQL databases and how they differentiate.

SQL versus NoSQL databases

In this section, we will explore these two types of databases and define their characteristics and differences. Learning about databases is crucial to understanding how to manage, query, and process data in the context of Grafana.

Let's start with **SQL databases**.

SQL databases

This type of database was invented in the 1970s, and it is widely used today.

A **relational database management system** (**RDBMS**) is a system that manages data according to a relational model. This type of database represents data in tables, where each of the rows has a unique ID, called an **index** or **ID**. This field serves to relate the information among the tables.

Imagine you have a user database for accessing a web application. One table can store all the information that belongs to a specific user. Another table can have the permissions granted to each user. In this case, the user ID is the link between both tables. So, you can relate each user with the corresponding access policies.

This type of database is the best option for well-structured data, such as customer information, sales data, flight schedules, student notes, and so on. Relational databases offer rigid but simple and reliable data management.

SQL

Whenever a database is called a SQL database, it refers to a relational database.

SQL is the language that developers use to manage data of relational databases. It offers a clean and easy way to interact with the data stored in a relational database. However, we will see that you can use it in combination with NoSQL databases, such as TSDBs.

Let's see some basic SQL commands:

```
SELECT - extracts data from a database
UPDATE - updates data in a database
DELETE - deletes data from a database
CREATE DATABASE - creates a new database
ALTER DATABASE - modifies a database
CREATE TABLE - creates a new table
CREATE INDEX - creates an index (search key)
INSERT INTO - inserts new data into a database
ALTER TABLE - modifies a table
DROP TABLE - deletes a table
DROP INDEX - deletes an index
```

In the following, you can see a typical SQL command to extract data from a database:

```
SELECT column1, column2, column3
FROM table_name
WHERE condition;
```

Here, `column1`, `column2`, and `column3` are the data that you want to obtain from the `table_name` table when the condition is satisfied.

Let's see an example of a SQL query.

Imagine that you have a database of IoT devices. These devices belong to different customers and are deployed across several sites.

Some fields (columns) of the database are `customer`, `device_location`, `serial_number`, and `type_of_sensor`.

If you want to know what sensors belong to a customer within a geographic area, you can use the following query:

```
SELECT serial_number, type_of_sensor
FROM devices
WHERE customer="your customer" AND device_location="site of
interest"
```

As you can see, SQL is very natural and easy to understand, yet powerful and efficient.

These are some of the SQL databases that you can use with Grafana:

- **Microsoft SQL Server (MSSQL)**
- **MySQL**
- **PostgreSQL**
- **SQLite**
- **Oracle Database (Enterprise Grafana version)**

In the next section, you will learn about NoSQL databases, and why they are a good choice for many IoT uses.

What are NoSQL databases

As you have seen in the previous section, relational databases and SQL are the right choices for well-structured data. However, in the IoT world, you will find that most of the data is not structured and not standardized.

For example, an IoT solution can have devices from different vendors. In this case, you will find that the data is delivered in incompatible formats. This leads to making the construction of a database table impracticable with fixed fields and types.

Let's see some examples.

Imagine that you have two sensors from different vendors. Suppose that both devices use JSON formatting for sending the data. However, the data they send is not the same. They even use different keys to represent the same data. On the other hand, one sensor provides data that is not delivered from the other.

You can see an example of this case in the following code:

```
##Sensor 1
{
     "sensor_type": "temperature",
     "reading": 25,
     "unit": "celsius",
     "serial_number": "a095cd87daf0"
}


##Sensor 2
{
     "sensor": "temp",
     "value": 31,
     "serial": "BD0159FF45",
     "location": [{"Country":"Argentina"}, {"State":"Capital"},
{"City":"Buenos Aires"}],
     "site": [{"latitude":-34.55937615855352},
{"longitude":-58.434491456032056}]
}
```

In a worst-case scenario, think about sensors that use different data formats. One could use JSON and the other XML or YAML. The management of such dissimilar data is a challenge that is hard to solve with relational databases.

Let's see how it looks for data from sensor 2 in XML format:

```
<?xml version="1.0" encoding="UTF-8"?>
<root>
   <location>
      <element>
         <Country>Argentina</Country>
      </element>
      <element>
         <State>Capital</State>
      </element>
      <element>
         <City>Buenos Aires</City>
      </element>
```

```
    </location>
    <sensor>temp</sensor>
    <serial>BD0159FF45</serial>
    <site>
        <element>
            <latitude>-34.559376</latitude>
        </element>
        <element>
            <longitude>-58.43449</longitude>
        </element>
    </site>
    <value>31</value>
</root>
```

By the way, you can play with data conversion using online converters, such as the ones provided at `https://www.freeformatter.com/`.

Anyway, converting data from one format to another is easy, but managing that data is a bigger problem.

Another drawback of using SQL databases is related to the type of data. Some types of data don't fit smoothly in relational databases.

Imagine geographical location coordinates. There is no easy method to get information from a geographic area using SQL commands. With NoSQL databases, you can even define areas to explore data conveniently.

Another example is when you want to get data from a specific period. There is no way of doing this in a relational database unless you have a field with timestamp data. This is solved naturally by the TSDB that we will see in the next section.

These are some of the NoSQL databases that you can use with Grafana:

- **MongoDB (Enterprise Grafana version)**
- **InfluxDB**
- **OpenTSDB**
- **ElastichSearch**
- **OpenSearch**

- **Apache Cassandra**

- **Prometheus**

- **Graphite**

Now, let's take a look at TSDBs.

What are TSDBs?

Every single IoT device out there is sending data to some IoT platform. As we have discussed in the previous section, this data can come in different types and formats. However, all this data shares one thing in common: the timestamp.

The timestamp is as valuable as the data itself. Each data point is associated with timestamp information, so you can see when it was created. Knowing every data point timestamp allows you to order the information and build a historical trend. Then, you can visualize it, run analytics on it, perform transformations, and so on. You can see an example in the following figure:

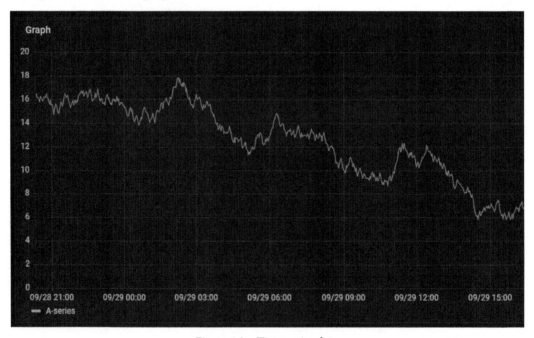

Figure 4.2 – Time series data

Although the previous discussion can seem a little obvious, it reveals the critical value of the timestamp in IoT applications.

A TSDB allows you to manage time-related data by just performing simple queries. Every record in the database is associated with a timestamp. So, you can obtain only the data that you need.

TSDB is a type of NoSQL database, and it is commonly used in IoT applications. TSDBs are tailored to store and manage large amounts of time series data and perform efficient real-time analysis.

In the next chapter, we will see two options in TSDB: **InfluxDB** and **OpenTSDB**.

Google Sheets and CSV files

Grafana not only allows you to connect to databases, but it also admits parsing files and cloud services, such as CSV files and Google Sheets.

In simple IoT applications, you may find that data is being saved in Google Sheets or text files. Also, you could have data stored on SD cards or in old files.

So, you can have either living data ingressing in a cloud spreadsheet or historical data stored in the cloud or local files.

In any case, you may want to build a dashboard with this information to analyze it or even show it to other people.

Google Sheets data source

Although you will see how to manage and install plugins in *Chapter 7, Managing Plugins*, let's see how to install the Google Sheets plugin.

You have two options: **local installation** and **cloud installation**.

Local installation

The Google Sheets plugin doesn't come by default with Grafana, so you have to install it.

In a local instance, you will have to use the **command-line interface** (**CLI**) tool, `grafana-cli`. You will be able to install the plugin by executing the following command in the console:

```
$ sudo grafana-cli plugins install grafana-googlesheets-
  datasource
```

The plugins are installed in the `/var/lib/grafana/plugins` Grafana plugins directory by default.

After the installation, you will have to restart Grafana for the change to take effect. Then, you will find the data source in the data source section of your instance.

> **Important Note**
>
> There is no version of this plugin to run on **Advanced RISC Machine (ARM)** devices. So, you will not be able to use it on a Raspberry Pi. However, you can install it on any AMD64 compatible system, including Windows, Linux, and Darwin.

Let's see now how to install the plugin in the Grafana Cloud instance.

Cloud installation

To install the plugin in your Cloud instance, you will need first to start it.

Then, you must go to the following URL and click on the **Install plugin** button, as you can see in *Figure 4.3*:

```
https://grafana.com/grafana/plugins/grafana-googlesheets-
datasource/?tab=installation
```

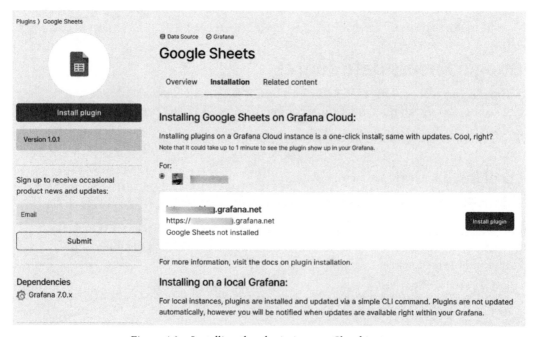

Figure 4.3 – Installing the plugin in your Cloud instance

Now, let's see how to connect the data source to the Google Sheets service.

Connecting to Google Sheets

Once you have installed the plugin, you will have to select it to configure it, as shown in the following figure:

Figure 4.4 – Selecting the Google Sheets plugin

There are two methods for accessing a Google Sheet, one for public spreadsheets and another for private spreadsheets.

Accessing public Google Sheets

If you want to get data from a public Google Sheet, you can use the API key method.

To interact with the Google Sheets API, you will have to have a Google Developer Profile. If you don't have one, you can easily create one with your Google user.

Then, you will have to follow these steps:

1. Go to the **Credentials** page in the Google API console using the following URL and enable the API: `https://console.cloud.google.com/apis/api/sheets.googleapis.com/`.

2. Click on **CREATE CREDENTIALS** (see *Figure 4.5*): `https://console.cloud.google.com/apis/credentials`.

3. Click on **API key**.

4.   Go to Grafana and ingress the key in the **API key** field on the plugin settings page.

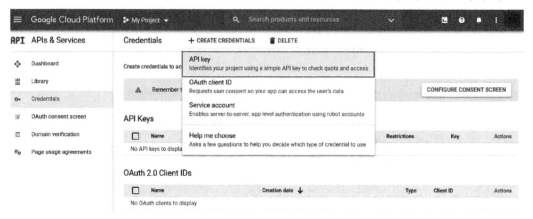

Figure 4.5 – API key generation

Once you have generated the key, you have to ingress it into the plugin **Settings** page, as you can see in the following figure:

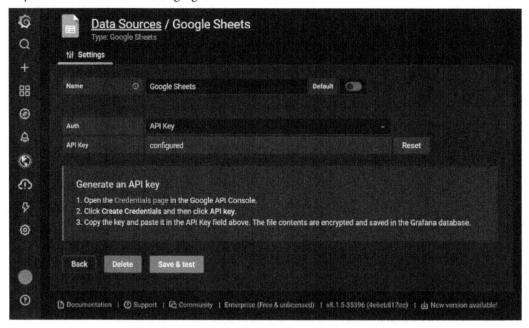

Figure 4.6 – Google Sheets data source configuration

Now, go to your Google Sheet and make it publicly available. Copy the link and allow any person with the link to read the data.

Now, return to Grafana and create a dashboard. Then, add a panel and use the Google Sheets data source for feeding the data. Also, take into account that you must enable your API at `https://console.cloud.google.com/apis/library/sheets.googleapis.com`. To do this, click on the **Manage** button and then on the **Enable API** button.

> **Important Note**
>
> The sheet must be a Google Sheet. Otherwise, it will not work. Take this into account and verify that you are not using another kind of spreadsheet, such as MS Excel or **Open Document Spreadsheet (ODS)**.

In the following figure, you can see a dashboard created from a Google Sheet. It shows environmental variables from historic weather data:

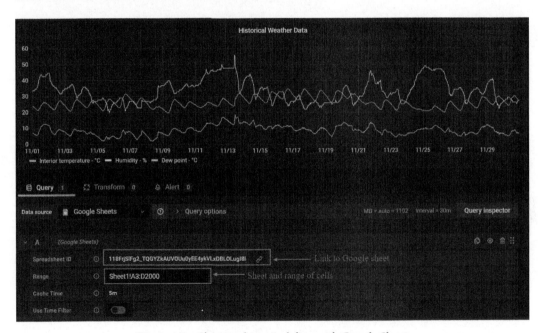

Figure 4.7 – Showing historical data with Google Sheets

Let's see how you can access private or protected Google Sheets.

Accessing private Google Sheets

If you need to get data from private Google Sheets, you will have to use a key JSON file. Let's see how to configure the plugin:

1. First, you have to open the **Credentials** page in the Google API console.

2. Then, click **CREATE CREDENTIALS** and **Service account**, as you can see in the following figure:

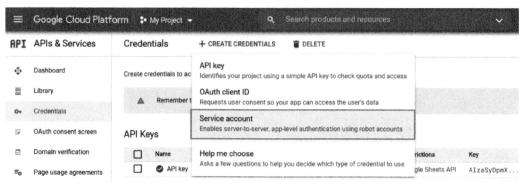

Figure 4.8 – Creating Service account credentials

3. On the **Service account** page, fill in the details for **Service account name** and **Service account ID** (you can use any name and ID). Ignore the service account permissions.

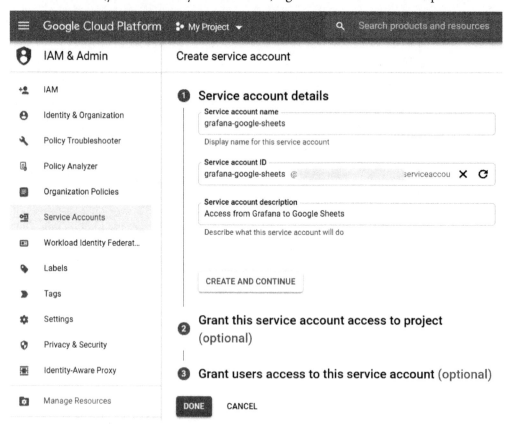

Figure 4.9 – Creating a service account

4. Now, go to the **KEYS** tab and create a JSON key, as you can see in the following figure:

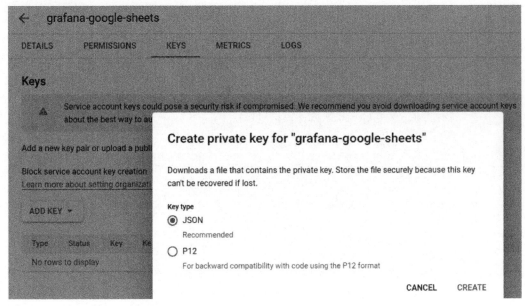

Figure 4.10 – Creating a private key

5. Open Google Sheets in the API library and enable access for your account. You can find the page at `https://console.cloud.google.com/apis/library/sheets.googleapis.com?q=sheet`.

6. Then, open Google Drive in the API library and enable access here too. In this way, you will have access to all the spreadsheets that you have in your Drive.

7. Change the authorization type to Google **JSON Web Token (JWT)** and drag and drop the JSON file to the dotted area in the Google Sheets data source configuration page.

8. Then, press **Save & test** to verify your settings.

9. Finally, you will have to share the Google spreadsheet with the email account generated in *step 3*. This procedure is identical to sharing the file with any Gmail user.

10. You will then be able to access the data of the spreadsheet, as you can see in the following figure:

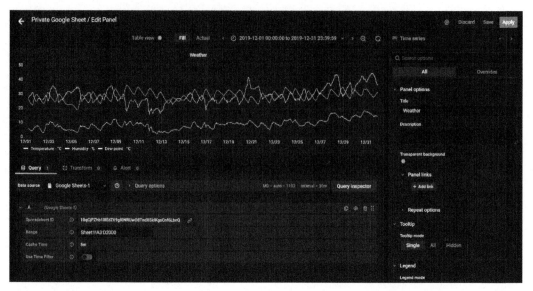

Figure 4.11 – Showing data from private Google Sheets

Besides cloud file services, you can use local files, as you will see next.

Using files as data sources

Currently, there are two plugins available for using files as data sources: **CSV** and **Infinity**. You can find the plugins at the following links:

- https://grafana.com/grafana/plugins/marcusolsson-csv-datasource/

- https://grafana.com/grafana/plugins/yesoreyeram-infinity-datasource/

With CSV, you can import just CSV files, whereas Infinity allows importing JSON, CSV, XML, GraphQL, and HTML.

Given that Infinity has many file options, let's see how to use it.

For installing in a local instance, run the following command:

```
$ grafana-cli plugins install yesoreyeram-infinity-datasource
```

If you want to install it in a Grafana Cloud instance, follow the same procedure as with the Google Sheets plugin.

Now, go to **Configuration | Data sources** and click on **Add data source**.

Then, select the Infinity plugin, as shown in the following figure:

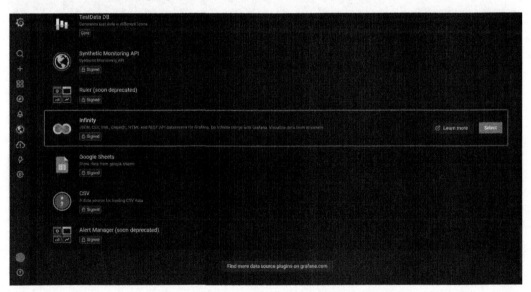

Figure 4.12 – Selecting the Infinity data source

After creating the data source instance, you can look at the configuration:

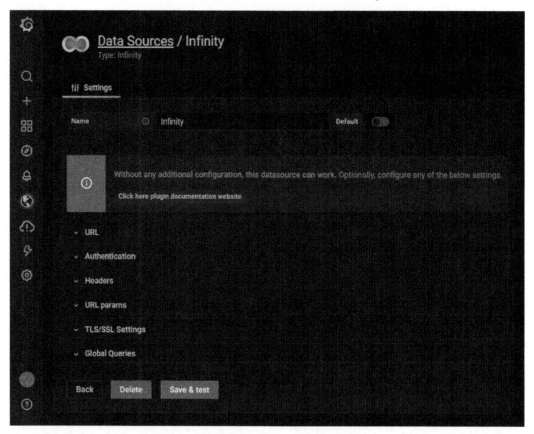

Figure 4.13 – Configuration settings of Infinity

This plugin works out of the box, but you can specify any setting that you need here. All these configurations will be applied to all the queries that use this data source instance. If you need different configuration settings, you will have to create more instances of this data source.

You can get datasets from `https://www.kaggle.com/datasets?search=iot` to experiment.

You can use this plugin to access remote data or simply copy the data in the dialog box of the query interface. Let's see an example of reading a remote CSV file, as shown in the following figure:

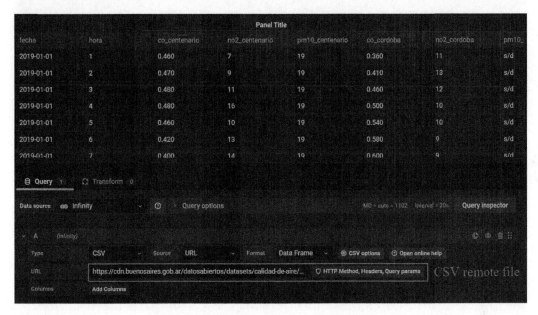

Figure 4.14 – Showing remote CSV data

In this case, you can see data published by the **Environmental Protection Agency (APA)** of the city of Buenos Aires about air contamination. You can obtain these datasets from `https://data.buenosaires.gob.ar/dataset/calidad-aire`.

In the next example, you can see how Grafana shows the data of the sensor example used earlier in this chapter:

Figure 4.15 – Showing JSON data locally

Beyond these examples, you can use any panel to show the data in different ways. You will have to match the data format with the required fields and types in the panel. Also, take into account that, sometimes, you will need to change panel options for showing the correct data units and data format.

Until now, we have seen how to get data from stored data sources. In the following sections, you will see how to send live data to Grafana.

How to use live data

Using live data is a must in any IoT project. Fortunately, Grafana allows using live data since version *8.0*. It uses **WebSocket** connections to exchange data in a quasi-real-time way.

This feature is enabled by default, with a maximum number of simultaneous connections of 100. WebSocket is a resource-intense protocol so it has to be used carefully. If you want to extend this feature to more clients, take into account the availability of resources (CPU and memory).

As we have seen in *Chapter 3, Connecting IoT Devices*, WebSocket initiates with an HTTP request, followed by an upgrade request. Then, the HTTP session remains open and data is exchanged between client and server using the WebSocket connection.

Features

Currently, Grafana supports the following features:

- It processes data as soon as it arrives. Instead of polling data from data sources at a specified polling period, it can manage asynchronous data in real-time.

- Whenever a dashboard changes, it is updated on all connected devices.

- Backend data source plugins can send data to frontend panels.

- You can send data to Grafana panels from Telegraf. The data sent from Telegraf arrives in Influx format, and Grafana converts it and sends it to channels.

Let's see how you can use live channels in Grafana.

Live channels

There are currently two types of channels, depending on the origin of the data: **data source backends** and via **PUSH endpoints (HTTP and WebSockets)**. One system that uses the second method is Telegraf.

Data source plugins

For data source plugin channels, Grafana uses a channel structure as follows:

```
ds/<DATASOURCE_UID>/<CUSTOM_PATH>
```

Where `ds` is the scope, `DATASOURCE_UID` is the channel ID, and `CUSTOM_PATH` is the path specified by the data source plugin.

Grafana creates `DATASOURCE_UID` at the moment of the data source creation.

The plugin developer specifies `CUSTOM_PATH`, which the plugin will use to publish the data.

You can see a live data example creating a dashboard and selecting Grafana as the data source. Then, you can choose **Live Measurements** and some of the available channels. You can see an example in the following figure:

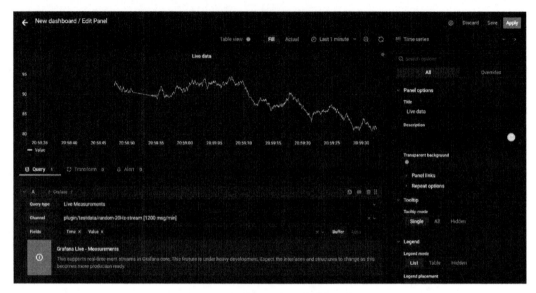

Figure 4.16 – Live data dashboard

Telegraf

You can use the PUSH feature from a Telegraf instance.

According to its GitHub repository, Telegraf is an agent for collecting, processing, aggregating, and writing metrics. It has been developed by **InfluxData** and it belongs to the **InfluxDB TICK Stack**, a platform to collect, store, visualize, and act on time series data.

Grafana accepts metrics data in Influx format at /api/live/push/:streamId.

Whenever Grafana receives data, it publishes it on stream/custom_stream_id/ measurement.

Where the stream scope is constant, custom_stream_id is the end of the API URL of Telegraf in this case, and measurement is the name of a measurement.

Let's see some considerations for using live data in Grafana.

Origin check

Grafana uses a mechanism to avoid the hijacking of WebSocket connections. To achieve this, Grafana checks the `Origin` request header that the client is using in the HTTP `Upgrade` request.

The default value of the `Origin` header matches `root_url` (public Grafana URL).

You can add other origins using the `allowed_origins` option in the configuration.

Use of resources

Each WebSocket connection consumes resources. You can take 50 KB of memory by connection as a rule of thumb.

Guessing CPU usage is not so easy, because it depends on the utilization of Grafana Live.

Maximum number of connections

Each new WebSocket connection uses a file descriptor. The number of file descriptors in operating systems is limited. Remember the default limit of 100 simultaneous connections that was mentioned before.

In an Ubuntu system, you can view the limit for a process with the following:

```
$ sudo cat /proc/<PROCESS_PID>/limits
```

The number of open files limit represents approximately how many connections you can manage in your server.

Summary

In this chapter, you have met Grafana data sources. We have explored the different types of data sources that you can use in Grafana. We have addressed some database concepts, and you have learned the difference between SQL and NoSQL databases. Finally, you have learned how to use files as data sources, from the cloud and locally. In the next chapter, you will learn about TSDBs.

5

Using Time Series Databases

Time series databases (TSDBs) are a must in any **Internet of Things (IoT)** platform. As we have seen in *Chapter 4, Data Sources for Grafana*, we need a way to store data from IoT devices.

IoT data is inherently associated with time because every measurement occurs at a specific time. So, we have a timestamp for each measurement.

The TSDB allows storing, managing, and querying time-series data easily.

Let's start learning how to install and configure an InfluxDB instance.

In this chapter, you will see the following topics:

- Installing and configuring InfluxDB
- Creating and managing an InfluxDB database
- Installing OpenTSDB
- Writing data in OpenTSDB

This chapter is a fundamental piece of this book because we will use TSDBs for building dashboards and performing analytics over the next chapters.

Installing and configuring InfluxDB

In this section, you will learn how to install and configure an **InfluxDB** instance. Also, you will learn the main concepts in InfluxDB databases.

Let's start with the installation process.

Installing InfluxDB

The following procedure is valid for any 64-bit **Debian systems**, such as **Ubuntu** and **Raspberry Pi OS** (previously **Raspbian**).

> **Important Note**
>
> Along with this chapter, we will be using InfluxDB version 2.0. Unlike the 1.x version, which was available for 32- and 64-bit systems, this version only supports 64-bit OSes. So, you will not be able to run on 32-bit systems, such as the Raspberry Pi 3. Instead, you can use a Raspberry Pi 4 or 400 with a 64-bit Ubuntu Server installed.

Before starting any installation, it is recommended to update the system:

```
$ sudo apt-get update && sudo apt-get upgrade -y
```

Now, let's download the correct version for your installation:

```
$ wget https://dl.influxdata.com/influxdb/releases/influxdb2-
2.x.x-xxx.deb
```

The x character indicates the version and the platform where you are going to install InfluxDB.

You can find a complete list at the following link: `https://portal.influxdata.com/downloads/`. In this page, you will also find alternative ways to install InfluxDB.

Now that you have downloaded the package, you can install it in your system:

```
$ sudo dpkg -i influxdb2_2.x.x_xxx.deb
```

After completing the installation, you can start the service with the following command:

```
$ sudo service influxdb start
```

And, you can check the service is running by executing the following:

```
$ sudo service influxdb status
```

Then, you will get information similar to the following screenshot:

```
ubuntu@primary:~$ sudo service influxdb start
ubuntu@primary:~$ sudo service influxdb status
 influxdb.service - InfluxDB is an open-source, distributed, time series database
   Loaded: loaded (/lib/systemd/system/influxdb.service; enabled; vendor preset: enabled)
   Active: active (running) since Thu 2021-10-14 15:29:54 -03; 2s ago
     Docs: https://docs.influxdata.com/influxdb/
  Process: 15304 ExecStart=/usr/lib/influxdb/scripts/influxd-systemd-start.sh (code=exited, status=0/SUCCESS)
 Main PID: 15305 (influxd)
    Tasks: 8 (limit: 1059)
   Memory: 57.6M
   CGroup: /system.slice/influxdb.service
           └─15305 /usr/bin/influxd
```

Figure 5.1 – Showing InfluxDB running as a service

When you install InfluxDB as a service, you obtain the following directories for storing InfluxDB data:

- Time series data: `/var/lib/influxdb/engine/`
- Key-value data: `/var/lib/influxdb/influxd.bolt`
- Influx **Command Line Interface** (**CLI**) configurations: `~/.influxdbv2/configs`

You have finished the InfluxDB installation. Let's see how to configure it.

Configuring the InfluxDB service

For configuring InfluxDB, you can use three different methods (ordered by precedence):

- Using `influxd` flags (command-line arguments)
- Using the `environment` variables
- Using the `configuration` file

Let's start with the `influxd` command.

influxd daemon

The `influxd` command is the daemon that runs and manages all the processes of the InfluxDB instance. You can run this daemon from the CLI.

The `influxd` daemon can be followed by two types of arguments: commands and flags.

The CLI looks as follows:

```
influxd [flags]
influxd [command]
```

Let's see the command options:

- `inspect`: This allows for the inspection of on-disk database data.
- `print-config`: This prints the complete `influxd` configuration.
- `run`: This starts the `influxd` instance (default behavior).
- `upgrade`: This allows us to upgrade from version 1.x to 2.0.
- `version`: This shows the current version.

In the following figure, you can see a partial screen of the `influxd print-config` command. It shows the configuration of the InfluxDB instance:

```
ubuntu@primary:~$ influxd print-config
INFO[0000]log.go:104 gosnowflake.(*defaultLogger).Infof reset OCSP cach
INFO[0000]log.go:104 gosnowflake.(*defaultLogger).Infof reading OCSP Re
ERRO[0000]log.go:120 gosnowflake.(*defaultLogger).Errorf failed to open
 directory
assets-path: ""
bolt-path: /home/ubuntu/.influxdbv2/influxd.bolt
e2e-testing: false
engine-path: /home/ubuntu/.influxdbv2/engine
feature-flags: {}
flux-log-enabled: false
http-bind-address: :8086
http-idle-timeout: 3m0s
http-read-header-timeout: 10s
http-read-timeout: 0s
http-write-timeout: 0s
influxql-max-select-buckets: 0
influxql-max-select-point: 0
influxql-max-select-series: 0
key-name: ""
log-level: info
metrics-disabled: false
nats-max-payload-bytes: 1048576
nats-port: -1
no-tasks: false
pprof-disabled: false
query-concurrency: 1024
query-initial-memory-bytes: 0
query-max-memory-bytes: 0
query-memory-bytes: 9223372036854775807
query-queue-size: 1024
reporting-disabled: false
```

Figure 5.2 – Output of the influxd print-config command

There are a lot of **flags**, one for every configuration option. You can find all the available flags at the following link:

```
https://docs.influxdata.com/influxdb/v2.0/reference/cli/
influxd/
```

Environment variables

You can configure the InfluxDB instance using **environment variables** (**EVs**), as you use them for other systems and applications.

Let's see it with an example. You can use the following command to set the URL and the port of the InfluxDB API and user interface:

```
$ export INFLUXD_HTTP_BIND_ADDRESS=YOUR_URL:8086
```

Let's see now how you can use a configuration file for configuring InfluxDB.

Configuration file

Finally, you can edit the configuration file to adapt the `influxd` daemon behavior to your needs.

The configuration file can have any of the following formats:

- YAML (`.yaml` and `.yml`)
- JSON (`.json`)
- TOML (`.toml`)

You have to specify the settings that you want to change. Otherwise, the default values will be applied.

When you run `influx`, it sees whether a file named `config.*` exists in the current working directory.

On the other hand, if you want to specify the location of the configuration file, you can run the following command:

```
export INFLUXD_CONFIG_PATH=/path/to/custom/config/directory
```

Let's see an example:

```
bolt-path: /users/user/.influxdbv2/influxd.bolt
query-concurrency: 25
flux-log-enabled: true
```

You can see all the configuration options in the following link:

`https://docs.influxdata.com/influxdb/v2.0/reference/config-options/`

Let's see now how to configure the InfluxDB database itself.

Configuring the InfluxDB database

Until here, you have seen how to use `influxd` to customize the behavior of the InfluxDB instance. It's important not to confuse `influxd` with `influx`.

In this section, you will learn how to manage the databases using `influx`.

The `influx` command allows you to manage organizations, buckets, users, tasks, and so on.

You can use the `influx` CLI either with flags or commands.

You can find the complete list of commands in the following link:

`https://docs.influxdata.com/influxdb/v2.0/reference/cli/influx/`

Let's see an example of the `influx` CLI. Using the following command, you can set the starting configuration for your database:

```
$ influx setup
```

After executing this command, you will have to follow these steps:

1. Ingress a primary username.
2. Enter the password for your user.
3. Confirm the password.
4. Ingress the name of your primary organization.
5. Enter the name of your primary bucket.
6. Enter the retention period.
7. Confirm all the ingress parameters.

After completing this process, you will have initialized the organization, user, bucket, and API token. You can see an example in the following figure:

```
ubuntu@primary:~$ influx setup
> Welcome to InfluxDB 2.0!
? Please type your primary username iot-user
? Please type your password **********
? Please type your password again **********
? Please type your primary organization name iot-company
? Please type your primary bucket name iot-bucket
? Please type your retention period in hours, or 0 for infinite 720
? Setup with these parameters?
  Username:          iot-user
  Organization:      iot-company
  Bucket:            iot-bucket
  Retention Period:  720h0m0s
  Yes
> Config default has been stored in /home/ubuntu/.influxdbv2/configs.
User            Organization      Bucket
iot-user        iot-company       iot-bucket
ubuntu@primary:~$
```

Figure 5.3 – Setup of an InfluxDB bucket

You can also see the current configuration by executing the following command:

```
$ influx config list
```

We will see the concepts of bucket, organization, retention period, and more in the next section.

Creating and managing an InfluxDB database

In this section, you will learn how to create a database, record values, and read them. But, before that, let's look at some important concepts of InfluxDB databases.

Main concepts of InfluxDB databases

In this subsection, you will learn about the data structure of InfluxDB databases.

Organization

The **InfluxDB organization** is the same concept that we have seen for Grafana. An organization is a workspace where you can group **users**, **dashboards**, **buckets**, and **tasks**.

Bucket

In InfluxDB, the data is stored in buckets. A bucket consists of a database that is related to a **retention period**. The retention period establishes the time that each data point persists in the database. Also, each bucket belongs to an organization.

In the next table, you can see an example of an InfluxDB bucket. This table will be useful for defining the rest of the concepts:

_time	_measurement	site	_field	_value
2021-18-18T00:00:00Z	freezertemp	lab	tempin	-19
2021-18-18T00:00:00Z	freezertemp	lab	tempout	18
2021-18-18T00:05:00Z	freezertemp	lab	tempin	-20
2021-18-18T00:05:00Z	freezertemp	lab	tempout	17

Table 5.1 – InfluxDB bucket example

In the following subsections, we will explore each of these items.

Timestamp

The InfluxDB database has a _time column. InfluxDB uses this column to store the **timestamp** of each data point. The timestamp information is stored on disk using the epoch nanosecond format. InfluxDB shows the time data using **RFC3339**, which is a human-readable format.

Measurement

A **measurement** is a group of **tags**, **fields**, and **timestamps**. You must specify a measurement to identify and describe your data. In the database, there is a column named _measurement for storing each of them.

Fields

Fields are pairs of **keys** and **values**. The keys are stored in the _field column, whereas the values are stored in the _value column.

The **field key** is a string that you can use to name the field, and the **field value** is the value itself of the associated field.

Finally, a **field set** is a group of fields that share the same timestamp. In *Table 5.1*, for example, you can see two pairs of values that share the same timestamp.

Tags

Tags are optional. You don't need to define tags in your bucket. However, as tags are indexed, queries on tags are faster than queries on fields. So, tags are a good option for grouping data and performing rapid queries on them.

A **tag key** is the name of the tag, in *Table 5.1*, for example, you can see `site` as the tag name. A **tag value** is the value of the tag, in this case, `lab`. A **tag set** is a group of key-value pairs that share the same key-value pairs.

Series

There are two types of series: **series key** and **series**.

A **series key** is a group of points that share measurement, tag set, and **field key**. In our case, a series key is as follows:

```
measurement:freezertemp, tag: site=lab, field:tempin
```

Notice that field values and timestamps are excluded from the series key.

A **series** is a group of timestamps and field values for a given series key. In the previous example, you get the following series:

```
2021-18-18T00:00:00Z     -19
2021-18-18T00:05:00Z     -20
```

Point

A **point** is a group of data that includes the series key, a field value, and a timestamp. You can see an example next:

```
2021-18-18T00:00:00Z   freezertemp   lab tempin -19
```

In other words, a point includes all the data related to a timestamp record.

In the next subsection, you will see how to create an InfluxDB bucket and store data in it.

Creating an InfluxDB bucket

Creating an InfluxDB bucket is an easy task, although there are a lot of options. We will see some examples, whereas you can find the full list of options in the following link:

```
https://docs.influxdata.com/influxdb/v2.0/reference/cli/
influx/bucket/create/
```

> **Important Note**
>
> Before you can create a bucket, you must run the `influx setup` command described in the previous section. With this command, you will create the organization that has precedence over the bucket.

Let's see how to create an InfluxDB bucket with the `influx` command.

Creating a bucket with an infinite retention period is as follows:

```
$ influx bucket create --name your-bucket-name
```

Creating a bucket with a retention period of 15 days is as follows:

```
$ influx bucket create --name your-bucket-name --retention 15d
```

Once you have created your bucket, you will be able to store data in it. You will learn how to do that in the following subsections.

Storing values in the bucket

There are many ways of storing data in the bucket. We will see some of them.

Using the CLI

You can write data in the bucket using the `influx write` command. This command allows using the **line protocol** and **annotated CSV**.

The `influx write` command admits flags for specifying several options. You can see the complete list at the following link: https://docs.influxdata.com/influxdb/v2.0/reference/cli/influx/write/#write-line-protocol-via-stdin.

Line protocol

The `influx write` command uses the line protocol for structuring the data that you want to store in the bucket. The scheme of the line protocol is as follows:

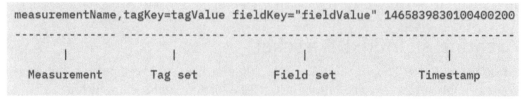

Figure 5.4 – Structure of the line protocol

So, when you use line protocol, you must specify the parameter in the following order:

1. First, you must include the measurement (required).

2. Then, you can include tags (optional) after the measurement, separated by a comma. Multiple tags are delimited by commas.

3. Then, you have to include a space for ingressing fields (required).

4. Last, you can include a timestamp (optional). You have to include a space between the key-value field and the timestamp. If you don't include the timestamp, the record will take the current timestamp from the system.

Let's see an example with data from *Table 5.1*:

```
influx write --bucket your-bucket "
freezertemp,site=lab tempin=-19
freezertemp,site=lab tempout=18
"
```

If you want to write data from a text file, you can run the following:

```
influx write \
  --bucket your-bucket \
  --file path/to/your/line-protocol/file.txt
```

And, if you want to get data from an URL, you can run the following:

```
influx write \
  --bucket your-bucket \
  --url https://yoururl.com/your-line-protocol.txt
```

Let's see what an annotated CSV is and how you can use it in Grafana.

An annotated CSV

You can use an annotated CSV to ingress data into a bucket. An annotated CSV can be passed as text in the command line or pointing to a file.

An annotated CSV is a table that has data rows at the beginning describing the properties of each column.

There are two types of annotated CSV:

- **Annotated CSV**: In this case, measurements, fields, and values are represented by `_measurement`, `_field`, and `_value` columns. The CSV annotations determine the types of data.

- **Extended annotated CSV**: In this case, measurements, fields, values, and their types are determined by CSV annotations. So, all the data and its types are specified with CSV annotations.

To write data to InfluxDB, you must include the following:

- Measurement
- Field set
- Timestamp (optional but recommended)
- Tag set (optional)

The table has the following structure:

- **Annotation rows**: Describes the properties of each column
- **Header row**: Describes the label of each column
- **Record row**: Describes the data itself

Let's see an example:

```
#datatype,dateTime:RFC3339,double,string,string
,_time,_value,_field,_measurement
,2021-12-18T18:16:11Z,-19,tempin,freezertemp
,2021-12-18T18:16:21Z,-20,tempin,freezertemp
,2021-12-18T18:16:31Z,-18,tempin,freezertemp
```

If you want to use a CSV file, just run the following command:

```
$ influx write \
  -b bucketName \
  -o orgName \
  -p s \
  --format=csv
  -f /path/to/data.csv
```

If you want to pass data in the command line, run this command:

```
$ influx write \
  --bucket example-bucket \
  --format csv \
  "#datatype,dateTime:RFC3339,double,string,string
,_time,_value,_field,_measurement
,2021-12-18T18:16:11Z,-19,tempin,freezertemp
,2021-12-18T18:16:21Z,-20,tempin,freezertemp
,2021-12-18T18:16:31Z,-18,tempin,freezertemp
"
```

For more options with annotated CSV, you can visit the following link: `https://docs.influxdata.com/influxdb/v2.0/reference/syntax/annotated-csv/`.

Let's now see other options for writing data in the bucket.

Client libraries

You can use client libraries to build scripts for writing and querying data.

You can use any of the following languages:

- Arduino
- C#
- Go
- Java
- JavaScript for browsers
- Kotlin
- Node.js
- PHP
- Python
- R
- Ruby
- Scala
- Swift

If you want to implement a client with any of these languages, please visit the following link: `https://docs.influxdata.com/influxdb/v2.0/api-guide/client-libraries/`.

We will not look at these libraries because it's beyond the scope of this book.

The InfluxDB API

Finally, let's see the InfluxDB API for writing and reading data from InfluxDB. This is the method that Grafana uses to interact with InfluxDB.

You can write data to InfluxDB using a `POST` request to the `/write` endpoint.

These are the parameters that you must use:

- **Organization**: You must use the `org` parameter in the URL.
- **Bucket**: You must specify the bucket in the URL.
- **Timestamp precision**: You may specify the precision in the URL. The default value is `ns`.
- **API token**: You have to use an authorization token in the header. You can create an API token with full permissions by running the following command:

  ```
  influx auth create \
      --org my-org \
      --all-access
  ```

  For the full documentation, go to `https://docs.influxdata.com/influxdb/cloud/security/tokens/create-token/`.

- **Line protocol**: You must pass the request body in plain text.

Let's see an example:

```
$ curl --request POST \
"http://your_dns_name_or_ip:8086/api/v2/write?org=YOUR_ORG&bucket=YOUR_BUCKET&precision=ns" \
    --header "Authorization: Token YOUR_API_TOKEN" \
    --header "Content-Type: text/plain; charset=utf-8" \
    --header "Accept: application/json" \
    --data-binary '
    freezertemp,site=lab tempin=-19,tempout=20
1630424257000000000
```

```
    freezertemp,site=lab tempin=-20,tempout=19
1630424257000000000
    '
```

Remember that the body is built using line protocol, as you have seen earlier in this chapter.

If you want to compress the data before sending it, you can use the following:

```
$ curl --request POST \
"http://your_dns_name_or_ip:8086/api/v2/write?org=YOUR_
ORG&bucket=YOUR_BUCKET&precision=ns" \
  --header "Authorization: Token YOUR_API_TOKEN" \
  --header "Content-Encoding: gzip" \
  --header "Content-Type: text/plain; charset=utf-8" \
  --header "Accept: application/json" \
  --data-binary @freezertemp.gzip
```

The `freezertemp.gzip` file must contain the data in line protocol format.

Reading data from InfluxDB

There are several methods for querying data from an InfluxDB bucket. However, we will concentrate on the methods that you can use with Grafana.

Adding the data source

Grafana uses the Web API for connecting to the InfluxDB bucket. For getting access to a bucket, you have to add an InfluxDB data source, as shown in the following screenshot:

Figure 5.5 – Adding an InfluxDB data source

Now, let's see how to configure the data source.

Configuring an InfluxDB data source

After you have added the data source, you will have to configure it. The first step is deciding what type of query language you will use.

You can see the two options available in the following figure:

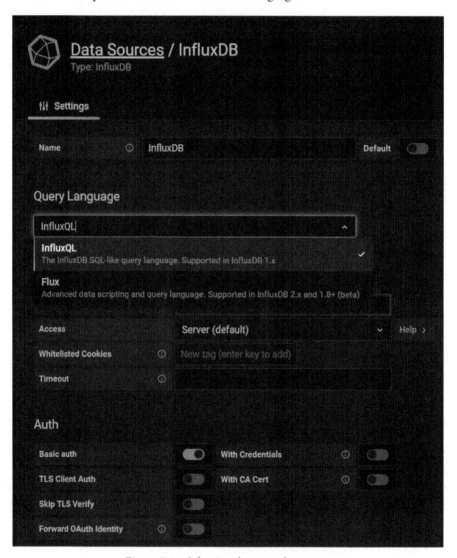

Figure 5.6 – Selecting the query language

Selecting the query language has some implications. Let's see what it is about.

InfluxDB query languages

There are two query languages:

- **InfluxQL**: This is a language that uses the same structure as SQL. You can use SELECT, FROM, WHERE, and GROUP BY as if you were using native SQL. This language is fully used in legacy versions (1. x), and with some restrictions in version 2.0.

- **Flux**: This offers more functionalities than InfluxQL, such as functions for data shaping, processing of time-series data, and string manipulation. You can write scripts in a JavaScript similar style. You can use Flux both in versions 1.x and 2.0.

Let's explore some considerations about InfluxQL and Flux:

- Grafana fully supports InfluxQL, whereas it offers a beta implementation of Flux at the time of writing this book.

- Grafana offers a graphical interface for building InfluxQL queries.

- You can use Flux scripts by writing them in a text dialog box in Grafana.

- InfluxQL queries can only perform reading operations in InfluxDB 2.0.

The last point implies that you can only run the following operations in InfluxDB 2.0:

- DELETE

- DROP MEASUREMENT

- EXPLAIN ANALYZE

- SELECT (read-only)

- SHOW DATABASES

- SHOW MEASUREMENTS

- SHOW TAG KEYS

- SHOW TAG VALUES

- SHOW FIELD KEYS

This limitation is not a problem for Grafana, as it only performs reading operations on the database. In this book, we will use the InfluxQL language for querying data.

> **Important note**
>
> All the concepts and instructions provided in this book are based on an InfluxDB 2.0 instance.

There is another point to take into consideration: the **data model**. Let's see what it is and how to deal with it.

The data model

Version 1.x is based on **databases and retention policies (DBRPs)**, whereas version 2.0 uses buckets, as we have seen earlier in this chapter.

InfluxQL uses the data model of version 1.x, so if you want to use InfluxDB 2.0 with InfluxQL, you have to map the bucket to a DBRP.

To verify that your bucket is being mapped, you can run the following:

```
$ influx v1 dbrp list
```

This will print all the mapped buckets if you have at least one.

If you want to map a bucket, you will have to run the following command:

```
$ influx v1 dbrp create \
    --org your-organization
    --token your-token
    --db your-mapped-db \
    --rp your-retention-policy \
    --bucket-id 00oxo0oXx000x0Xo \
    --default
```

To run this command, you have to specify the following parameters:

- `org` and `token` for authentication.
- Database name: The name of the mapped database.
- Retention policy: The name of the new retention policy.
- Bucket ID: The ID of the bucket to be mapped.
- Default flag: Use this flag to optionally set the provided retention policy as default.

To find the bucket ID, use the following command:

```
$ influx bucket list
```

To see the complete list of DBRP options, visit the following link: `https://docs.influxdata.com/influxdb/v2.0/reference/cli/influx/v1/dbrp/create/`.

Now that you have mapped the bucket, you can access the database from Grafana using the InfluxQL language.

Configuring the rest of the parameters

Once you have the InfluxDB database in a compatible format, you can proceed to configure the rest of the parameters.

In the following screenshot, you can see part of the configuration options:

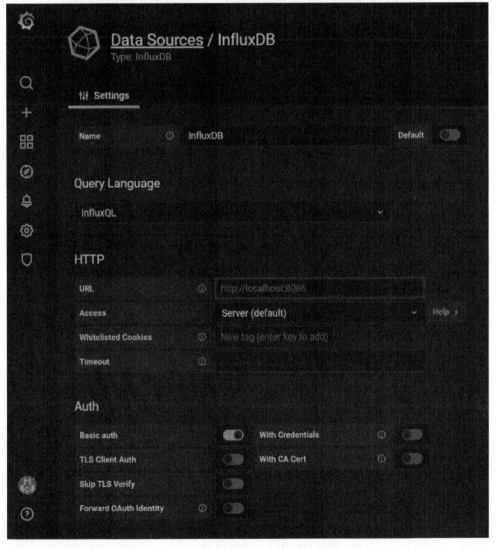

Figure 5.7 – Configuring the InfluxDB data source

The following screenshot shows the rest of the configuration:

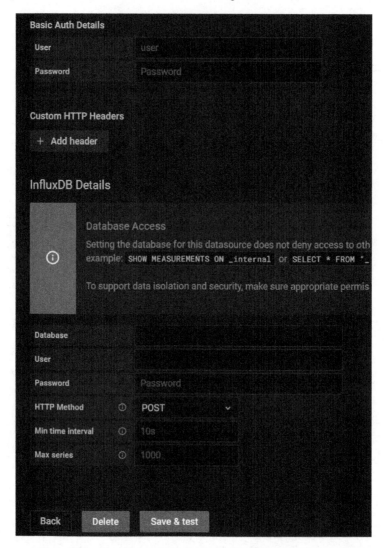

Figure 5.8 – Configuration options of the InfluxDB data source

Refer to your InfluxDB configuration to complete all the fields on the data source configuration page. At the very least, you will have to provide an URL to the InfluxDB instance, a database, and a user for accessing it. You may or may not use basic authentication, encryption, and custom HTTP headers.

We have seen all the main concepts regarding the InfluxDB. In the next section, you will learn about another TSDB: **OpenTSDB**.

Installing and configuring OpenTSDB

Although we will work with InfluxDB databases during the rest of this book, this section presents an alternative TSDB. The implementation of **OpenTSDB** can be laborious, so we will use a basic approach to it.

Installing OpenTSDB

To run OpenTSDB, you need these dependencies:

- Java Runtime Environment 1.6 or later
- HBase 0.92 or later
- gnuplot 4.2 or later (if you want to use its graphical interface)

For installing and running OpenTSDB you need **HBase**. HBase is an open source non-relational, distributed, scalable, and big data store.

Like OpenTSB, HBase runs on Java.

HBase is used for managing data of very large tables, offering fault-tolerant capabilities.

For full specifications and installation instructions, visit `https://hbase.apache.org`.

Unfortunately, there are no packages of OpenTSDB in the Linux repositories, so you will have to install it from the source.

Besides the requirements described earlier, you will need the following software:

- Autotools
- Make
- Python
- Git

Then, you must download and build OpenTSDB as follows:

```
$ git clone git://github.com/OpenTSDB/opentsdb.git
$ cd opentsdb
$ ./build.sh
```

This command will generate a `.jar` file in the `/build` directory. Then, you can run OpenTSDB executing the `tsdb` script. You can also install it in the system using `make install`.

If you prefer to build a Debian package, you can execute the following:

```
$ sh build.sh debian
```

This will generate a Debian package in the `./build/opentsdb-2.x.x/` directory, which you can install in your system as follows:

```
$ dpkg -i opentsdb-2.x.x_all.deb
```

After the installation, you will obtain the following directories:

- `/etc/opentsdb`: Configuration files
- `/tmp/opentsdb`: Temporary cache files
- `/usr/share/opentsdb`: Application files
- `/usr/share/opentsdb/bin`: The `tsdb` startup script that launches a TSDB or command line tools
- `/usr/share/opentsdb/lib`: Java JAR library files
- `/usr/share/opentsdb/plugins`: Location for plugin files and dependencies
- `/usr/share/opentsdb/static`: Static files for the **Graphical User Interface (GUI)**
- `/usr/share/opentsdb/tools`: Scripts and other tools
- `/var/log/opentsdb`: Logs

The installation process will set up an `init` script at `/etc/init.d/opentsdb`.

Then, you will be able to start and stop the services using the following commands:

```
$ sudo service opentsdb start
$ sudo service opentsdb stop
```

Let's see how you can perform the configuration of an OpenTSDB instance.

Configuring OpenTSDB

You can perform the configuration of OpenTSDB using configuration files, command-line arguments, or both.

The configuration file uses the Java properties specification. The names are lowercase, dotted strings without spaces. All the names start with `tsd`. You can comment on any configuration by adding a hash symbol (#).

The configuration methods have the following precedence:

1. OpenTSDB uses the default values.
2. The values of the configuration file will override the default values.
3. The command-line parameters override the configuration file and default values.

You can specify the location of the configuration file using the `--config` command-line argument.

If you haven't specified the path, OpenTSDB will search for a valid configuration file in the following directories:

- `./opentsdb.conf`
- `/etc/opentsdb.conf`
- `/etc/opentsdb/opentsdb.conf`
- `/opt/opentsdb/opentsdb.conf`

If OpenTSDB doesn't find any configuration file and can´t load the required properties, it will not start.

The required properties are as follows:

- `tsd.http.cachedir`: The path to the location of the temporary files (such as `/tmp/opentsdb`)
- `tsd.http.staticroot`: The path to the location where OpenTSDB stores static files, such as the web interface or JavaScript files
- `tsd.network.port`: The TCP port for listening to connections

You can find the full properties list at the following link: `http://opentsdb.net/docs/build/html/user_guide/configuration.html`.

Let´s now see how you can write data in an OpenTSDB database.

Writing data in an OpenTSDB database

In this section, we will see the data schema of an OpenTSDB database. You will also learn how to write data.

Data schema

The data schema of OpenTSDB is based on the following elements:

- **metric**: This is a name that is used to identify TSD, for example, `lab.freezer.sensor`, `server.cpu.user`, or `asset.location`.

- **timestamp**: As its name implies, this is a timestamp in seconds or milliseconds.

- **value**: This is a numeric value that represents some variable and it's stored associated with a timestamp. It can be an integer or a floating-point value.

- **tags**: These are a key-value pair. All the data points must have at least one tag assigned.

Let's see how metrics and tags work together.

Imagine that you have a fleet of trucks and you want to store data on location, speed, and fuel consumption. Then, you can create the `truck.location`, `truck.speed`, and `truck.fuel` metrics.

But, how do you identify each of the trucks? Easy, use tags.

So, you can have a tag such as `truckID`. Now, you can identify each data point associated with a metric and a tag.

If you want, for example, to see the location of the truck with ID 21, you can run a query with the following arguments:

```
truck.location truckID=21
```

For complete documentation about OpenTSDB queries, go to the following link: `http://opentsdb.net/docs/build/html/user_guide/query/`.

Let's now see how you can write data in an OpenTSDB database.

Writing data

There are three methods for writing data in an OpenTSDB database. Let's see each of them.

Telnet

You can connect to OpenTSDB using **Telnet**. Then, you can run a `put` command to ingress data into the database. The command format is as follows:

```
put <metric> <timestamp> <value> <tagk1=tagv1[ tagk2=tagv2
...tagkN=tagvN] >
```

Let's see an example:

```
put truck.speed 1635260345 95 truckID=21
```

Take into account that you can use put only for one data point at a time. Then, you have to ingress a new line character (\n) to write a new data point.

The HTTP API

Since version 2.0, HTTP can be used to send data to OpenTSDB. You can send unrelated data points in a single HTTP POST request.

The **HTTP API** is the easier method to integrate OpenTSDB with other systems. You can perform any operation using the HTTP API, such as querying TSD, managing metadata, and storing data points.

You can view all the details about the OpenTSDB API at http://opentsdb.net/docs/build/html/api_http/index.html.

Batch import

You can import data using the import CLI utility. This utility allows importing one or more files.

OpenTSDB will parse the files and load the data. The data must be formatted using the Telnet put style that we saw earlier. Also, each file can be compressed in gzip format.

Let's see an example:

```
$ import /your/path/to/file/your_file
$ import /your/path/to/file/your_file.gz
```

Now, let´s see how to add the data source to Grafana.

Adding the data source to Grafana

As we have seen with other data sources, adding them is a very straightforward procedure.

OpenTSDB comes with the core plugins of Grafana, so you only have to select, add, and configure it.

You can see the configuration options in the following screenshot:

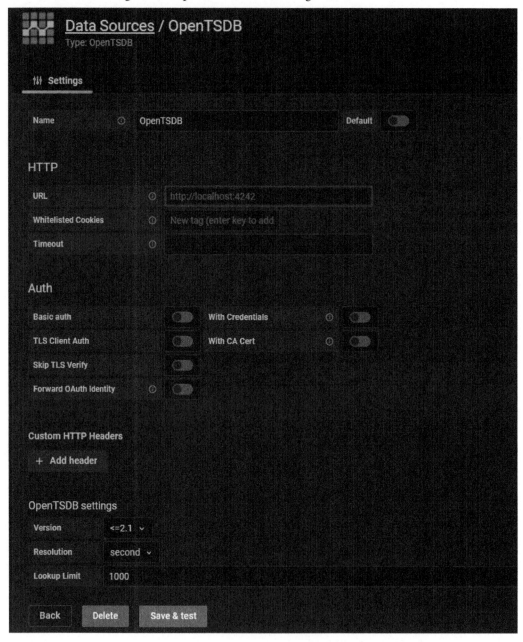

Figure 5.9 – Configuration settings of the OpenTSDB data source

As you can see in the screenshot, all the configuration options are quite self-explanatory. As soon as you fill the required fields, you will be able to use this data source in Grafana.

At the very least, you have to specify the URL and the version of the database. Authentication and encryption are optional but recommended.

Summary

In this chapter, you have learned about TSDBs. These are fundamental pieces of any IoT system. They allow you to store streams of data according to the timestamp of each point. Then, you can process, analyze, and visualize the data using Grafana.

We have seen the main concepts related to TSDBs, and two different implementations: InfluxDB and OpenTSDB.

You have learned how to store and read data using these databases.

In this book, we are going to use InfluxDB to show how to implement some examples. InfluxDB is easy to install and use and you can even take advantage of the ready-to-go service provided by InfluxData.

In the next chapter, we will see how to use data from TSDBs for building different types of dashboards.

Invitation to join us on Discord

Read this book alongside other Grafana users and the author Rodrigo Juan Hernández.

Ask questions, provide solutions to other readers, chat with the author via Ask Me Anything sessions and much more.

SCAN the QR code or visit the link to join the community.

https://packt.link/iotgrafana

Part 3: Connecting Data Sources and Building Dashboards

This part of the book covers several subjects related to dashboards, data sources, and plugins. You will learn how to get and use data from many data sources and how to show it using different types of panels. Also, you will learn how to install and manage plugins. Finally, you will learn how to organize and manage dashboards, including permissions, properties, annotations, and links.

This part contains the following chapters:

- *Chapter 6, Getting Data and Building Dashboards*
- *Chapter 7, Managing Plugins*
- *Chapter 8, Organizing and Managing Dashboards*

6
Getting Data and Building Dashboards

In the previous chapters, you have learned about data sources, **SQL** and **NoSQL databases**, and **time-series databases**.

In this chapter, you will see how you can use these data sources for feeding data into **Grafana** and building impressive dashboards.

Grafana offers a variety of panels for representing different types of data. In this chapter, you will learn how to perform data visualization using several of these panels.

In particular, you will learn about the following:

- Getting data from time-series databases
- Showing time-series data in graph panels
- Building table data panels
- How to show categorical data
- Showing text data
- Building a georeferenced map
- How to make a heatmap

This is a highly practical chapter, where you will be able to build dashboards from scratch. While the previous chapters prepared the terrain for the installation, administration, and managing of data, this chapter goes directly to the final objective of this book – the graphical representation of Internet of Things (IoT) data using Grafana.

So, let's start right now.

Getting data from time-series databases

In *Chapter 4, Data Sources for Grafana*, you learned about the concepts related to this type of database. You have seen two open source projects – **InfluxDB** and **OpenTSDB**.

In this chapter, all the operations are performed on an InfluxDB database. In the following screenshot, you can see the basic parameters (delimited by red squares) that you have to ingress for accessing an InfluxDB database from Grafana.

Any other additional configuration is related to a particular implementation of InfluxDB, such as **Transport Layer Security** (**TLS**) settings, timeouts, or custom HTTP headers. So, you will have to adapt the configuration of the InfluxDB data source to your particular installation.

Naturally, it's always a good idea to use secure connections, so TLS encryption is a must in production systems.

You can see the configuration settings page of the InfluxDB data source in the following screenshot:

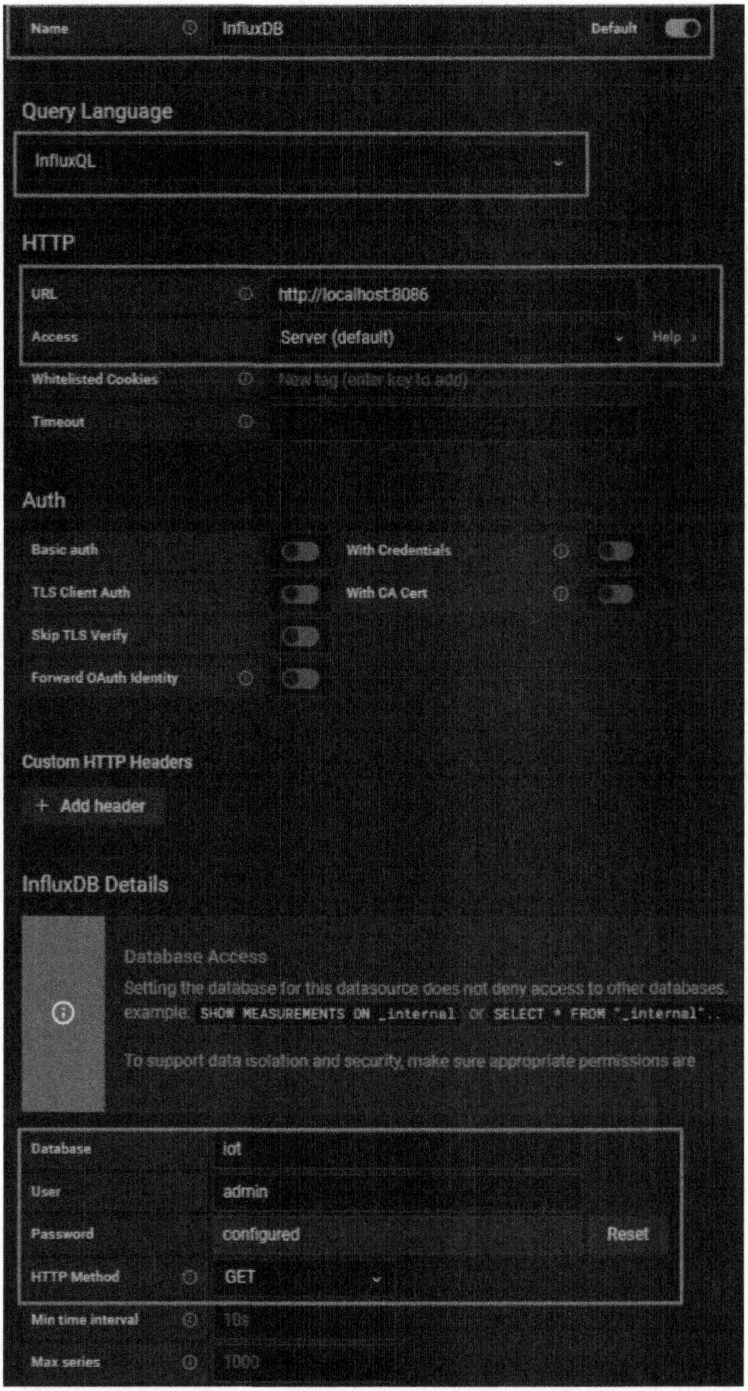

Figure 6.1 – A basic InfluxDB data source configuration

Regarding the reading of the data, the query language used in this book is InfluxQL.

Grafana offers a very clean and easy-to-use interface for running querying operations. You can see an example in the following figure:

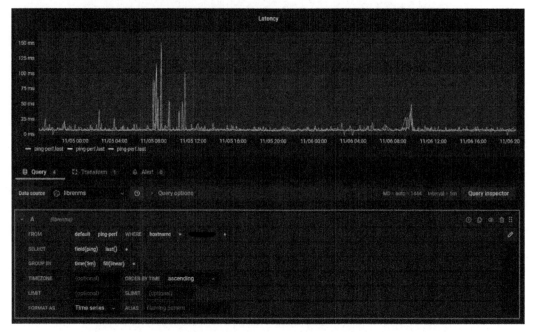

Figure 6.2 – The Query Inspector

The region boxed by the red square is the Query Inspector. This allows you to perform queries graphically, although you can also write a query by clicking on the pencil on the right side of the box.

Anyway, using the graphical interface is the recommended method. By clicking on each of the items, you can select the bucket, the measurement, the fields, the tags, the transformations, and the grouping.

Each of these clickable elements will show you a list of available options. So, you can select the correct values and see the results in the panel.

The Query Inspector is the tool that allows you to query the data that you need to build your dashboards.

Let's explore the previous example in detail. You can see it in the following figure:

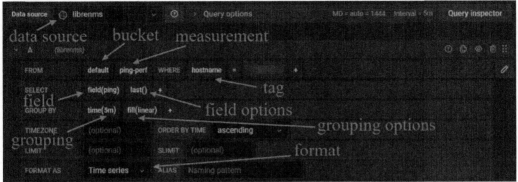

Figure 6.3 – Query parameters

Here, you can see all the options of the query.

Let's look at each of them in detail:

- **Data source**: First, at the top, you have to select the data source. Remember that you can have more than one data source of the same type. For example, you can have two InfluxDB data sources, each of them accessing different InfluxDB instances.

- **Bucket**: Then, you have to select the correct bucket. An InfluxDB instance can manage several buckets.

- **Measurement**: After you have selected the bucket, you have to specify the measurement.

- **Tags**: If there are tags in the bucket, you can select them here. Remember that tags allow you to perform efficient queries.

- **Field**: Then, you can choose the field that you are interested in. The field is associated with the field value that you want to display in the dashboard.

- **Field options**: The field options let you apply different types of numeric transformations. You can select them from several menus – **Aggregation**, **Selectors**, **Transformations**, **Predictors**, **Math**, **Aliasing**, and **Fields**. We will take a look at all these options later in this book.

- **Grouping and options**: Here, you can select the granularity of data and the way that you want to connect data points. In the example in *Figure 6.2*, the data is connected by linear interpolations, but you can let them be unconnected.

- **Format**: This option lets you specify how you want to see the data. You could choose between **Time series**, **Tabular**, and **Logs**.

- **Other options**: Finally, you can name the pattern using **ALIAS**, and you can specify some other parameters related to the type of data source that you are using. In this case, you have the following options – **TIMEZONE, ORDER BY TIME, LIMIT**, and **SLIMIT**.

We have now covered the basics of getting data from a time-series database, specifically using an InfluxDB data source. In the next section, you will learn how to create dashboards using data obtained from an InfluxDB bucket.

Showing time-series data in graph panels

Showing time-series graphs is possibly the main objective of any Grafana implementation. Using this type of graph not only allows you to see a clear picture of the evolution of some variables but also gives you the option of performing analytics on the data.

In this section, you will learn how to create your first graph panel using a time-series data source. So, let's start with the dashboard creation, as you can see in the following screenshot:

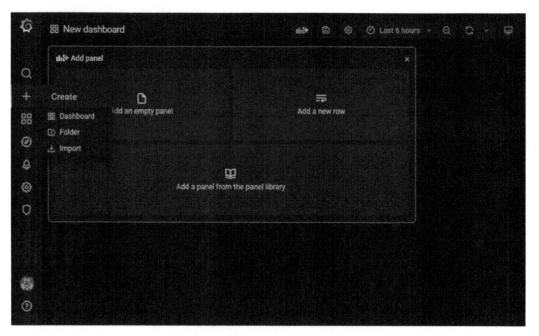

Figure 6.4 – The creation of a dashboard

To create a dashboard, you have to go to the *plus sign* in the left menu and click on **Dashboard**. A new, empty dashboard will be created.

From here, you will have to create **panels**, where you will be able to specify the type of visualization that you need. So, click on **Add an empty panel** to explore the available options. You will get a view similar to the one shown in the following screenshot:

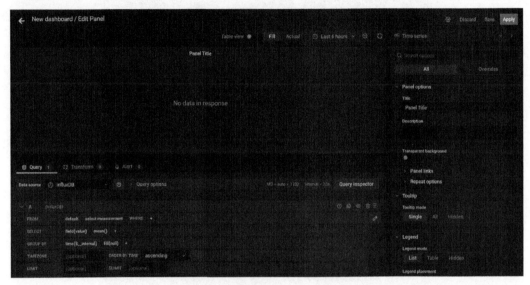

Figure 6.5 – Creating a new panel

As you can see, Grafana selects the data source that you have set as the default data source. Also, it selects by default a time-series panel. Clicking on **Time series** will show you a drop-down menu, where you can select another type of panel, as shown in the following screenshot:

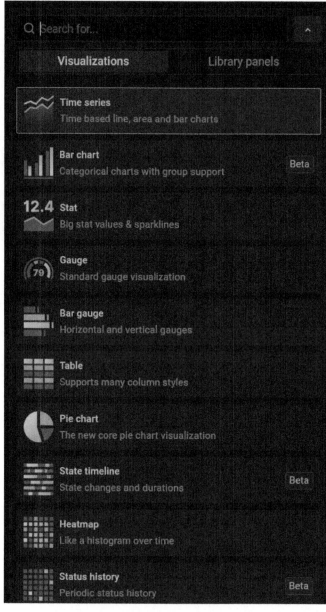

Figure 6.6 – The list of panels available

There are a lot of panel types available for use with the default installation of Grafana. But for now, we will focus on the **Time series** panel.

Panel options

Panel options are common to all types of panels. You can see all these fields in the following screenshot.

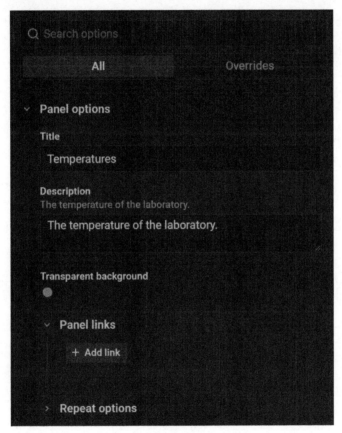

Figure 6.7 – Panel options

Now, let's see what these panel options are:

- **Title**: You can and should specify a title for each of your panels. This way, you will be able to identify each panel and avoid confusion.

- **Description**: Even when the purpose of some panels is quite evident, it is always a good idea to describe the objective and characteristics of a panel.

- **Transparent background**: Enabling this option, you can set the transparency of the panel background.
- **Panel links**: You can specify links to any valid URL, including websites, other dashboards, or panels. The links will be shown in the upper-left corner of the panel.

Time-series panel options

Whenever you create a panel, Grafana creates a time-series panel by default. There are three types of graphs available – dots, lines, and bars. Let's look at the other options that you can set in this panel.

Tooltip

This option lets you choose the visualization of tooltips in the panel. There are three options:

- **Single**: When you hover your cursor over the visualization, it shows only one series of values, depending on which visualization you are hovering over.
- **All**: When you hover your cursor over the visualization, the tooltip shows all the series.
- **Hidden**: If you select this option, the tooltip will not display any series.

Let's now look at the **Legend mode** options.

Legend mode

Using this option, you can specify how to display the legends in your visualization. Again, you have three options available:

- **List**: This shows the legends as a list, putting all of them on the same line.
- **Table**: This displays the legends as a table, putting them in different rows.
- **Hidden**: This hides the legends.

Now, let's learn how to place the legends.

Legend placement

You can choose where to show the legends. There are two options:

- **Bottom**: This shows the legends below the graph.
- **Right**: This shows the legends on the right of the graph.

Let's look at the final option for legend visualizations.

Legend calculations

You can display standard calculations next to the legends. To see all the available calculations, visit the following link: `https://grafana.com/docs/grafana/latest/panels/calculations-list/`.

You can see an example of legend calculations in the following screenshot, where the mean value is displayed next to the legends:

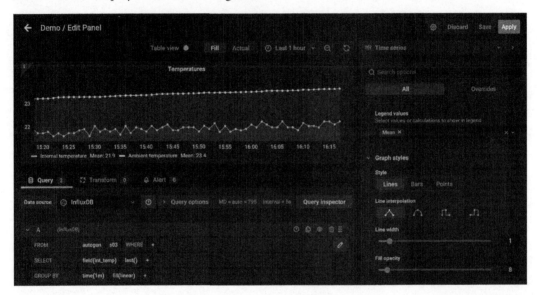

Figure 6.8 – An example of legend calculation

Let's continue with the rest of the options.

Graph styles

You can choose between three graph styles:

- **Lines**: By selecting this option, you can connect the data points using lines. When you use lines, you can choose the interpolation method among four techniques – linear, smooth, step before, and step after. Play with these options and select the one that best suits your needs.

- **Bars**: If you prefer using bars instead of continuous lines, you can select this option. When you use bars, you can choose one of three bar alignments – before, center, and after.

- **Points**: If you simply want to show the data points unconnected, choose this option. When using points, you can modify the point sizes.

When you use lines or bars, you have some additional appearance settings:

- **Line width**: You can specify the line thickness, from 0 to 10 pixels.

- **Fill opacity**: With this option, you can set the opacity of the areas below the curves.

- **Gradient mode**: This feature allows you to add a gradient effect to the painted areas.

- **Line style**: You can choose between solid, dash, and dots.

- **Connect null values**: With this option, you can specify whether you want to connect null values or not. You can choose from **Never**, **Always**, or **Threshold**.

- **Show points**: You can choose between showing and hiding data points. This option lets you choose between **Auto**, **Always**, or **Never**.

- **Point size**: This option lets you specify the size of the data points. This configuration is available for point graphs too.

- **Stack series**: With this feature, you can stack the values. This means that the series are stacked with one on top of another.

Let's see how you can configure the axis.

Axis

This configuration section allows you to customize the axis of the time-series panel. **Axis** lets you choose between the following options:

- **Placement**: You can select where you want to place the Y axis. You can choose between **Auto**, **Left**, **Right**, and **Hidden**.

- **Label**: This option lets you write a label for the Y axis.

- **Width**: With this option, you can specify the width of the axis.

- **Soft min and soft max**: With this feature, you can control the range of the Y axis for a better visualization experience.

- **Scale**: Here, you can choose between a linear and a logarithmic scale.

Let's explore the numerical options.

Standard options

Here, you can specify the options related to units and numbers. These options apply to several types of panels, not only time-series panels:

- **Unit**: This option lets you select the unit of the value that you are displaying. There is a large list of units – area, length, pressure, radiation, temperature, velocity, and so on. You can explore all the available units by selecting the drop-down list menu.

- **Min and Max**: Here, you can specify the minimum and the maximum values of the *Y* axis. If you leave this field blank, it will adjust automatically.

- **Decimals**: You can use a fixed amount of decimals or leave it in automatic mode.

- **Display name**: You can assign a name to the series. This will replace the name of the series obtained from the data source.

- **Classic palette**: Here, you can select a color palette, according to your needs or likes.

- **No value**: You can choose the value that will be displayed when there is no value present.

- **Thresholds**: You can specify thresholds and associate them with different colors. You can also choose between absolute and percentage thresholds.

Value mappings

This option lets you map values or ranges to words or emojis. This feature is very useful when you want to build an easy-to-visualize dashboard. For instance, you can map values to low level, warning, alert, and so on.

Data links

Here, you can specify links that include a series name. You can use this feature to provide context or more data related to the current dashboard.

Let's see an example with some of the configurations mentioned in this section.

Figure 6.9 shows the following features:

- **Title: Temperatures**
- **Description: The temperature of the laboratory (not shown)**
- **Tooltip: All**
- **Legend: List, Bottom, and Legend values (mean)**

- **Graph styles: Lines, Line interpolation (smooth), and Fill opacity**
- **Line width: 1**
- **Fill opacity: 8**
- **Gradient mode: Opacity**
- **Line style: Solid**
- **Connect null: Never**
- **Show points: Auto**
- **Point size: 5**
- **Stack series: Off**
- **Axis placement: Auto**
- **Scale: Linear**
- **Unit: Celsius (°C)**
- **Color scheme: Classic palette**
- **Show thresholds: Off.**

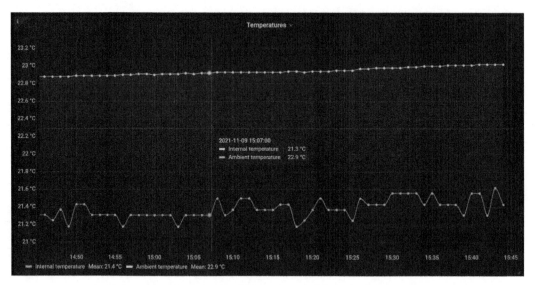

Figure 6.9 – An example of time-series dashboard customization

You have now learned how to build time-series panels. In the next section, we will look at how to build table data panels.

Building table data panels

Time-series panels are an excellent tool for showing time-series data, but sometimes, it can be useful to use table data panels.

The table data panel allows you to show data in a table, ordered by time. In the following figure, you can see an example of one of these panels:

Signal strenght	
Time ↓	RSSI
2021-11-09 16:26:00	-66 dB
2021-11-09 16:25:00	-67 dB
2021-11-09 16:24:00	-65 dB
2021-11-09 16:23:00	-76 dB
2021-11-09 16:22:00	-84 dB
2021-11-09 16:21:00	-82 dB
2021-11-09 16:20:00	-82 dB

Figure 6.10 – A table data panel

The table panel comes with the basic installation of Grafana, and you can select it in the visualization menu.

Table panel options

Besides the common panel options, the table panel offers a few more customization settings. Let's look at them.

Table options

These configuration settings have the following options:

- **Show headers**: This allows you to show or hide the names imported from the data source.
- **Column width**: Here, you can specify the column width in pixels. By default, Grafana calculates it based on the table size and the minimum column width. The minimum column width by default is 150, but when you specify the column width, you override this value.

- **Cell display mode**: This field lets you choose different display options – color text, color background, gradient gauge, LCD gauge, JSON view, and image.

- **Column filter**: This option enables or disables a filter on each column. You can then choose to show or hide certain values.

Let's see how to build a table with multiple queries.

Building and customizing a table with multiple queries

In a table, you can show data from multiple queries. The following screenshot shows two queries running on an InfluxDB data source:

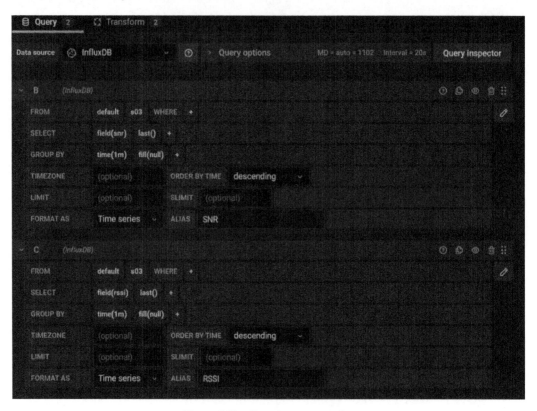

Figure 6.11 – Running two queries

Note that both queries have an alias. This makes it easier to reference these values.

Applying transformations

To show two or more queries in the same table, you have to use **transformations**. This feature is available beside the query interface, as you can see in the following screenshot:

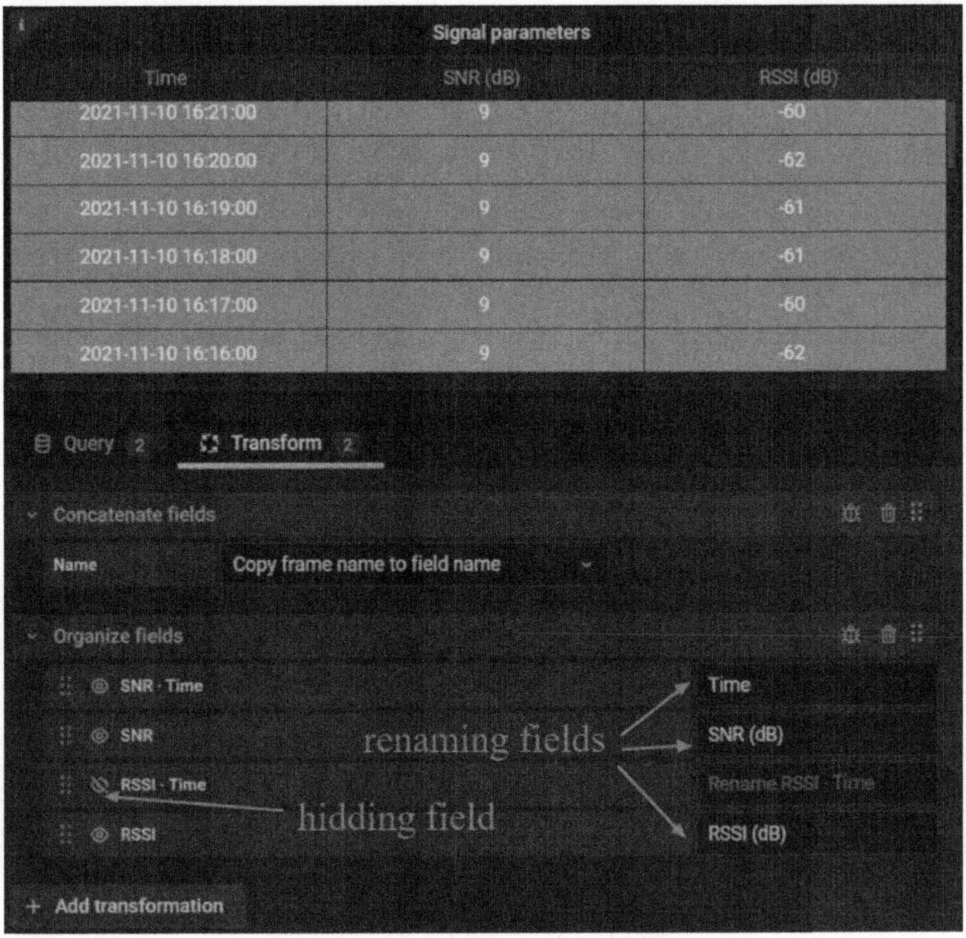

Figure 6.12 – Showing two queries in a table

In the preceding screenshot, you can see two transformations.

Using the first one (**Concatenate fields**), you can show the two queries, copying the frame name to the field name.

Applying the second transformation (**Organize fields**), you can choose what fields you want to show and whether you want to change their names.

You can apply successive transformations to shape and transform the visualization of the data.

Overriding panel properties

In *Figure 6.12*, you can see that all of the table is colored blue. This is because the field color scheme in **Standard options** is set to a single color (**blue**). Whenever you change the standard options, the changes are applied to the entire table unless you override the panel properties.

You can customize the appearance of each of the fields independently. You can see an example in the following screenshot:

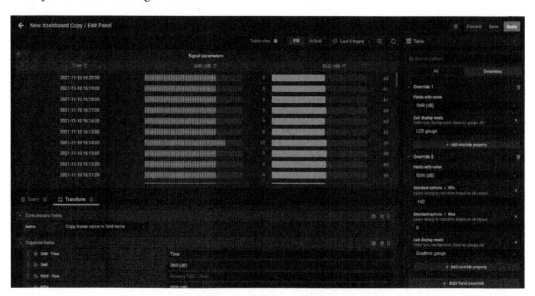

Figure 6.13 – Overriding the table properties

In this case, the properties of the **SNR (dB)** and **RSSI (dB)** fields were set to override the general options. The **Cell display mode** field of the **SNR (dB)** was set to **LCD gauge**, while the **Min** and **Max** options of the **RSSI (dB)** were set to **-140** and **0** respectively, and the **Cell display mode** field was set to **Gradient gauge**.

As you can see, overriding properties brings you great flexibility for customizing your panels.

In the next section, you will learn how to display categorical data.

How to show categorical data

Sometimes, you need to know whether a pump is working or not, or if a light is on or off.

On the other hand, sometimes, it is useful to perform the classification of some data. Think about the number of times that each IoT device sent data, or the number of devices that have a specific version of the firmware.

In this section, you will learn how to build visualizations of categorical data.

Using stat panels

When you want to show the state of a thing, a machine, a process, and so on, you can use a stat panel. This panel allows you to show any number or text associated with the state that you want to show.

For instance, you can show whether the power mains of an **Uninterruptable Power Supply** (**UPS**) is present or not, or whether its batteries are okay or need to be replaced.

You can convert numerical data to categorical data, performing a mapping between data values and categories. For example, you can map a low level of liquid in a tank with the word *empty* and a high level with the word *full*. We have seen this feature in the *Standard options* section of this chapter. The following screenshot shows a UPS state that has been mapped to text:

Figure 6.14 – Mapping numerical data to categorical data

In a stat panel, you can handle data that includes any number of categories. Think about the identification of a type of vehicle. The images coming from a camera could be analyzed to determine whether a vehicle is a truck, a car, a motorcycle, or anything else.

The categorical data can be combined and customized, as shown in the previous section.

If you want to show the evolution of states across time, you can use the **State timeline** panel. You can see an example in the following figure:

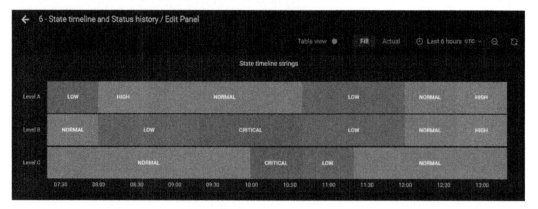

Figure 6.15 – The State timeline panel

Now, let's take a look at bar charts.

Using bar charts

You can use bar chart panels to show categorical data. At least one of the fields must contain string data to be used as the category name. The following figure shows an example:

	A	B	C	D
1	device	bluetooth	wifi	lorawan
2	end_devices	50	40	70
3	gateways	20	10	8
4				

Figure 6.16 – Categorical data in a Google spreadsheet

You can use this data in Grafana for building categorical dashboards, such as the one shown in the following screenshot:

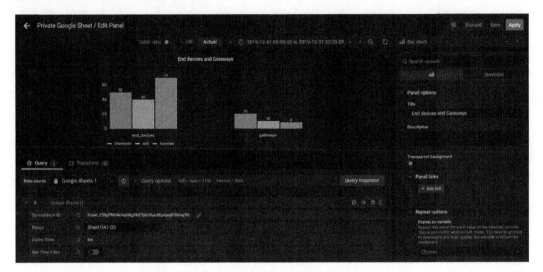

Figure 6.17 – Showing categorical data in a bar panel

As you can see, it is very easy to show categorical data using bar panels. Also, you can customize the visualization using all the standard settings.

In the following section, you will learn how to build georeferenced maps.

Building a georeferenced map

Showing assets, persons, animals, or vehicles on a map is a common use of IoT. In this section, you will see how to build georeferenced maps using Grafana.

The Geomap panel

The best option for showing georeferenced data in Grafana is **Geomap**. This plugin comes installed by default, so you will only have to configure it. Let's see the configuration options.

Map view

This setting allows you to specify the starting coordinates and zoom of the panel. You can choose from preloaded regions or write down coordinates. You can see an example in the following screenshot:

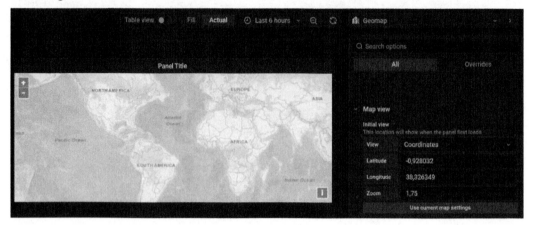

Figure 6.18 – A map view of Geomap

Let's see how you can configure the base layer.

The base layer

This panel offers several base layers for showing world maps. By default, Grafana loads the CartoDB base map.

Each of the base maps brings specific options to change the style of the map. You can define base layers in the .ini configuration file.

You can see all the options in the following screenshot:

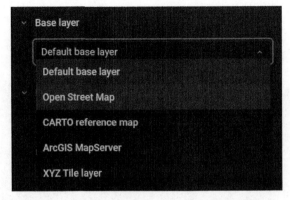

Figure 6.19 – The base layers of the Geomap panel

To visualize the data, you have to use the data layer.

The data layer

The data layer allows you to visualize your data on top of the base map.

Location

There are four methods for specifying the location of the data:

- **Auto**: Grafana determines the correct option for showing the data – **Geohash**, **Latitude**, **Longitude**, and **Lookup**.

- **Coords**: With this option, you can use numerical coordinate data. You will have to select the fields corresponding to the latitude and the longitude from your database.

- **Geohash**: You can use **geohash** data to get the coordinates. A geohash is a unique identifier of a specific region of Earth. There are online geohash calculators that you can use for free. You will have to select the string data field from your database.

- **Lookup**: With this method, you can use a location name and convert it to a location value. You will have to enter the **Lookup** field from the database and a **gazetteer**. The gazetteer is the directory that you are using to map the data to a geographic region.

Let's see now how you can represent your data over the map.

The Markers layer

With the **Markers** layer, you can show the data points as different shapes – circles, squares, triangles, stars, and so on. You can see the configuration menu in the following screenshot:

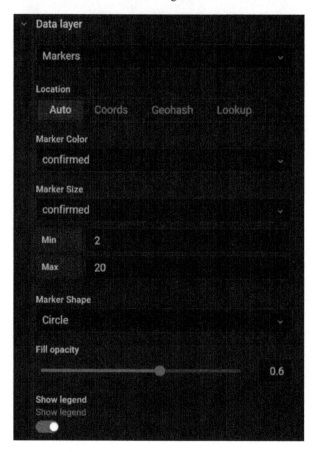

Figure 6.20 – The Markers layer menu

In the **Markers** layer menu, you can select the following options:

- **Marker Color**: You can choose between a fixed color or a varying color, according to the value of data points. If you select the latter, you have to specify the thresholds in the **Thresholds** section.

- **Marker Size**: Here, you can set the size of the markers. Like **Marker Color**, you can choose between fixed or variable settings. In the second case, greater values will be displayed with larger markers. Also, you can specify **Min** and **Max** sizes, defining the range of the size.

- **Marker Shape**: You can select any of these shapes – circle, square, triangle, star, cross, and X.

- **Fill opacity**: With this option, you can specify the opacity of the markers.

In the following screenshot, you can see an example of using markers in a **Geomap** panel:

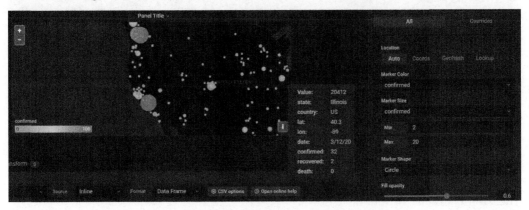

Figure 6.21 – Using markers in a Geomap panel

In this case, the size and color of the markers are determined by the **confirmed** fields, which represent the confirmed cases of COVID-19 in a specific location.

Let's see now how you can use heatmaps to show data in a **Geomap** panel.

The Heatmap layer

You can create heatmap visualizations over a map by selecting the option in the data layer menu, instead of the default option (the **Markers** layer).

The heatmap visualizes clusters data points according to their values. A heatmap is useful when you want to view densities or levels over a map.

In the following screenshot, you can see an example that shows COVID-19 cases using a heatmap:

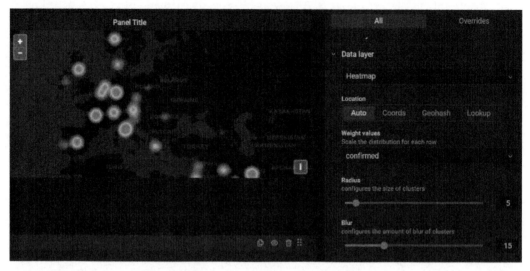

Figure 6.22 – Heatmap visualization

The setting of this visualization is similar to the **Markers** layer.

The parameters are the following:

- **Weight values**: This option lets you specify the weight of each data point. A fixed value brings a constant weight to all the data points. On the other hand, you can scale the weights according to a particular data value, as you can see in the preceding figure.

- **Radius**: Here, you can specify the sizes of the clusters.

- **Blur**: This option lets you set the amount of blur.

Now, you know how to build georeferenced dashboards using Grafana. In the next section, you will learn about histograms and heatmaps.

Histograms and heatmaps

In this section, we will explore two visualization panels – **Histograms** and **Heatmaps**. Let's start with histograms.

The Histogram panel

You can use histograms to represent the distribution of numerical data. In a histogram, the data points are grouped into buckets (like discretized intervals) and then counted.

So, for each X-axis bucket, the count of data points is displayed on the Y axis. You can use time series or table data with numerical fields.

Display options

Let's see the options of the **Histogram** panel. They allow us to set how we group, calculate, and show the data.

- **Bucket size**

  This option lets you specify the size of the bucket. If you leave it empty, the bucket size will be approximately 10 percent of the full range of the data.

- **Bucket offset**

  You can set a value here between 0 and the bucket size for shifting the aggregation window. In general, you will use this option when you specify the bucket size (and don't use the automatic setting).

- **Combine series**

  This option lets you merge all the series and fields to build a combined histogram.

- **Line width**

  With this option, you can set the line width of the bars. You can make them thicker or thinner, depending on your visualization needs.

- **Fill opacity**

  Here, you can set the opacity of the bars. This option lets you modify the transparency of the bars.

- **Gradient mode**

  This option lets you specify the gradient of the fill. To change the color, you can use the standard color scheme field option. Also, you can change the appearance of the gradient with the fill opacity settings – **None, Opacity, Hue, and Scheme**.

- **Tooltip, legend mode, and legend placement**

  You can customize the visualization of tooltips and legends, as you saw in the first section of this chapter.

You can see an example of a histogram in the following screenshot:

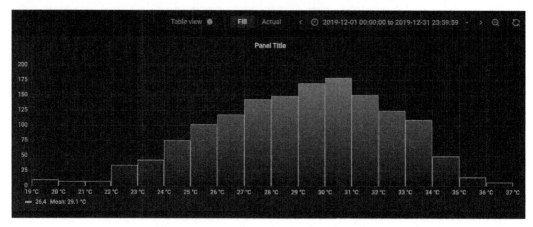

Figure 6.23 – A Histogram panel example

Now, let's see look at heatmaps.

The Heatmap panel

First, don't get confused with the Geomap heatmap. This one is a panel itself and serves to represent the variation of data across time.

A heatmap is the variation of a histogram through time. In the following screenshot, you can see the evolution of the distribution of ambient temperature:

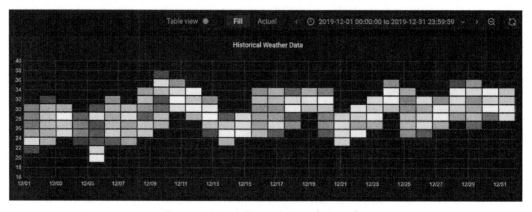

Figure 6.24 – A Heatmap panel example

Heatmap panels have a variety of options. Let's look at them.

Axes options

You can customize your visualization using the following options.

The Y axis

This option lets you specify the following settings:

- **Unit**: Here, you can set the unit for the Y axis.

- **Scale**: You can choose between linear and logarithmic.

- **Y-Min** and **Y-Max**: These are the minimum and maximum values for the Y axis respectively.

- **Decimals**: This is the number of decimals you want to use on the Y axis.

Let's see how to configure the buckets.

Buckets

This section has the following options:

- **Y Axis – Buckets**: The number of buckets the Y axis will be split into.

- **Size**: The size of each Y-axis bucket. This option overrides the **Y Axis – Buckets** setting. This option is only available when the scale is linear.

- **Split Factor**: This is visible when the scale is logarithmic. Grafana splits the Y values by log base by default. You can use this option to split each bucket into smaller buckets.

- **X Axis – Buckets**: The number of buckets that you want to split the X axis into.

- **Size**: The size of each X-axis bucket. You can specify a number or a time interval (1 second, 3 minutes, 2 hours, and so on). This option overrides **X Axis – Buckets**.

Let's explore more bucket options.

Bucket bound

This option applies when the data format is time-series buckets. This type of data has a series with names that represent the bucket bound. However, depending on the data source, a bound can be upper or lower. You can set the bound type with this option.

Bucket size

With this option, you can specify the size of cells in the heatmap. You can set the bucket size, either by count or by defining a size interval.

Data format

There are two data formats:

- **Time-series**: The buckets are defined over the entire time-series data values. You can specify the buckets' sizes and intervals in the **Buckets** options.
- **Time-series buckets**: Each time series has a defined Y-axis bucket. The time series name (**ALIAS**) is a numeric value that represents the upper or lower interval for the bucket.

Display options

You can customize even more of your dashboard with these options. They allow you to build more clear visualizations.

Colors

This option lets you map values to colors. The leftmost color corresponds to the minimum count, whereas the rightmost color maps to the maximum count.

The color mode setting allows you to choose between opacity and spectrum options.

Color scale

This option lets you define minimum and maximum values for mapping the cell colors.

Buckets

This setting allows you to specify the following options:

- **Hide zero**: Do not show cells with zero values.
- **Space**: The space between cells.
- **Round**: The roundness of the cells.

Finally, you have the **Legend** and **Toolpit** options.

Legend and Toolpit

These settings are common to all panel types. However, they are repeated here for convenience.

This option lets you choose a visualization of tooltips in the panel. There are three options:

- **Single**: When you hover your cursor over the visualization, it shows only one series of values, depending on which visualization you are hovering over.
- **All**: When you hover your cursor over the visualization, the tooltip shows all the series.
- **Hidden**: If you select this option, the tooltip will not display any series.

And that concludes heatmap panels.

Summary

In this chapter, you have learned how to build several types of dashboards using different panels. You have learned how you can customize each of these panels and adapt them to your needs.

The panels presented in this chapter are tailored for use with different types of data – time-series, categorical, text, georeferenced, and statistical. With all this information, you can now build any type of dashboard for your IoT projects.

In the next chapter, we will see how to install and manage plugins in Grafana.

7
Managing Plugins

Plugins are pieces of software that allow adding different features to **Grafana**. From data sources to panels and applications, plugins offer a large variety of functionalities.

In the previous chapters, we have explored some of the plugins included in the core installation of Grafana. You have learned how to use data source plugins such as **InfluxDB**, **Google Sheets**, and a **CSV plugin**.

In the panel plugins, you have used Time series, Histogram, Geomap, Text, and many others.

In this chapter, you will learn how to manage the plugins in your instance of Grafana. This includes several methods of installation, types of plugins, signed and unsigned plugins, and user permissions for managing plugins.

In this chapter, we'll cover the following topics:

- How to install and manage plugins
- All the flavors of plugins

Technical requirements

To get the most out of this chapter, I recommend you have any or all of the following resources:

- A Grafana Cloud instance.
- A Grafana instance running on your own server. In this chapter, all the examples refer to Ubuntu Server, but you can use any system or distribution.

Let's start this chapter with plugin administration.

How to install and manage plugins

There are different methods for installing plugins. You learned how to install some plugins in *Chapter 4, Data Sources for Grafana*. In this chapter, you will learn the general procedures.

First, let's see how to install a plugin on your own server.

Installing a Grafana plugin on your server

There are two methods for installing a plugin in a Grafana instance: the Grafana CLI and manual installation.

Installing a plugin with the Grafana CLI

The easiest method for installing a plugin is using the Grafana CLI. With this tool, you can install, upgrade, and remove plugins.

Let's see all the available commands.

This command installs the latest version of a plugin:

```
$ grafana-cli plugins install <the-plugin-id>
```

This command specifies the version to install:

```
$ grafana-cli plugins install <the-plugin-id> <version>
```

This one lists the plugins available for installing:

```
$ grafana-cli plugins list-remote
```

This command lists the installed plugins:

```
$ grafana-cli plugins ls
```

This command updates one plugin:

```
$ grafana-cli plugins update <plugin-id>
```

This one updates all the installed plugins:

```
$ grafana-cli plugins update-all
```

Finally, this command removes one plugin:

```
$ grafana-cli plugins remove <plugin-id>
```

Now that you have learned how to install plugins using the CLI tool, let's see how to do it manually.

Installing plugins manually

Sometimes, it is not possible to install a plugin using the Grafana CLI. For example, you might have a server that is not connected to the internet. Also, you might want to install a plugin not listed in the official repository of Grafana plugins.

In these cases, you can install any plugin manually. To do that, all you have to do is copy the plugin files to the Grafana plugins directory.

By default, the Grafana plugins directory is located in the following path: /var/lib/ grafana/plugins.

The plugins include several files and directories and are packed in a compressed file (.zip). So, after you download the plugin, you have to copy it to the plugins directory and unzip it there, as you can see in the following command:

```
$ unzip your-plugin-0.1.0.zip -d YOUR_PLUGIN_DIR/your-plugin
```

Remember that the path to your plugin directory is specified in the configuration file of Grafana. Also, take into consideration the user permissions of this directory. They must be the same as the default directory.

Installing plugins in a Grafana Cloud instance

Installing a plugin in a Grafana Cloud instance is a very easy procedure. Let's see each of the steps:

1. First, go to your instance and select the **Plugins** tab in the **Configuration** section, as you can see in the following screenshot:

Figure 7.1 – Plugins available in a Grafana Cloud instance

2. In the upper sector of the screen, you can see several options for filtering the results. You can select the type of plugin: **All**, **Data sources**, **Panels**, and **Applications**. Also, you can choose between **All** and **Installed**.

3. To install a plugin, you have to select the plugin that you want to install. This will lead you to the plugin, as you can see in the following screenshot:

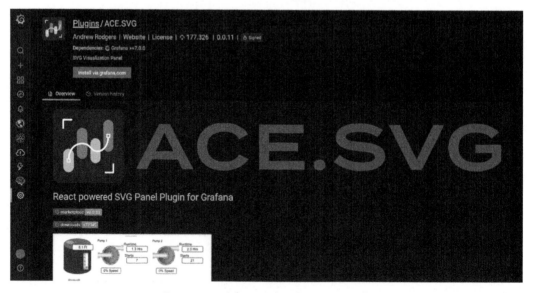

Figure 7.2 – Selecting the plugin to install

4. Then, you have to click on the **Install via grafana.com** button, which will take you to the installation page:

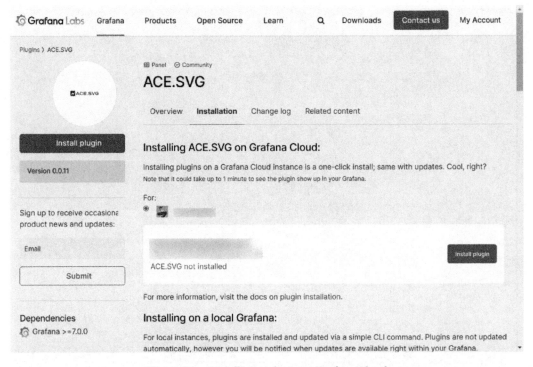

Figure 7.3 – Installing a plugin in Grafana Cloud

5. If you want to update or uninstall a plugin in a Grafana Cloud instance, you have to go to the plugin page, as you can see in the following screenshot:

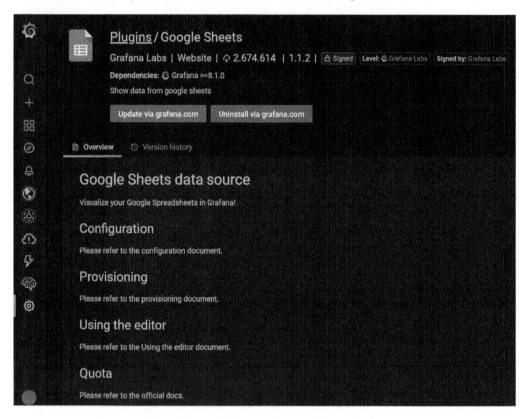

Figure 7.4 – Updating and uninstalling a plugin

6. Once you are on the plugin page, updating or uninstalling is as easy as clicking on the corresponding button.

Now that you have learned the three methods for installing a plugin, let's see the permissions that you will need to manage them.

Plugins administration permissions

As we have seen earlier, you can manage the plugins from the plugin catalog of Grafana. To perform the administration of the plugins, you have to be a Grafana administrator or an organization administrator.

Let's see these permissions in detail:

- If you are both a server admin and an organization admin:
  - You can configure app plugins.
  - You can install, uninstall, and update plugins.
- If you are not a server admin, but you are an organization admin:
  - You can configure app plugins.
  - You cannot install, uninstall, and update plugins.
- If you are a server admin, but not an organization admin:
  - You cannot configure app plugins.
  - You can install, uninstall, and update plugins.

So far, we have seen how to manage plugins. In the next section, you will learn all the flavors of Grafana plugins.

All the flavors of plugins

You can see the complete list of available plugins in the following link:

`https://grafana.com/grafana/plugins/`.

The plugins are classified into several categories, depending on various factors. Let's explore them.

Signed versus unsigned plugins

Grafana validates each plugin by means of a signature. Grafana uses this signature for verifying that a plugin is original and has not been modified.

When Grafana starts, it checks the signature of each of the plugins in the plugin directory. If a plugin is not signed, Grafana will not load it.

You can see the verification of the plugins by going to the **Configuration | Plugins** page.

There are several statuses for the signature of a plugin:

- **Core**: When the plugin is included in the Grafana code.
- **Invalid signature**: When the plugin doesn't have a valid signature.
- **Modified signature**: When the plugin suffered modifications after its signature. This can be a security issue.
- **Unsigned**: When the plugin is not signed.
- **Signed**: When the plugin signature has been verified.

Now that you understand what a plugin signature is, let's see when it is recommended to use unsigned plugins.

Allowing unsigned plugins

Because of security risks, it is not recommended to use unsigned plugins. However, you may want to use an unsigned plugin for many reasons.

One of them could be that you are developing a plugin and you want to try it in a test environment. In this case, you will have to allow the use of unsigned plugins in the configuration settings, as follows:

```
[plugins]
allow_loading_unsigned_plugins
```

Here, you have to enter a comma-separated list of the identifiers of each unsigned plugin.

When you enable the loading of unsigned plugins, Grafana will write a warning message in the server log.

> **Important Note**
>
> Even if you allow the use of unsigned plugins, Grafana will not load plugins with modified signatures.
>
> Also, take into consideration that unsigned plugins are not allowed in the Grafana Cloud service.

Now, let's see the signature levels of plugins.

Signature levels

The plugins have signature levels to determine how they can be distributed.

There are three levels:

- **Private**: If you want to develop your plugin and use it only in your Grafana server, this is the level of signature that you should use. It will be not distributed to the Grafana community and it will not be published in the Grafana catalog.
- **Community**: These are open source plugins that are published in the Grafana catalog and are distributed in the community.
- **Commercial**: These are based on closed source technologies. However, they are still published in the Grafana catalog and are available to the community.

Now, you will see the three types of plugins available.

Types of plugins

As we have seen in previous chapters, there are three types of plugins. These are panel plugins, data source plugins, and application plugins. Let's see each of them.

Panel plugins

These plugins allow you to build different types of visualizations, as you saw in *Chapter 6, Getting Data and Building Dashboards*.

The functions of these plugins are as follows:

- Showing data through different types of visualizations
- Browsing dashboards
- Performing actions on remote systems

So, this type of plugin offers all the functionalities for building the graphical user interface of the dashboards.

Data source plugins

The data source plugins allow getting data from different types of data repositories.

As we have seen in previous chapters, you can get data from relational databases, non-relational databases, and even text files.

Each of these data stores has different APIs and data structures. The data source plugins establish the communication with the data management systems and return the data in the Grafana format.

So, using a data source plugin, you can access and use the data quickly and easily. In other words, you don't have to bother with the implementation of the communication with the data sources.

App plugins

With app plugins, you can build dashboards for specific applications in a matter of minutes. These plugins can have their own custom panels and data sources too.

The app plugins are generally used for monitoring purposes.

Let's summarize what you have learned in this chapter.

Summary

In this chapter, you have learned how to install, update, and remove plugins in different environments.

Also, you have learned about the signatures of the plugins, and why they are important in a production environment.

Finally, you have explored all the features and functionalities that the plugin ecosystem offers.

In the next chapter, you will learn how to organize and manage dashboards to offer a better experience to the final user.

8

Organizing and Managing Dashboards

A **dashboard** must provide a clear picture of the data. So, it is important to keep things clean and organized, showing neat dashboards with relevant information.

In previous chapters, you have learned how to build dashboards using different types of data sources and visualization panels. In this chapter, you will learn how to organize, manage, and share dashboards.

Grafana offers several tools for organizing dashboards and making insights.

In this chapter, you will learn about the following:

- Organizing panels and dashboards
- Properties of dashboards
- Annotations and variables
- Linking and sharing dashboards
- Exporting and importing dashboards

First, let's see how you can organize your panels and dashboards.

Organizing panels and dashboards

In this section, you will learn how to manage dashboards and control visualizations.

Building dashboards is not just about showing data in visualization panels. You will have to provide an easy-to-understand user interface, where people can observe the data they need.

Controlling the visualization

Let's start looking in detail at all the options available in a Grafana dashboard. In the following figure, you can see the upper-right menu, where you can control many aspects of the visualizations:

Figure 8.1 – Visualization controls

From left to right, you can see the following controls:

- *Add panel button*: With this button, you can add a new panel to the dashboard.

- *Save dashboard*: This button allows you to save the dashboard with the current name.

- *Dashboard settings*: This option leads you to the configuration settings of the dashboard. We will see it later in this chapter.

- *Time range drop-down*: Here, you can select the time range of your interest. You can set relative values (such as last hour, last seven days, and so on) or specific dates and times.

- *Update visualizations*: This button allows you to force the update of the data. Also, you can specify the update period by clicking on the *arrow* beside it.

- *Playlist control*: You can use this to show a dashboard in different ways: **Normal**, **Kiosk**, and **TV**. We will see more of this later in this chapter.

Now that you have met the controls of a dashboard, let's see how you can modify your dashboard.

Adapting a dashboard to your needs is as easy as moving panels and resizing them using drag and drop operations. You can see an example of this in the following screenshot:

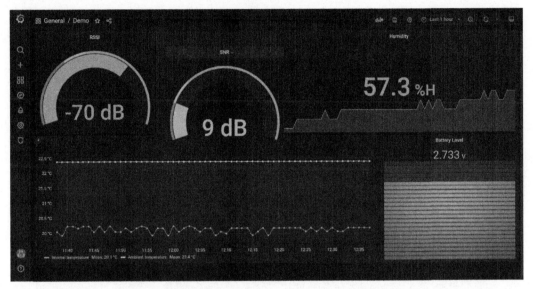

Figure 8.2 – Resizing and moving panels in a dashboard

Now, let's see how to build playlists.

Building and showing playlists

A playlist is a series of dashboards that are shown in sequence. They are used to show several dashboards on the same screen.

Playlists are useful, for instance, for showing information to visitors or for bringing relevant data to monitoring operators. So, playlists can be a very interesting feature in **Internet of Things (IoT)** projects. Let's see how to create one.

Creating, editing, and deleting a playlist

To create a playlist, do the following:

1. Go to **Dashboards | Playlists** and click on **Create Playlist**. This will lead you to the **New Playlist** page, as you can see in the following screenshot:

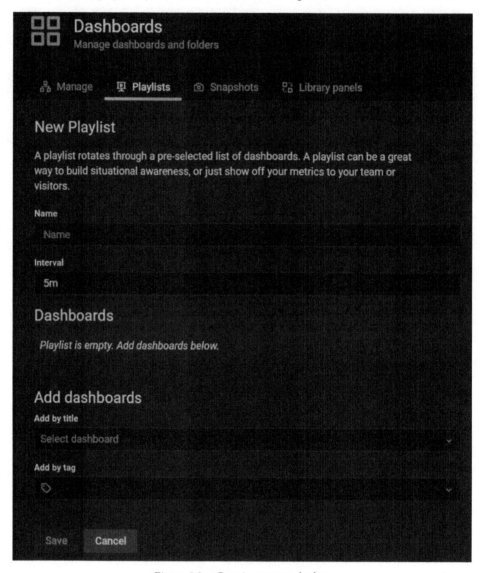

Figure 8.3 – Creating a new playlist

On this page, you have to specify some parameters for building a new list. First, you have to give a name to the list. This name will let you select the playlist when you want to run it.

2. Then, you have to specify a time interval. This value determines the time each dashboard will be shown before passing to the next one.

3. The **Dashboards** section shows the dashboards included in the list. As this is a new playlist, there are no dashboards listed here yet.

4. To add dashboards to the playlist, you have two options: **Add by title** and **Add by tag**. Each of these allows you to select the dashboards from drop-down lists where all the available dashboards are shown.

5. Whenever you add a dashboard, it appears in the list after the last one. However, you can reorder them later. Also, you can remove any dashboard from the playlist.

6. After you have selected the dashboards, you have to save the playlist by clicking on the **Save** button.

7. Finally, you can edit or delete any playlist. To edit, you have to select the playlist from the **Playlists** page and click on **Edit playlist**.

To delete a playlist, you just have to click on the **Delete playlist** button and confirm the action. You can see all these options in the following screenshot:

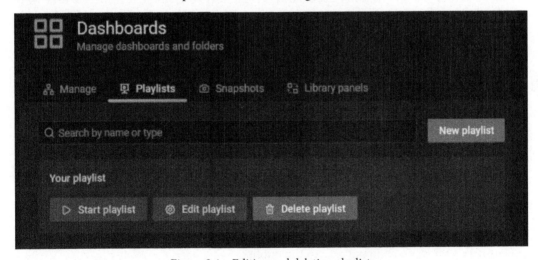

Figure 8.4 – Editing and deleting playlists

Let's see how you can start a playlist.

Starting a playlist

As you can see in *Figure 8.4*, there is a **Start playlist** button to start the playlist. However, there are many ways of playing a playlist, as shown in *Figure 8.5*:

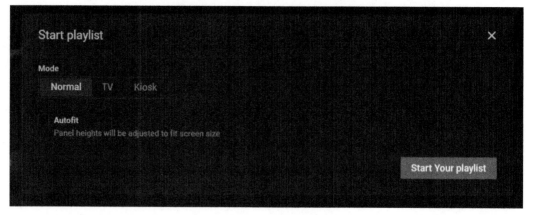

Figure 8.5 – Starting a playlist

Let's explore each of the visualization modes that you can use.

Normal mode

In this mode, all the menus and panel controls remain visible on the screen. The user will see exactly the same menus and panels that you see.

The available options will depend on the user permissions.

TV mode

In this mode, the side menu is hidden, whereas the navbar, row, and panel controls are shown at the top.

This mode is enabled after a minute of inactivity. Also, you can enable it manually by adding the `?inactive` parameter to the URL. As soon as you press any key or move the mouse, this mode is disabled.

Kiosk mode

In this mode, all the menus, navbar, and panel controls are completely hidden. This is the preferred option when showing data to the public.

Controlling a playlist

When the playlist is in the **Normal** or **TV** mode, you can control it using the navbar at the top of the screen.

The following are the available options:

- *Next* (double-right arrow): Advance to the next dashboard.
- *Back* (left arrow): Go back to the previous dashboard.
- *Stop* (square): Stop the playlist.
- *Cycle view mode* (monitor icon): You can change the view mode using this button.
- *Time range*: Here, you can specify the time range that you want to visualize. You can choose between five minutes to five years.
- *Refresh* (circle arrow): This element allows you to update the data. Also, you can configure it to update automatically from five seconds to one day.

Now that you know how to create and play a playlist, let's see how you can share one.

Sharing a playlist

You can share a playlist in view mode to show it to operators, the public, managers, and so on.

To share a playlist, you can just copy the URL from a view mode visualization.

The procedure is as follows:

1. Go to the **Dashboards** submenu and click on **Playlists**.
2. Click **Start playlist** on the playlist you want to share.
3. Click the view mode you want to use.
4. Copy the URL to your clipboard. The URL will look like `https://your-grafana-domain/playlists/play/1?kiosk` (where `1` is the first playlist, and `kiosk` refers to kiosk mode).
5. Finally, share the link.

So far, you have learned about the basic management of dashboards. In the next section, you will learn about the properties of dashboards.

Properties of dashboards

Dashboards have many properties, which you can configure to control the way they behave. Let's see each of them.

General dashboard properties

In *Figure 8.6*, you can see the settings page of the **General** dashboard properties:

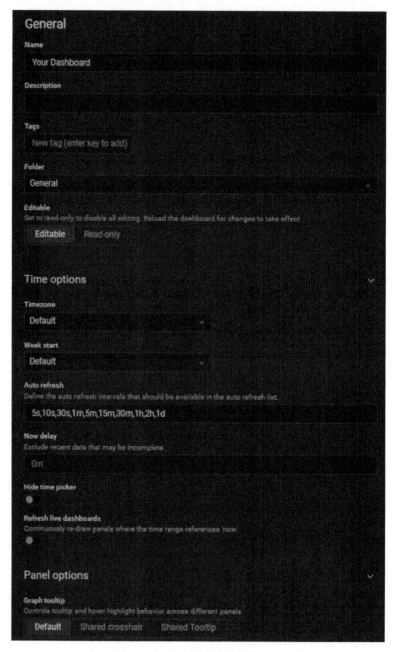

Figure 8.6 – Setting the dashboard properties

Now, let's explore all the fields shown in the preceding figure:

- **Name**: As you can guess, this is the name of the dashboard. You can give the dashboard any meaningful name.

- **Description**: Here, you can include a helpful text to describe the purpose of the dashboard.

- **Tags**: Tags are useful for identifying the features and objectives of the dashboards. You may put here things such as type of sensor, location, type of hardware, type of use, and so on. Then, you can group dashboards in a playlist according to their tags.

- **Folder**: Inside an organization, you can use folders to group dashboards into different categories. This allows you to keep things ordered in a logical structure. To assign a dashboard to a folder, you need to have created the folder previously.

- **Editable**: You can set whether the dashboard is editable or not.

- **Time options**: Here, you can set the following options:

  - **Timezone**: Here, you have two options in the drop-down list:

    - **Default:** The dashboard will use the time zone configured for the user profile, team, or organization if used. If this option is not configured, Grafana will use the local browser time.

    - **Local browser time**: In this case, the dashboard will use the time zone configured in the browser.

  - **Week start**: You can select the start day of the week.

  - **Auto refresh**: Here, you can build a list of the periods that will be available in the refresh list of the dashboard.

  - **Now delay**: You may prefer to delay the visualization of the data in certain cases. This option lets you do it.

  - **Hide time picker**: With this option, you can hide the time picker in the upper part of the screen.

  - **Refresh live dashboards**: This option lets you continuously refresh the dashboard when the time range includes *now*.

Now that you know the general properties of a dashboard, let's explore the topics of annotations and variables.

Annotations and variables

In this section, you will learn about two important features of Grafana: **annotations** and **variables**. First, we will explore annotations.

Annotations

Annotations are a great tool for building insights into the data. With annotations, you can mark data points according to specific criteria.

Then, when you hover a data point, you will see the annotation description and the associated tags (if available).

Grafana makes it easy to add annotations. You can do it directly from the graphical user interface. The annotations can be related to a data point or a range of data. In *Figure 8.7*, you can see an annotation related to a data range.

To add a data range annotation, press *Ctrl/Cmd* + click to select the region with the mouse. If you just want to select a data point, use *Ctrl/Cmd* + click with the mouse.

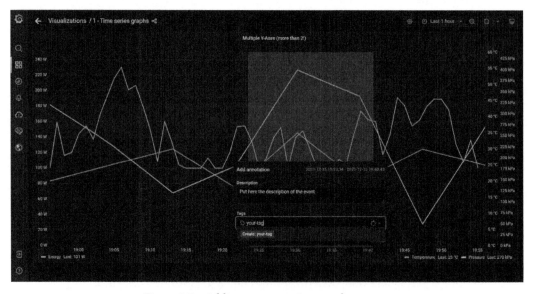

Figure 8.7 – Adding an annotation to a data range

Once you have added an annotation, it will remain visible in the panel. Grafana has a built-in annotation query that runs on all the dashboards. This query searches all the annotation events of the current dashboard and shows them on the panels.

If you want to stop the queries in a dashboard, you can go to the **Annotations** settings on the dashboard **Settings** page, as you can see in *Figure 8.8*:

Figure 8.8 – Built-in annotation query

Then, click on the query, which will lead you to the annotation configuration (see *Figure 8.9*):

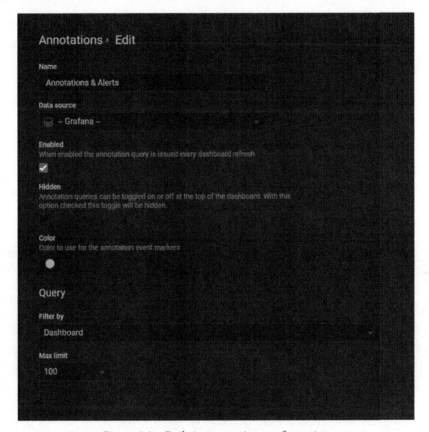

Figure 8.9 – Built-in annotation configuration

Let's see each of the options available on the annotation configuration page.

First, you have the name of the annotation, which you can change to anything meaningful for your annotation.

Then, you have to select the data source. In this case, we are using **Grafana**, because we are generating the annotations from Grafana. You can switch this between all the data sources that you have available.

With the **Enabled** option, you can enable (or not) the annotation on the dashboards.

You can hide (or not) the annotation queries toggle in the dashboard using the **Hidden** option on this configuration page.

With the **Color** option, you can choose the color of the annotations on the dashboards.

Finally, you can filter the annotation using two types of filters: dashboards and tags. If you choose dashboards, all the annotations belonging to the current dashboard will be shown. On the other hand, if you select tags, all the annotations related to specific tags will be displayed.

So far, you have learned about annotations and how to use them. In the following section, you will learn about variables.

Variables

You can use variables in Grafana to store values of metric queries and panel titles. This allows you to use a drop-down menu to select the metrics that you want to visualize in your dashboard.

Using variables allows you to build dynamic dashboards, where the user can select the metrics that will be shown. The variables are available in drop-down menus at the top of the dashboard. You can see an example in the following screenshot:

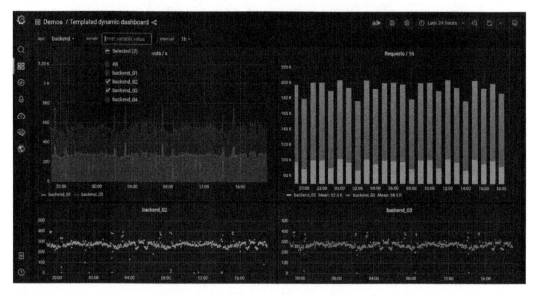

Figure 8.10 – Using variables in a dashboard

Before learning about variables, let's see what templates are.

Templates

A template is any query that contains a variable. You can use these queries to show specific data in panels. Variable values are always synced to the URL using the var-<varname>=value syntax.

Now, let's see how you can build your variables.

Creating a variable

To create a new variable, go to **Dashboard settings | Variables,** and click on **New**. This will lead you to the **Variables** page, as you can see in the following screenshot:

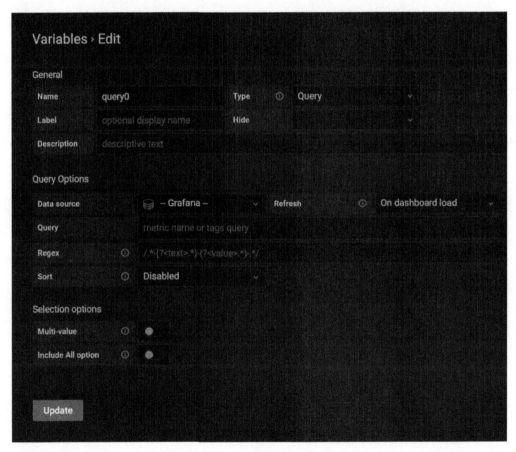

Figure 8.11 – Variable configurations

There are many options to configure a variable. Let's start with the **General** options.

General options

Let's explore all the options available:

1. First, give a name to your variable.
2. Then, select the type of variable. You can choose from the following options: **Query**, **Custom**, **Text box**, **Constant**, **Data sources**, **Intervals**, and **Ad hoc filters**. We will see each of these options later.
3. You can assign a label to the variable for easy identification. However, this is optional and if you leave this field blank, the variable will show its name instead.
4. In the **Hide** option, you can choose between the following:

    I.   **No selection**: This is the default option. In this case, the drop-down menu will show the label or name of the variable.

    II.   **Label**: The variable drop-down menu only shows the selected variable value.

    III. **Variable**: In this case, the drop-down menu will be not shown.

5. In the **Description** field, you can type any text that helps to understand the meaning and use of the variable.

As we have seen in a bullet point earlier, there are many types of variables. Let's start with the **Query** variables.

Query variables

This type of variable is the first option available in the list. The **Query** options let you specify the query that you want to use in your variable.

These are the options available:

- In the **Data source** list, choose the data source you want to use for the query.
- In the **Refresh** list, specify the way that variables should update. There are two options:

    - **On dashboard load**: If you choose this option, the query will run every time the dashboard loads.
    - **On time range change**: In this case, the query will be executed when the dashboard time range changes.

- Ingress a query in the **Query** field. Here, you can ingress the text of the query. All queries depend on the type of data source that you are using.
- Then, you can optionally add a regex expression in the **Regex** field. This is useful if you want to capture and filter some data from the query result.

- The **Sort** option lets you specify the order of the values in the drop-down list. The default option is **Disabled**, in which case the order will be determined by the result of the query.
- Then, you can set **Selection options**, which you can use for managing variable option selections:

  - **Multi-value**: If you choose this, the user will be able to select multiple options at the same time.
  - **Include All option**: In this case, Grafana will add the **All** option to the variable drop-down list.

- Finally, you can see a preview of the query in the **Preview of values** section.

Now, let's see each one of the remaining variables.

Custom variables

The **Custom** variables allow you to store values that don't change, such as names, regions, clusters, sensor IDs, and so on.

You can see the configuration page in the following screenshot:

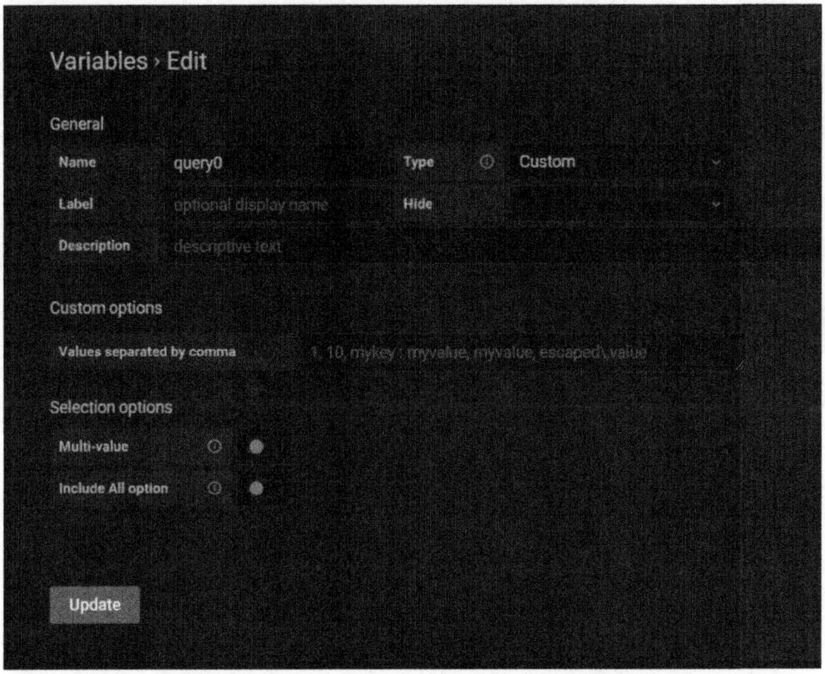

Figure 8.12 – Configuring custom variables

To configure a custom variable, follow these steps:

- For the **General** options, you can apply the same instructions that you have seen earlier in this section.

- In the **Values separated by comma** field, you can enter the values in a comma-separated list. You can use numbers, strings, or key/value pairs, for example, `key1 : value1` and `key2 : value2`.

Now, let's see the **Text box** variable.

Text box variable

You can use a text box variable to show free text on your dashboard. Here, you can enter any type of data.

You can specify a default text or you can leave it blank, in which case the user will be able to input any text. You can see the **Text box** variable configuration page in the following screenshot:

Figure 8.13 – Configuration of text box variables

Let's continue with the **Constant** variables.

Constant variables

You might think that a constant variable is a contradictory idea because a variable is the opposite of a constant. However, it makes sense in this case.

Constant variables allow you to assign to variables values that don't change over time. Think about serial numbers, device addresses, and so on.

You can use constant variables in queries, avoiding writing complex values. You can see the **Constant** variable configuration page in the following screenshot:

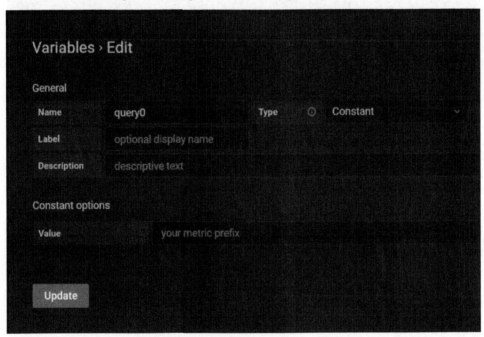

Figure 8.14 – Configuring constant variables

Now, let's look at the **Data source** variables.

Data source variables

Data source variables let you specify different data sources for a dashboard. For example, you can have several instances of InfluxDB data sources and you want to switch between them on the same dashboard.

In the following screenshot, you can see the configuration page for the **Data source** variables:

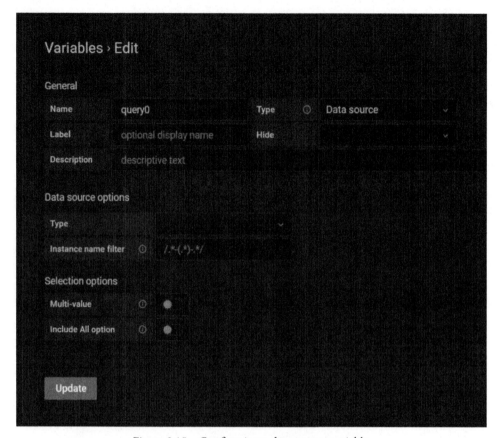

Figure 8.15 – Configuring a data source variable

To configure a data source variable, follow the next steps:

- In the **Type** list, select the type of data source that you want to use.
- In the **Instance name filter**, you can optionally specify a regex filter to choose the data source instances for the specified type. If you leave this field empty, it will display all the instances.

Let's continue with the **Interval** variables.

Interval variable

You can use interval variables to set time ranges, such as 1s, 1m, 1h, and 1d. With interval variables, you can change the grouping of the data in the visualization.

You can see the **Interval** variables configuration page in the following screenshot:

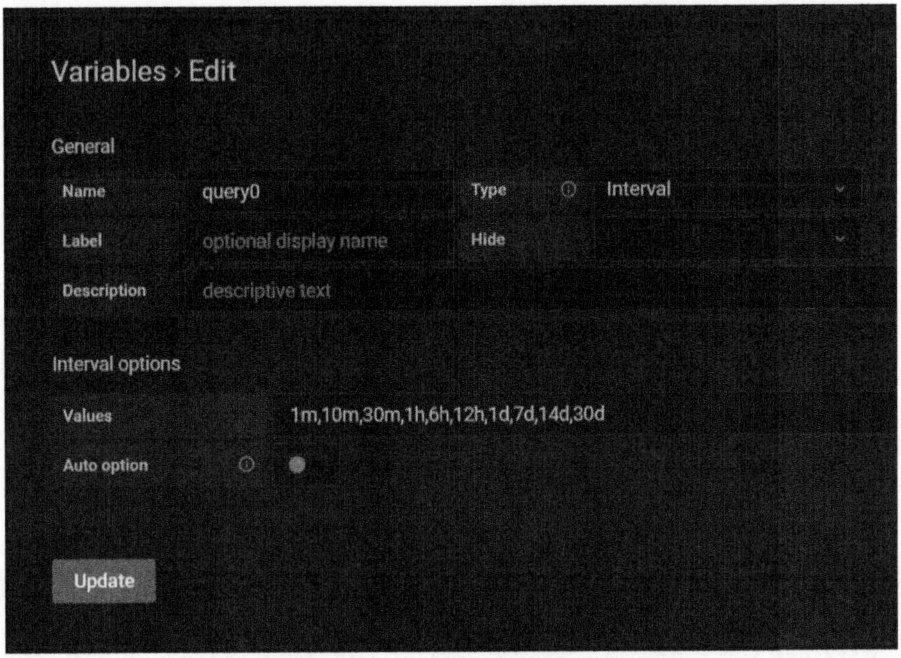

Figure 8.16 – Configuring interval variables

To configure an interval variable, follow these steps:

- In the **Values** field, specify the time ranges that you want to show in the variable drop-down list. You can choose any or all of the following options: **s** (seconds), **m** (minutes), **h** (hours), **d** (days), **w** (weeks), **M** (months), and **y** (years). You can edit the default values: **1m**, **10m**, **30m**, **1h**, **6h**, **12h**, **1d**, **7d**, **14d**, and **30d**.

- Optionally, you can enable **Auto option** if you want to add the auto option to the list. With this option, you can specify the number of divisions of the current time range. When you enable it, two more options appear:

  - **Step count**: In this field, you can specify the number of divisions. For example, if the visible time range is 60 minutes, then the auto interval will group the data into 30 two-minute parts. The default value of step count is **30**.

- **Min Interval**: In this field, you can limit the minimum division allowed. For example, if you have a 40-minute range and you set this option to **2m**, then you will obtain 20 two-minute increments.

Now, let's look at **Ad hoc filters**.

Ad hoc filters

With ad hoc filters, you can create key/value filters that you can use in any metric query for a specific data source. Ad hoc filters are not a query expression. Instead, you use ad hoc filters to run filters in existing queries.

The only parameter that you have to specify in **Ad hoc filters** is **Data source**, as you can see in the following screenshot:

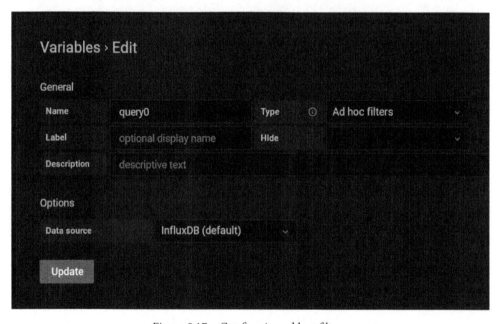

Figure 8.17 – Configuring ad hoc filters

In the example in the previous screenshot, **InfluxDB (default)** is selected as the data source. In this case, you can build queries based on tags.

You can build very complex queries using ad hoc filters. They are the more flexible type of variable in Grafana.

Now that we have seen all the types of variables, let's learn about global variables.

Global variables

In Grafana, there are built-in variables that you can use in your queries.

Let's see each of these variables:

- `$__dashboard`: This variable lets you specify the name of a dashboard.
- `$__from` and `$__to`: These are time range variables. They are specified as epoch milliseconds by default, but you can change the formatting with the following options: `${__from:date}`, `${__from:date:iso}`, `${__from:date:seconds}`, and `${__from:date:YYYY-MM}`. The same applies to `${__to}`. You can also use these variables in the URL of a dashboard (for example, `https://play.grafana.org/d/000000012/grafana-play-home?viewPanel=2&orgId=1?from=now-6h&to=now`).
- `$__interval`: This variable lets you specify the grouping of data points. Grafana calculates the interval according to the time range and the resolution of the screen. If there are more data points than the number of pixels in the panel, Grafana will group them to fit the visualization. So, if you want to see four months of data, a one-day interval will be more convenient than one hour. The automatic calculation performed by Grafana approximates to *(to – from)/resolution*.
- `$__interval_ms`: This variable is the `$__interval` variable, but in milliseconds. So, if `$__interval` is `60s`, then `$__interval_ms` is `60000`.
- `$__name`: This variable is used only with the Singlestat panel. You can use it in the prefix or suffix fields on the **Options** tab. The variable will be replaced with the series name or alias.
- `$__org`: This variable represents the ID of the organization. For example, to obtain the name of the current organization, you can use `${__org.name}`.
- `$__user`: This variable provides the following: `${__user.id}` is the ID of the current user, `${__user.login}` is the login handle, and `${__user.email}` is the email of the user.
- `$__range`: This variable is only supported by Prometheus and Loki data sources. It is related to the `rate` function.
- `$timeFilter` or `$__timeFilter`: This variable returns the current time range as an expression. For example, if you have **Last 12 hours**, the expression is `time > now() - 12h`.

To see some variable examples, go to the following URL: `https://grafana.com/docs/grafana/latest/variables/variable-examples/`.

So far, we have looked at annotations and variables. Now, let's see how to link and share panels and dashboards.

Linking and sharing dashboards

In this section, you will learn how to link dashboards to achieve better navigation. You will also learn how to share dashboards.

Linking dashboards and panels

You can use links to navigate between dashboards, panels, and even external sites. Links allow you to build a better experience for the user. For example, you may have related data distributed among several dashboards. In this case, links are a good tool for rapid and easy navigation.

In Grafana, you can use dashboard links, panel links, and data links. Dashboard links are shown at the top of the dashboard, whereas you can see panel links in the top-left corner of the panel.

Dashboard links

In a dashboard link, you can include the time range and variables, so the user can see the right data. Let's see how to create a dashboard link.

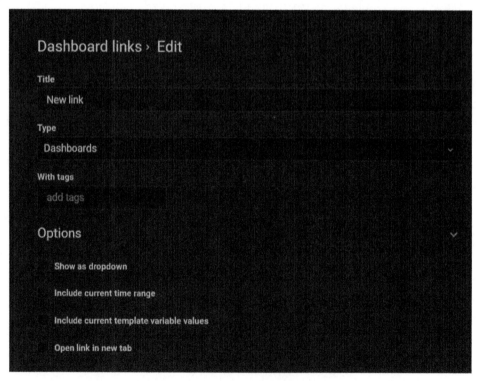

Figure 8.18 – Creating a dashboard link

To add links to dashboards, follow these steps (see *Figure 8.18*):

- In the dashboard, go to the **Dashboard settings** page.
- Click on **Links** and then click on **Add Dashboard Link** or **New**.
- In **Type**, choose **Dashboards**.
- Now, you have to the set the link options:

  - **With tags**: Here, you can specify all the tags related to the dashboards that you want to see. In this way, you can filter dashboards. If you don't include tags, Grafana will include links to all the dashboards.
  - **Show as drop-down**: When you have a lot of dashboards, you can use this option to have a better user interface. With this option, you can include the dashboard links in a drop-down list.
  - **Include current time range**: You can select this option to include the time range in the link.
  - **Include current template variable values**: You can select this option to include variable templates.
  - **Open link in new tab**: Select this if you want to open the dashboard in a new tab.

Now, let's see how to add a URL link.

URL links

With URL links, you can link any type of URL, including dashboards, panels, and external sites.

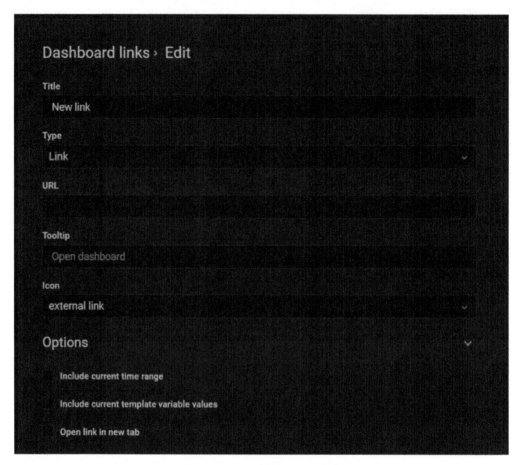

Figure 8.19 – Adding a URL link

To add a URL link, do the following:

- Go to the link page and select **Link** under **Type** (see *Figure 8.18*).

- In the **Title** field, enter the title you want to use.

- In the **URL** field, ingress the full URL.

- In the **Tooltip** field, ingress the tooltip you want to show when the user hovers the mouse on it.

- In the **Icon** field, select the type of icon you want to display from the drop-down list.

- For time range, template variables, and open in a new tab, apply the same as we applied for dashboard links (see the *Dashboard links section*).

So far, you have learned about dashboard and URL links. Now, let's learn about panel links.

Panel links

Panel links are pretty much the same as dashboard links. You can link to dashboards, panels, and external sites. You can also control the time range.

In *Figure 8.20*, you can see the Panel links section:

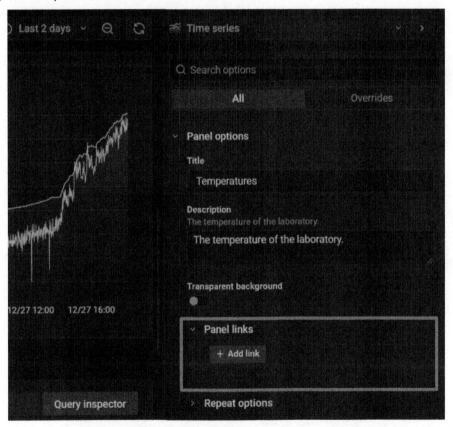

Figure 8.20 – Adding a panel link

To add a panel link, do the following:

- First, go to the panel and click on **Edit Panel**.
- On the panel configuration, go to the **Panel links** section (see *Figure 8.19*).

- Click on **Add link**.
- Enter a title for the link.
- Enter the URL of the link. You can add template variables and a time range.
- Choose whether you want to show it in a new tab.
- Finally, save the link.

Now, let's look at data links.

Data links

With data links, you can show more specific data. You can pass names, values, templates, global variables, and many more options.

To add a data link, go to the panel settings and look for the **Data links** section (see *Figure 8.20*). Then, click on **Add link**.

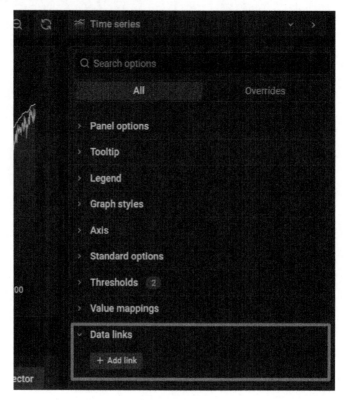

Figure 8.21 – Adding a data link

When you click on **Add link**, a new dialog box will appear, where you can ingress the data link parameters. You can see this in *Figure 8.21*:

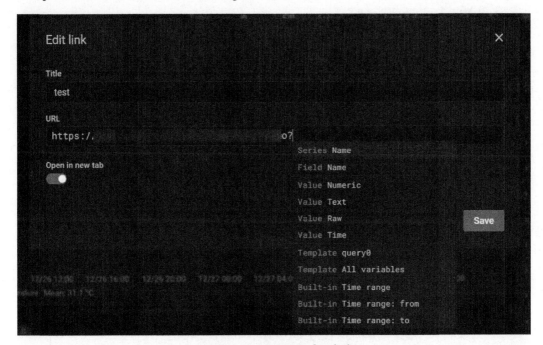

Figure 8.22 – Setting a data link

To see the available variables, you can press *Ctrl/Cmd* + spacebar. After you have added the data link, you can access it by clicking on the data points of a time-series visualization. In Singlestat, Gauge, Bar Gauge, or similar panels, you can click on any pixel of the panel.

Now, let's see how you can share a dashboard.

Sharing dashboards and panels

In Grafana, you can share your dashboards and panels with other users within an organization and even with the public on websites.

There are four methods of sharing a dashboard:

- A direct link
- A snapshot
- An embedded link
- An export link

Note that you have to grant viewer permission (at least) to the user to see a direct link visualization. The same applies to embedded links, although you can enable anonymous access for your Grafana instance.

On the other hand, a snapshot can be viewed by anybody that has the link. Snapshots don't need any authorization. Because of this, Grafana cuts any sensitive data related to the account, the data, and the instance.

Now, let's see how to share a dashboard.

Sharing a dashboard

You can share a dashboard with a direct link or a snapshot. Also, you can export it.

To share a dashboard, you have to go to your dashboard and click on the *share* icon at the top of the screen.

Once you have clicked on the *share* icon, the **Share** dialog box will be shown (as you can see in *Figure 8.22*):

Figure 8.23 – Sharing a dashboard

To use a direct link, you only have to copy the URL. This URL contains the current time range, template variables (if any), and the theme that you are using. You can also choose to shorten the URL.

If you want to publish a snapshot, select the second option (**Snapshot**) in the dialog box (see *Figure 8.23*):

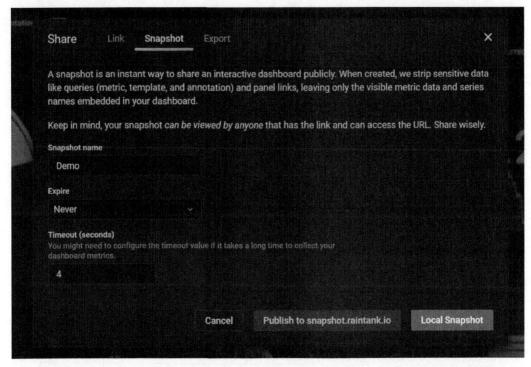

Figure 8.24 – Sharing a snapshot

You can share a dashboard publicly using a snapshot. All the sensitive data will be cut off: queries (metric, template, and annotation), and panel links. The user will be able to see just metric data and series names.

You can set the expiration of the dashboard by choosing one of four options: **Never**, **1 Hour**, **1 Day**, and **7 Days**.

Also, you can specify a timeout value if the dashboard takes a long time to load.

Finally, you can publish the snapshot on your local instance, or use `snapshot.raintank.io`. This last option is a free service offered by Grafana Labs. You can use it to publish snapshots to an external Grafana instance.

Once you click on any of the two options, a link is generated, as you can see in *Figure 8.24*:

Figure 8.25 – Generating a snapshot link

To share the snapshot, you only have to copy the URL and paste it.

Now, let's see how you can share a panel.

Sharing a panel

Sharing a panel is quite similar to sharing a dashboard, but with some minor differences. To share a panel, click on the panel title to open the menu and click on **Share**. The dialog box will appear, as you can see in *Figure 8.25*:

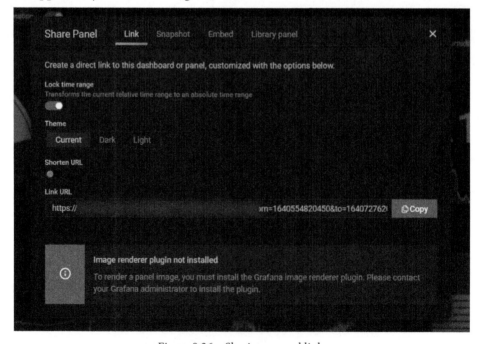

Figure 8.26 – Sharing a panel link

The first option for sharing a panel is a direct link. You can do it in the same way as for dashboards (see the *Sharing dashboards* section).

The next option is taking a snapshot. The procedure is the same as for dashboards.

The third option is to embed the panel. This option allows you to embed the panel using an iframe on a website. However, a user must be logged in to Grafana to be able to see the graph.

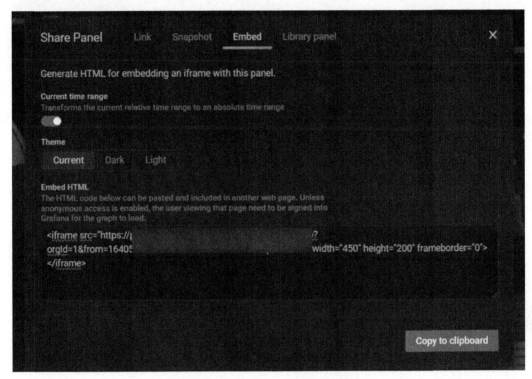

Figure 8.27– Sharing an embedded panel

The embedded HTML generates an interactive panel.

Finally, you can create a library panel. You can use library panels to reuse panels across different dashboards. Any change in the library panel will be reflected on all the dashboards in which the panel is used.

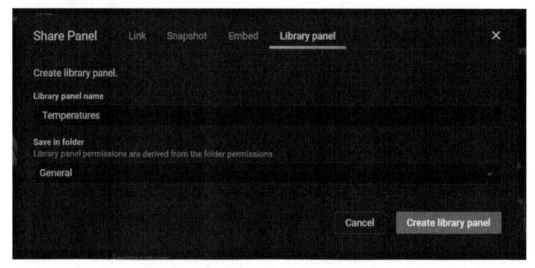

Figure 8.28 – Creating a library panel

To create a library panel, write a title and choose the folder where you want to save it.

So far, we have seen how to share dashboards and panels in different ways. Now, let's see how to export and import a dashboard.

Exporting and importing dashboards

The dashboards in Grafana are based on a JSON structure. This object includes all the information about properties, panel data, variables, and queries.

To see the JSON of a dashboard, go to the top of the screen, click on **Dashboard settings**, and click on **JSON Model**. You will see something similar to the following code:

Figure 8.29 – JSON model of a dashboard

As the JSON model has all the data needed to represent a dashboard, if you want to export one, you only need to copy this model and store it in a text file.

Let's see how you can export a dashboard easily from Grafana.

Exporting a dashboard

First, click on the *share* icon at the top of the screen, and select the **Export** tab in the dialog box, as you can see in *Figure 8.29*:

Figure 8.30 – Exporting a dashboard

Then, you can choose to view the JSON object on the screen or click on **Save to file** to generate a JSON file that will be downloaded to your device.

Importing a dashboard

To import a dashboard, the procedure is as follows:

1.   Click on the + icon on the left side menu.

2.   Click on **Import**. The page shown in *Figure 8.30* will appear.

3.   Here, you have three options:

  • Import the dashboard by uploading a JSON file.

  • Import the dashboard using a URL from `grafana.com`.

  • Copy the JSON model in the text box and click on **Load**.

On `grafana.com`, you have a lot of dashboards available, designed by Grafana Labs or by the community. To explore them, go to `https://grafana.com/dashboards`.

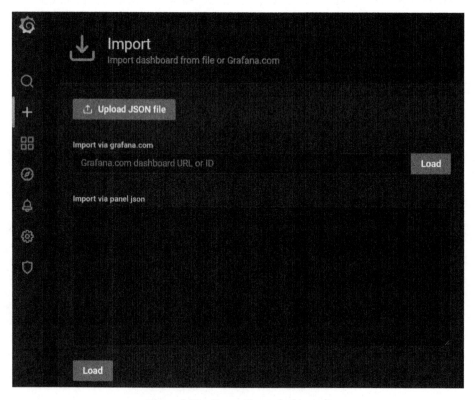

Figure 8.31 – Importing a dashboard

As you have seen, exporting and importing a dashboard are easy tasks in Grafana.

Summary

This has been a long chapter, in which you have learned a lot of things. First, you saw how to manage and organize dashboards and panels. Then, you learned everything about dashboard properties. After that, you learned about two important features of Grafana: annotations and variables. Then, you learned how to build links to other dashboards and how to share them with users inside and outside of the organization. Finally, you learned how to export and import dashboards.

That's all for now. The next chapter starts a new and very interesting part of the book: performing analytics and notifications. We will start by seeing how to perform advanced analytics using some plugins in Grafana.

Part 4: Performing Analytics and Notifications

In this part, you will learn how to use different tools to apply analytics.

You will learn how to perform numerical operations on data, including statistical analysis. Based on conditions and analytics, you will configure alerts and notifications using different communication channels.

This part contains the following chapters:

- *Chapter 9, Performing Analytics in Grafana*
- *Chapter 10, Alerting and Notifications in Grafana*

9
Performing Analytics in Grafana

In this chapter, you will learn how to transform data and perform calculations on it. You will use some built-in **Grafana** functionalities, **InfluxQL** capabilities, and the **Plotly** plugin.

First, you will learn how to use numerical manipulations on an **InfluxDB** data source. Then, you'll learn about transformations in Grafana.

These calculations include statistical, derivative, integral, and mathematic functions.

You will also learn how to embed Plotly dashboards in Grafana panels.

The topics that are covered in this chapter are the following:

- InfluxDB calculations
- Transformations in Grafana
- Building advanced plots with Plotly

After finishing this chapter, you will be able to perform all kinds of calculations on data and build complex visualizations.

Technical requirements

To apply the techniques shown in this chapter, you will need the following:

- A running instance of Grafana

- An InfluxDB data source with historical data

- The Plotly plugin installed in Grafana

Let's start by looking at InfluxDB calculations.

InfluxDB calculations

In InfluxDB, you can perform calculations on the data. In this section, you will learn how to apply them from the graphical query section of Grafana.

First, let's identify the section on the panel edition screen. *Figure 9.1* shows the query editor, which you already know about from previous chapters:

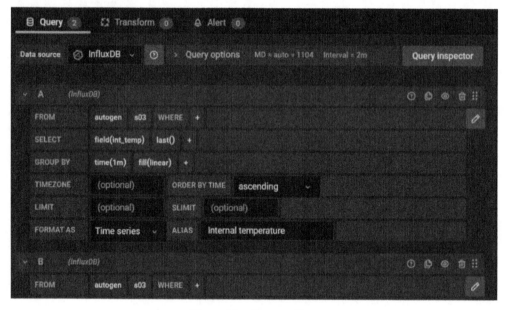

Figure 9.1 – Query editor

Recall from *Chapter 5*, *Using Time Series Databases*, that InfluxDB has two query languages: **InfluxQL** and **Flux**. In that chapter, you learned that versions 1.x of InfluxDB use InfluxQL, whereas versions 2.x of InfluxDB use Flux.

However, you can also use InfluxQL in versions 2.x. Please refer to *Chapter 5*, *Using Time Series Databases*, for more information.

In the end, Grafana fully supports InfluxQL, so we will work with that. So, let's start by looking at functions in InfluxQL.

InfluxQL functions

InfluxDB offers you a wide range of calculations. It's important to note that each of these calculations can be performed from the Grafana graphical interface. This makes it easy to try it with different computations and transformations.

In this section, we will explore some of the most useful functions for IoT projects.

Each of these functions allows the use of tags and **regular expressions (regexes)**.

Selectors

This group of operators lets you select specific data according to some criteria. Let's see some of them:

- BOTTOM (): This function returns the N smallest field values. As usual, you can filter by tags or period. You can see an example of this function in *Figure 9.2*.
- FIRST (): This function returns the first field value, taking into account the timestamp.
- LAST (): This returns the last field value, according to the last timestamp.
- TOP (): This returns the maximum N field values.

- MAX() and MIN(): These functions return the maximum and minimum absolute values, respectively. They differ from BOTTOM() and TOP() because they return a single value.

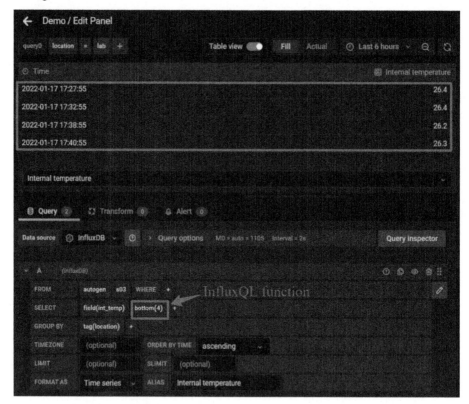

Figure 9.2 – Example of a selector function in an InfluxDB data source

Now, let's look at aggregation functions.

Aggregations

These functions let you perform some numerical and statistical computations. Let's see each of them:

- COUNT(): This counts the number of non-zero field values. It can be useful for counting events, such as a door opening or closing or people passing by a gate.

- DINSTIC(): This counts the number of unique values of a field.

- INTEGRAL(): This function lets you calculate the area below the curve of subsequent values. You could use it, for example, to calculate the energy provided by a solar panel for a period.

- `MEAN()`: This function returns the average arithmetic value of field values.

- `MEDIAN()`: This returns the middle value of a set of field values.

- `MODE()`: This function returns the most frequent value of a field value set.

- `SPREAD()`: This returns the difference between the minimum and maximum field values.

- `STDDEV()`: This function calculates the standard deviation of the field values.

- `SUM()`: This calculates the sum of all of the field values. You could use it, for example, to add up the weights of goods on a scale.

Some of these functions, such as `MEAN()`, `MEDIAN()`, `SPREAD()`, and `STDDEV()`, can be useful for building some basic analysis, or even an anomaly detection system.

Let's look at transformation functions.

Transformations

The group of transformation functions in InfluxQL allows you to apply several mathematical functions to data. Let's explore some of them:

- `ABS()`: This function lets you calculate the absolute value of the field value.

- `ACOS()`: With this one, you can calculate the arccosine (in radians) of the field value. Take into account that the field values must be between -1 and 1.

- `ASIN()`: This function returns the arcsine of the field value. It also applies the limit of -1 to 1.

- `ATAN()`: This returns the arctangent of the field value. Remember that you have to have values between -1 and 1.

- `CEIL()`: This function lets you round up the field value to the nearest integer.

- `COS()` and `SIN()`: You guessed it. These return the cosine and the sine of the field value, respectively.

- `CUMULATIVE_SUM()`: This function lets you perform a cumulative sum of subsequent field values.

- `DERIVATIVE()`: With this function, you can calculate the rate of change between subsequent field values.

- `DIFFERENCE()`: This performs the subtraction of subsequent field values.

- `ELAPSED()`: This function returns the difference between subsequent field values' timestamps.
- `EXP()`: With this function, you can calculate the exponential of the field value.
- `FLOOR()`: This function lets you round down the field value to the nearest integer.
- `LN()`, `LOG()`, `LOG2()`, and `LOG10()`: With these functions, you can perform logarithmic calculations on the field values.
- `MOVING_AVERAGE()`: You can use this function to calculate the rolling average in a window of subsequent field values.
- `POW()`: This function calculates the power, x, of the field values.
- `ROUND()`: This function lets you round the field values to the nearest integer.
- `SQRT()`: With this function, you can calculate the square root of the field values.
- `TAN()`: This function lets you calculate the tangent of the field values.

As you can see, InfluxQL lets you apply a wide range of functions to data. You can use these to perform basic analytics, avoiding the use – in many cases – of more complex tools.

For a complete description of all the InfluxQL functions available, check out the following link: `https://docs.influxdata.com/influxdb/v1.8/query_language/functions/`.

Now, let's see what transformations are in Grafana, and how you can use them.

Transformations in Grafana

You can use **transformations** in Grafana to process the data from a query before Grafana shows it. With transformations, you can join queries, rename fields, perform mathematical operations, and so on.

To access the transformation feature, go to the **Transform** tab in the panel editor, as you can see in *Figure 9.3*:

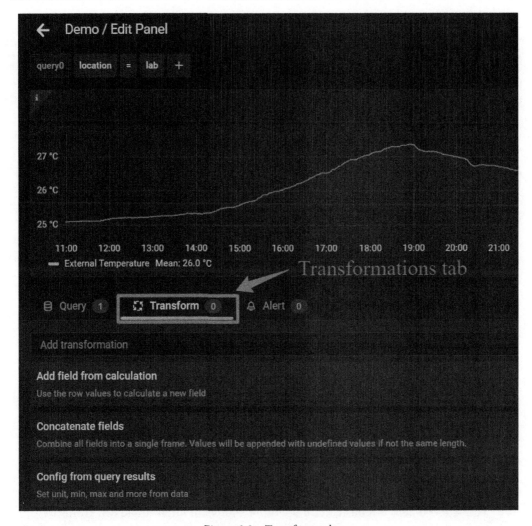

Figure 9.3 – Transform tab

Take into account that, sometimes, the resulting data isn't shown in the panel because of some incompatibility with the type of panel. In these cases, you can switch the panel to **Table view** at the top of the screen. In this mode, you will be able to see the results as a table and analyze whether they are what you are looking for.

If you apply more than one transformation, the order of them is important. Each transformation passes the result to the next, forming a pipeline. So, changing the order can modify the final result.

Finally, to apply transformations, you need a working data source and a valid query. Remember that transformations run between the query and the visualization.

Let's see each of the available transformations.

Add field from calculation

You can use this transformation to generate a new field calculated from the other two. You can concatenate this transformation to add more fields.

Let's see the options for this transformation:

- **Mode**: You can select between two modes:

  - **Reduce row**: Select this if you want to apply the calculation on each row of the selected fields in an independent way.

  - **Binary option**: This lets you perform basic math operations in a single row on the values of two fields.

- **Field name**: Here, you can select the names of the fields that you want to include in the calculation.

- **Calculation**: When you select **Reduce row** mode, the **Calculation** field shows up. Clicking on it lets you view the list of calculations available. See the full list at the end of these bullet points.

- **Operation**: When you select **Binary option** mode, the **Operation** field appears. This lets you perform basic math operations on values in a single row from two selected fields.

- **Alias**: This is optional, but it can be useful in many cases. It allows you to change the name of the new field. If you leave it blank, the new field will match the name of the calculation.

- **Replace all fields**: You can hide all the fields and show only the calculated one using this option.

In *Figure 9.4*, you can see an example where the new field is calculated in **Reduce row** mode and a sum is applied to all the fields:

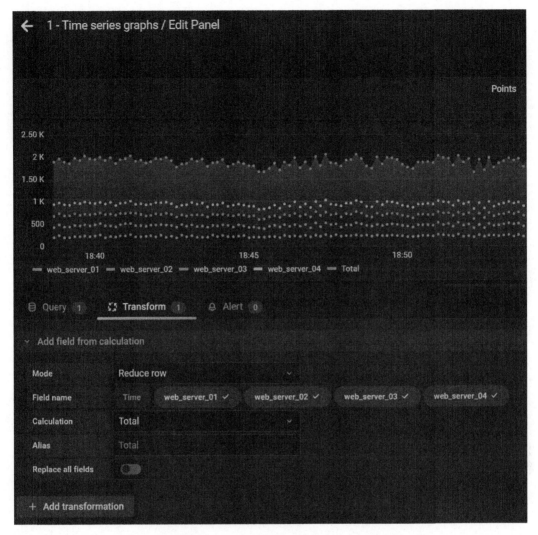

Figure 9.4 – Example of an add field calculation

You can see all the calculations available in the following list. You may notice that some of them are quite similar to the ones used by InfluxQL.

You can use these calculations in many panels, such as stat visualizations, gauges, and bar gauges.

Let's see the full list:

- `All nulls`: This is **true** when all values are null.
- `All zeros`: This is **true** when all values are zero.
- `Change count`: This counts the number of times that the field value changes.
- `Count`: This counts the number of values in a field.
- `Delta`: This calculates the cumulative change in field values and only counts increments.
- `Difference`: This calculates the difference between the first and last values of a field.
- `Difference percent`: This is the same as the previous calculation but in percentage form.
- `Distinct count`: This counts the number of unique values.
- `First (not null)`: This returns the first non-null value in a field.
- `Max, Min`: This returns the maximum and minimum values of a field, respectively.
- `Mean`: This returns the mean value of all values in the field.
- `Min (above zero)`: This returns the minimum positive value of a field.
- `Range`: This calculates the difference between the maximum and minimum values of a field.
- `Step`: This finds the minimum interval between values of a field.
- `Total`: This calculates the sum of all values in a field.

Now, let's see the next transformation.

Concatenate fields

This transformation allows you to concatenate the values of the fields, one after the other. See the following example:

The first query returns the humidity and the temperature values.

Temperature	Humidity
25	35

Table 9.1 – Query A

Another query returns the pressure value:

Pressure
1015

Table 9.2 – Query B

Then, by applying the **Concatenate** fields transformation, you will obtain the following:

Temperature	Humidity	Pressure
25	35	1015

Table 9.3 – Concatenated queries

Let's see the **Convert field type** transformation.

Convert field type

You can use this transformation to change the field type of a field.

Let's explore the options:

- **Field**: Here, you can select from the available fields.

- **as**: This lets you select the field type to convert to:

  - Numeric: This will try to convert values to numbers.

  - String: This converts the values to strings.

  - Time: This will try to parse the values as time.

  - Boolean: This converts the values to Booleans.

This transformation can be useful if you have, for example, values in a database stored as strings, but they are numbers.

Filter data by name

You can use this transformation to display only the data that you need. Grafana shows the name of the fields and you can select which one you want to show.

You can use regexes too.

You can see an example in *Figure 9.5*:

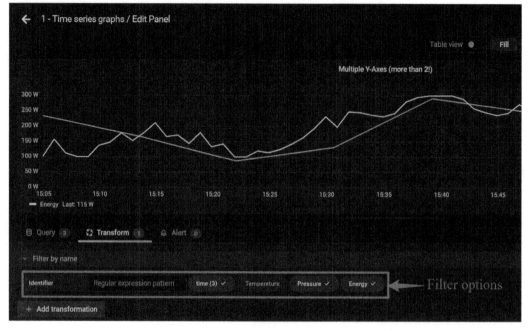

Figure 9.5 – Filter by name

Notice that only the metrics of **Pressure** and **Energy** are selected and displayed in the visualization panel.

Now, let's see how to filter data by query.

Filter data by query

If you have more than one query, as generally occurs, you can use this transformation to select which of them you want to display.

You can select the desired queries using the same procedure as for the filter by name transformation.

If the letters are white, the queries are shown, whereas if the letters are dark gray, the queries are hidden.

Let's see how you can filter data by value.

Filter data by value

With this transformation, you can select what data points you want to show from your query result. You can choose whether to include or exclude the data points that match your filter. All the conditions will be applied to the selected field.

This transformation can be very useful if your data source doesn't have native filters.

The general filter conditions are the following:

- Regex: This lets you use a regex.
- Is Null: This filter applies if the value is null.
- Is Not Null: This filter applies if the value is not null.
- Equal: This filter applies when the value is identical to the specified value.
- Different: This matches any value that is different from the specified value.

If you have numerical values, you can use any of the following conditions:

- Greater: This filter applies if the field value is greater than the one specified.
- Lower: This filter applies if the field value is lower than the specified value.
- Greater or equal: This filter applies if the field value is greater than or equal to the specified value.
- Lower or equal: This applies if the field value is lower or equal to the specified value.
- Range: Here, you can specify a range between the min and max. Any value in the range will be shown – including the min and max.

As you can see, this transformation brings you great flexibility.

Let's explore another useful transformation.

Group by

With this transformation, you can group the data by a specific column value. Then, you can apply calculations to this grouped data.

Let's see an example. Suppose you have the following original data – I have removed timestamp data for more clear visualization:

Location	Temperature	Humidity
Office	23	41
Lab	22	39
Storage	25	40
Office	22	42
Lab	21	38
Storage	20	37

Table 9.4 – Original data

Now, suppose that you want to group by `Location`. Then, the data will be ordered like the following:

Location	Temperature	Humidity
Lab	22	39
Lab	21	38
Office	23	41
Office	22	42
Storage	25	40
Storage	20	37

Table 9.5 – Grouped data

Now that you have grouped the data, you can apply any calculation to it. For example, you may want to calculate the average value of the temperature for each location. Then, you can use the **Mean** calculation on the `Temperature` field. You can even add more calculations to the groups.

Labels to fields

This transformation lets you change time series results that have labels or tags to a table format. The generated table will have a structure where each label or tag is a row or a column – depending on what type of visualization you choose.

Let's see an example where we use tags for storing the location and the number of a sensor:

Series 1 tags: Location=Office, Sensor=s01

Series 2 tags: Location=Lab, Sensor=s03

When you apply **Columns** mode, you will see something like the following:

Time	Location	Sensor
2022-01-25 11:55:10	Office	s01
2022-01-25 11:55:10	Lab	s03

Table 9.6 – Labels to fields transformation in Columns mode

On the other hand, if you use **Rows** mode, you will get a table for each series:

Tag	Value
Location	Office
Sensor	s01

Table 9.7 – Labels to fields transformation in Rows mode (table 1)

Tag	Value
Location	Lab
Sensor	s03

Table 9.8 – Labels to fields transformation in Rows mode (table 2)

Let's see the **Merge** transformation next.

Merge

You can use the **Merge** transformation to combine the results from multiple queries. If the values can be merged, they will appear in the same row.

To be mergeable, the shared fields must contain the same type of data.

Let's see an example:

The first query returns the location and the temperature values.

Time	Location	Temperature
2022-01-25 11:55:10	Office	25
2022-01-25 11:56:10	Lab	23

Table 9.9 – Data from query A

The second query returns the location and the humidity values.

Time	Location	Humidity
2022-01-25 11:55:10	Office	40
2022-01-25 11:56:10	Lab	39

Table 9.10 – Data from query B

When you merge these queries, you obtain the following:

Time	Location	Temperature	Humidity
2022-01-25 11:55:10	Office	25	40
2022-01-25 11:56:10	Lab	23	39

Table 9.11 – Result of merging the two queries

Let's see now how you can organize fields with transformations.

Organize fields

With this transformation, you can change the names, the order, or the visibility of the fields returned by the query. Take into account that this transformation can be used only in panels with a single query.

You can see an example of this transformation in the following figure:

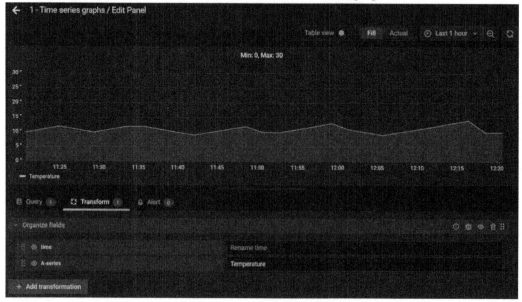

Figure 9.6 – Organize fields transformation

Let's explore the **Join by field** transformation.

Join by field (outer transformation)

You can apply this transformation to the results from several time series queries.

This lets you combine the results and show them in a single visualization. You can see an example of this in the following figure:

Figure 9.7 – Join by field transformation

Let's see how to apply the **Reduce** transformation next.

Reduce

With this transformation, you can apply a calculation to each field and return the results in a table. This transformation removes the time fields.

You can see an example in the following figure:

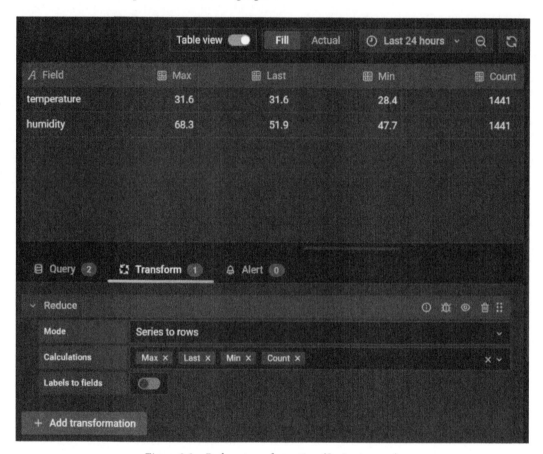

Figure 9.8 – Reduce transformation (Series to rows)

This transformation offers two modes:

- **Series to rows**: In this mode, it creates a row for each field and a column for each calculation – as in the previous example.

- **Reduce fields**: This keeps the structure from the queries and creates a frame for each of them, showing the calculated values of each field. You can see an example in the following figure:

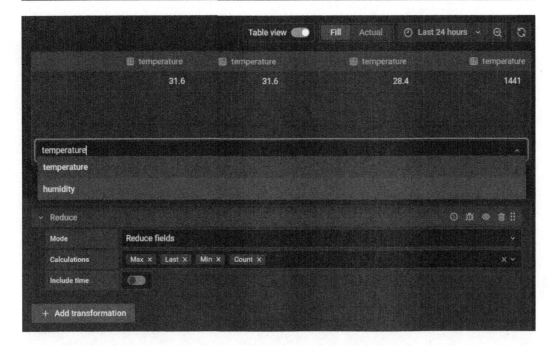

Figure 9.9 – Reduce transformation (Reduce fields)

We have now explored most of the transformations available in Grafana. In the next section, you will learn how to use the Plotly library inside Grafana.

Building advanced plots with Plotly

According to the GitHub description, **Plotly** is a standalone JavaScript data visualization library. This library is also available in **Python** and **R**.

With Plotly, you can build a wide range of basic and advanced visualizations, such as 3D graphs, SVGs, and statistical charts.

There are two plugins for running Plotly scripts at the time of writing this book. However, one of them seems to have some issues. In this book, we will work with the Plotly panel, whose source code is available in the following GitHub repository:

`https://github.com/ae3e/ae3e-plotly-panel`

You can find the plugin page on the Grafana Labs site, at the following link: `https://grafana.com/grafana/plugins/ae3e-plotly-panel/`.

To install this plugin, you can follow the same procedure described in *Chapter 7, Managing Plugins*.

In particular, you can install this plugin with the CLI tool, using the following command:

```
$sudo grafana-cli plugins install ae3e-plotly-panel
```

Now, let's see at the Plotly panel interface in Grafana. In the following figure, you can see how it looks:

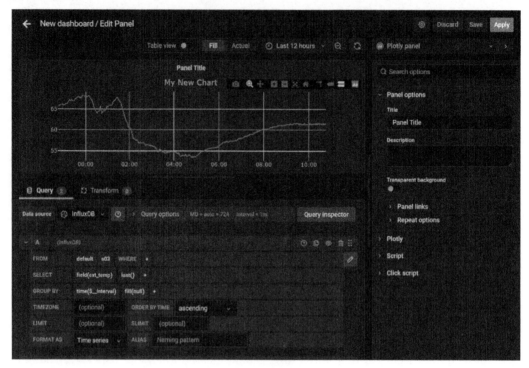

Figure 9.10 – Plotly panel

As you can see in the screenshot, the panel has three specific configuration sections: **Plotly**, **Script**, and **Click script**. Let's explore each of them.

In the **Plotly** section, you will find three textboxes: **Data, Layout,** and **Configuration**. They correspond to the three configuration options for displaying data using the Plotly library. Take into account that you must fill these fields with JSON format parameters.

Let's see the meaning of each of them:

- **Data**: In this field, you can specify the data that Plotly will use for drawing the plots. You can specify static or dynamic data. In general, you will use dynamic data provided by the data source, but you may want to display fixed values too.

- **Layout**: This field lets you specify how to display the plot. Here, you can introduce, for example, the title of the plot, the legend, and the font.

- **Configuration**: Finally, this field allows you to set many configurations in Plotly. You can, for example, show buttons to change the appearance of the plot or specify exporting options.

To see a complete list of options and examples, you can visit the following links:

`https://plotly.com/javascript/configuration-options/`

`https://plotly.com/javascript/plotly-fundamentals/`

If you prefer, you can use the **Script** textbox instead of the three textboxes described before.

In the following figure, you can see an example using the **Script** textbox:

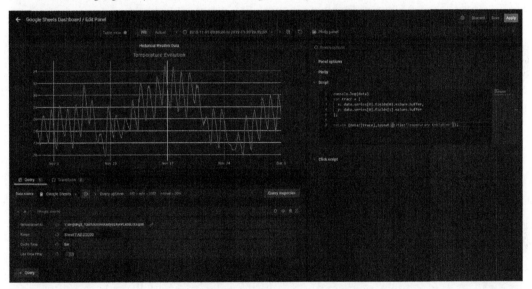

Figure 9.11 – Script in the Plotly panel

In this example, a Google Sheet is used, but the same code can be applied to any type of data source. That is because Grafana uses the same variables for accessing the data. So, the script becomes data source agnostic, making it easy to get the data.

Let's explore the code:

```
var trace = {
  x: data.series[0].fields[0].values.buffer,
  y: data.series[0].fields[1].values.buffer
};


return {data:[trace],layout:{title:'Temperature Evolution'}};
```

As you can see, the `trace` object has two variables: `x` and `y`. These variables get the values from the data variables defined in Grafana.

The `x` variable corresponds to the timestamp and `y` to the values of the selected field in the query.

The `series` array lets you select the query, whereas the `fields` array allows you to specify the field. So, in this example, it selected the first query and its fields.

Also, you can see in the last line a `layout` setting. This parameter allows you to specify the appearance of the visualization. In this case, it specifies the title of the plot.

To sum up, the Plotly panel plugin works with two types of arguments:

- `data`: This lets you access the data provided by the data source.

- `variables`: You can access any Grafana variable available in the dashboard. This includes global variables such as `__from`, `__to`, `__interval`, and `__interval_ms`.

Then, the script returns an object with at least one of the following properties: **data**, **layout**, **config**, or **frames**.

Although the example covered here is quite simple, take into account that Plotly allows you to build very complex plots, such as level plots and 3D plots, in a very easy way. You can see a histogram of temperature values evaluated in the last month in the following figure:

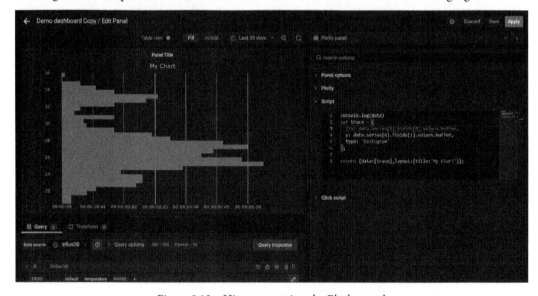

Figure 9.12 – Histogram using the Plotly panel

In this case, we just commented on the x variable and set the `type` variable of trace to `histogram`. In the same way, you can try and experiment with different graphs, layouts, and configurations.

Summary

In this chapter, you have seen how to perform basic analytics using the InfluxQL language, just before the data is displayed on the dashboard.

Also, you have learned how to use Grafana transformations to perform calculations, group data, modify data structure, and more. All these transformations allow you to arrange the data before displaying it on the dashboard.

Finally, you have seen how to use the Plotly library utilizing a plugin. This library brings you great versatility, allowing you to build things from simple plots to advanced visualizations.

In the next chapter, you will learn how to set alerts and notifications, something that is very important on any IoT platform.

Invitation to join us on Discord

Read this book alongside other Grafana users and the author Rodrigo Juan Hernández.

Ask questions, provide solutions to other readers, chat with the author via Ask Me Anything sessions and much more.

SCAN the QR code or visit the link to join the community.

https://packt.link/iotgrafana

10

Alerting and Notifications in Grafana

Alerting and notification features are an important part of any **Internet of Things (IoT)** platform. Fortunately, **Grafana** includes both. The alerting system included in Grafana allows you to specify very precise alert conditions based on your data. On the other hand, the notifications integrations let you send messages across many communication channels.

In this chapter, we will see all the options for generating alerts in Grafana. You will also learn how to integrate different notification systems.

In this chapter, you will see the following:

- How Grafana manages alerts
- Building numerical-based alerts
- Configuring notifications
- Connecting alerts and notifications

With Grafana, you can configure alerts and notifications in a matter of minutes. On the other hand, alert conditions can be as complex as you need. In this chapter, you will obtain the tools for creating your alerts and connecting to internal and external notification systems.

Technical requirements

To get the most out of this chapter, you will need the following:

- A running instance of Grafana

- A data source with numerical and categorical data

- An email service

- External notification services, such as Slack, Telegram, Discord, or general Webhooks

How Grafana manages alerts

From version *8.0*, Grafana manages alerts in a centralized way, so you can create, manage, and view alerts in the same place, as you can see in the following screenshot:

Figure 10.1 – Alerting manager in Grafana

This alerting system is enabled by default.

When the alerting manager is enabled, you can do the following:

- Create alert rules.
- View current rules and manage their state.
- View the state and health of rules.
- Add or modify contact points (notification systems).
- Add or modify notification policies.
- Add or modify silences.

Grafana uses **Alertmanager** from **Prometheus** for managing alerts. Alertmanager is embedded in Grafana, so you don't have to install it separately. If you want to learn about Prometheus Alertmanager, you can go to the following page: `https://prometheus.io/docs/alerting/latest/alertmanager/`.

Now, let's see how you can use Alertmanager.

Using Alertmanager in Grafana

To access Alertmanager, you have to click on the **Alerting** menu – the bell icon – on the left side of the screen, and then on **Alert rules**. You can see the menu in *Figure 10.2*. This will lead you to the **Alerting** page:

Figure 10.2 – Alerting menu

If it's your first time using the Alertmanager, you will see a blank page with a big blue button showing **New alert rule**. When you click on it, Grafana will lead you to the creation page, where you can choose between three options: **Grafana managed alert**, **Cortex/Loki managed alert**, and **Cortex/Loki managed recording rule**. In this book, we will just use the first option. You can see the rule creation page in *Figure 10.3*:

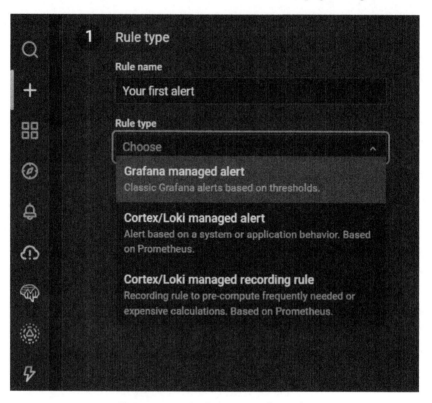

Figure 10.3 – Creating a new alert rule

Creating an alert involves five steps. Let's see each of them:

1. After you click on **New alert rule** on the **Alerts rules** page, a series of steps are shown on the screen:

    A. Give a name to the rule and select **Grafana managed alert** in the drop-down menu.

    B. As soon as you choose the rule type, new options appear on the screen – see *Figure 10.4*. The first of them is the folder where you want to store the alert rule. If you don't specify it, Grafana will use the general folder.

2. In this step, you can select the data source, specify the queries, and write the expressions that you want to use to evaluate the alert. You can see this step in *Figure 10.4*:

A. You can keep the default name of queries and expressions or edit them by hovering and clicking on them.

B. For queries, you have to select the desired data source in the drop-down list. It will show all the available data sources.

C. You can add all the queries and expressions needed.

D. For each expression, you will have to select the **Operation** type: **Classic condition**, **Math**, **Reduce**, or **Resample**. With **Classic condition**, you can create a single alert rule, whereas **Math**, **Reduce**, and **Resample** allow you to create separate alerts for each series.

E. After setting all the parameters, you can run the query to verify that it's working.

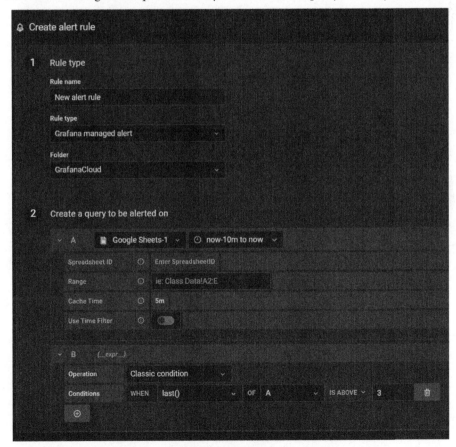

Figure 10.4 – Configuring a new alert rule

3. In this step, you can define the alert conditions – see *Figure 10.5*:

    A. Using the **Condition** drop-down list, select the query or expression that you want to use to trigger the alert.

    B. In the **Evaluate** option, specify two settings:

        i.   **Evaluate every** determines the frequency the alert rule will be evaluated. It must be a multiple of 10 seconds.

        ii. **Evaluate for** is the time that the condition must remain `true` before an alert is generated.

    C. In **Configure no data and error handling**, you can define how to proceed in case of a lack of data.

    D. Clicking on **Preview alerts** enables you to verify the result of the query.

4. In this step, you can add metadata associated with the rule – see *Figure 10.5*:

    A. You can add a description and a summary to add more information to the alert messages.

    B. You can also add a runbook URL, panel, dashboard, and alert IDs.

    C. You can also add custom labels.

5. Finally, you can click on **Save** to save the rule, or **Save and exit** to save the rule and exit the configuration page.

The following screenshots show the configuration sections of the alert rule. *Figure 10.4* shows the first and second steps.

In the following screenshot, you can see the alert conditions and details of the alert rule configuration:

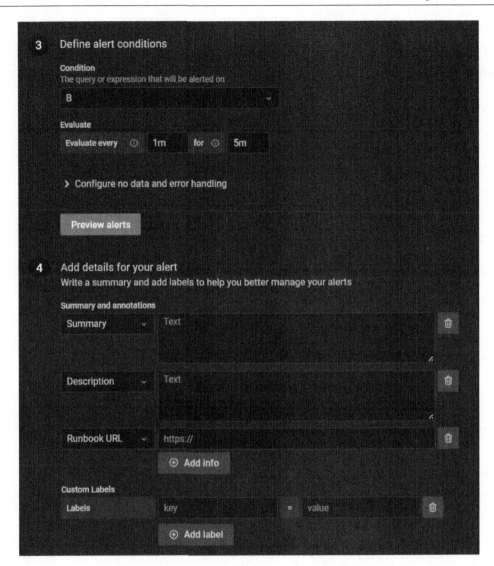

Figure 10.5 – Steps 3 and 4 of the alert configuration

Let's see how to process alerts in Grafana.

Alert rule types

In Grafana, you can create two different types of rules: **single** or **classic** condition, and **multidimensional**.

Classic condition rule

This type of rule triggers a single alert when the condition occurs. If your query returns more than one series, Grafana doesn't pay attention to the alert of each of them. So, Grafana will send only a single alert, even when several series are satisfying their alert conditions.

If you need to generate separate alerts for each series, then you have to use multidimensional rules.

Multidimensional rule

To generate a multidimensional rule, you have to use `Math`, `Reduce`, or `Resample` expressions.

You can learn about expressions at the following link, where you will find similar concepts to the ones developed in *Chapter 9, Performing Analytics in Grafana*:

`https://grafana.com/docs/grafana/latest/panels/query-a-data-source/use-expressions-to-manipulate-data/about-expressions/`

Now, let's see how to deal with no data or data errors.

No data and error handling

Sometimes, you can get errors because of a lack of data or connection issues with the data sources. In these cases, you can configure the behavior of the alerting system.

If there is no data available, you have three options:

- **No Data**: You can create a new alert, `DatasourceNoData`, with the name and **unique identifier (UID)** of the alert rule, and the UID of the data source.
- **Alerting**: You can set the rule state to `Alerting`.
- **OK**: You can ignore it and set the state to `Normal`.

If you have problems connecting to the data source (error or timeout) you can choose between any of the following options:

- **Alerting**: You can set the rule state to `Alerting`.

- **OK**: You can ignore it and set the state to `Normal`.

- **Error**: You can create a new alert, `DatasourceError`, using the name and UID of the alert rule, and the UID of the data source.

Now that you have learned about alert management in Grafana, let's see how to build numerical-based alerts.

Building numerical-based alerts

Grafana manages alerts using queries in the following data sources:

- All the data sources integrated by Grafana Labs: **InfluxDB**, **Graphite**, **Prometheus**, **Loki**, **Elasticsearch**, **Google Cloud Monitoring**, **Cloudwatch**, **Azure Monitor**, **MySQL**, **PostgreSQL**, **MSSQL**, **OpenTSDB**, and **Oracle**. In all the cases, the alerting must be enabled.

- All the community-developed data sources that have alerting enabled.

Besides data sources alerting, Grafana has its internal alerting metrics. You can see all the internal metrics in the following table:

Metric Name	Type	Description
grafana_alerting_alerts	gauge	It counts the alerts by state.
grafana_alerting_request_duration	histogram	It shows a histogram of requests to the alerting API.
grafana_alerting_active_configurations	gauge	It displays the number of active non-default Alertmanager configurations.
grafana_alerting_rule_evaluations_total	counter	It counts the number of rule evaluations.
grafana_alerting_rule_evaluation_failures_total	counter	It counts the number of evaluation failures.
grafana_alerting_rule_evaluation_duration	summary	It shows the duration of rule execution.
grafana_alerting_rule_group_rules	gauge	It displays the number of rules.

Table 10.1 – Internal metrics for Grafana alerts

Time-series and tabular data

In this book, we have focused mainly on **time-series data**. When you use time-series data, each record must be reduced to a single number, so alert rules can be applied.

On the other hand, if you have tabular data, you only have to compare the value obtained by the query.

You can process alerts in tabular data with the following data sources:

- SQL data sources: MySQL, MSSQL, Postgres, and Oracle.
- The Azure Kusto-based services.

To process alerts with Grafana on tabular data, you have to set the **Format AS** option to **Table** in the query.

The result of the query must only include a numerical data column, and eventually string columns.

When the query returns string columns, they are used as labels. The name of each column is the label name, and the values become the values of each label.

Let's see an example of tabular data.

Suppose you have the following SQL tabular data called `Sensors`:

Time	Site	Sensor	Value
2022-02-19 10:30:15	office	temperature	22
2022-02-19 10:30:15	lab	temperature	18
2022-02-19 10:40:00	storage	temperature	28

Table 10.2 – Example of SQL tabular data from Sensors

You can run the following query to select temperatures above 25 degrees:

```
SELECT Site, Sensor, CASE WHEN Value > 25.0 THEN Value ELSE 0
END FROM (
   SELECT
       Site,
       Sensor,
       Avg(Value)
```

```
FROM Sensors
Group By
    Site,
    Sensor
Where __timeFilter(Time))
```

Then, you will obtain the following:

Site	Sensor	Value
office	temperature	0
lab	temperature	0
storage	temperature	28

Table 10.3 – Results from the previous query

If you use this query inside an alerting rule, you will get the next result:

Labels	Status
{Site=office,Sensor=temperature}	Normal
{Site=lab,Sensor=temperature}	Normal
{Site=storage,Sensor=temperature}	Alerting

Table 10.4 – Results from an alerting rule

So far, you have learned how to manage and configure alerts. In the following section, you will see how to configure and use notifications in Grafana.

Notifications in Grafana

In the newest versions of Grafana, notifications are implemented using **contact points**. These contact points determine how the users will be notified when an alert triggers.

You can have several contact point types for the same contact point. For instance, you may have email and Slack. If an alert is triggered, all the contact point types included in the contact point will be used. You can also customize each notification message for every contact point type.

Let's see how you can create a contact point.

Adding a contact point

To add a contact point, you have to go to the **Contact points** tab on the **Alerting** page, as you can see in *Figure 10.6*.

Once there, you can perform the following steps:

1. Click on the **New contact point** button.

2. Give a name to your new contact point.

3. From the drop-down list, select **Alertmanager**.

4. Click on the **New contact point type** button.

5. In the **Contact point type** section, select the one you want to use. You will have to fill out the mandatory field for each contact point type – see *Figure 10.7*.

6. In some contact point types, you have optional settings. Those are configuration settings for the specified contact point type.

7. In the **Notification settings** section, you can tick **Disable resolved message** if you prefer not to be notified every time the alert clears.

8. If you want to add more contact point types, just repeat steps 4 to 7.

9. Finally, click on **Save contact point** to save your changes.

The following screenshot shows the **Contact points** page:

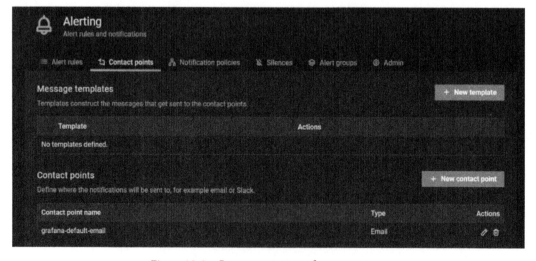

Figure 10.6 – Contact points configuration page

You can see the configuration page of a contact point in *Figure 10.7*. In this case, you can see **Email** as a contact point type:

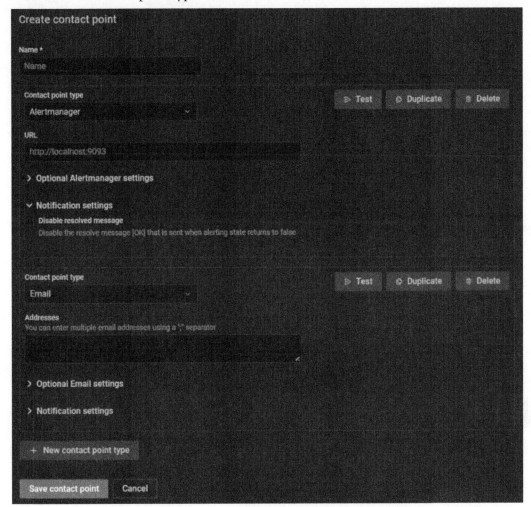

Figure 10.7 – Contact point configuration page

You can find the list of available contact point types at the following link: https://grafana.com/docs/grafana/latest/alerting/unified-alerting/contact-points/.

Some contact points worth mentioning are email, Discord, Telegram, Slack, Webhooks, Prometheus Alertmanager, Microsoft Teams, and Google Hangouts Chat.

To connect alerts with contact points, you have to use **notification policies** in Grafana. You will learn about this in the following section.

Connecting alerts and notifications

So far, you have learned how to build alerts and manage them. Also, you have seen how to create contact points to deliver alert notifications to the users.

In this section, you will learn how to connect both parts. So, you will be able to send notifications of specific alerts, in a specific way, to specific users. You can do this in Grafana using notification policies.

By using notification policies, you can define how the alerts will be routed to the contact points. These policies are built on a tree structure, where each policy can have one or more child policies.

With the exception of the root policy, all the policies can match specific alert labels. Every time an alert occurs, it is evaluated by the root policy first, and then by each child policy. If you enable the **Continue matching subsequent sibling nodes** option for a policy, the evaluation will continue even after one or more matches.

Policies have a hierarchical behavior. Any parent policy governs the behavior of an alert that doesn't match any child policy. In the last instance, a root policy governs the alerts that don't match a specific policy. Take this hierarchy into consideration when you are designing the notification policies.

For access to the **Notification policies** configuration page, go to **Notification policies** on the **Alerting** page. You can see this page in *Figure 10.8*:

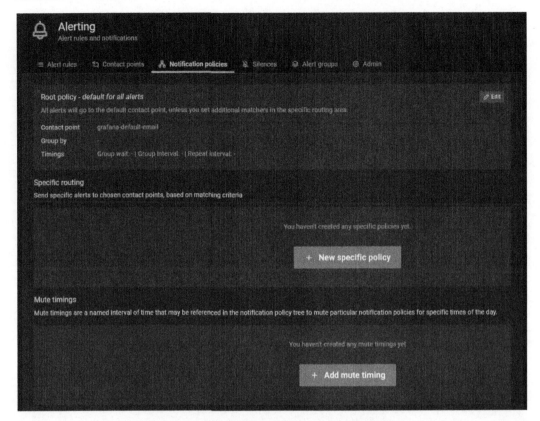

Figure 10.8 – Notification policies configuration page

Let's see how to create and configure notification policies in Grafana.

Grouping notification policies

In Grafana, you can use groups to gather alerts of the same nature or origin. Grouping allows you to route alert notifications in an efficient way when large amounts of alerts occur.

Suppose you have hundreds of devices distributed among several sites. You could group the alert notifications by site using a label – remember that you can create labels in alert rules. Doing this will help you to rapidly identify the source of notifications and the probable cause of them.

Adding notification policies

To add a new notification policy, do the following:

1. Go to the **Notification policies** tab on the **Alerting** page.
2. Go to the **Specific routing** section and click on **New specific policy**.
3. In the **Matching labels** section, add all the matching rules that you want to use.
4. In the **Contact point** drop-down list, select the one that you want to use for this policy.
5. You can also, optionally, enable the **Continue matching subsequent sibling nodes** option. With this option, you can receive more than one notification because the alert will be matched even after it has matched the parent policy.
6. You can optionally enable the **Override grouping** option to use the same grouping as the root policy. Otherwise, the root policy grouping is used.
7. You can optionally enable the **Override general timings** option to override the timing options set in the group notification policy.
8. Finally, you have to click on **Save policy** to save the changes.

You can see a screenshot of the **Notification policies** configuration page in *Figure 10.9*:

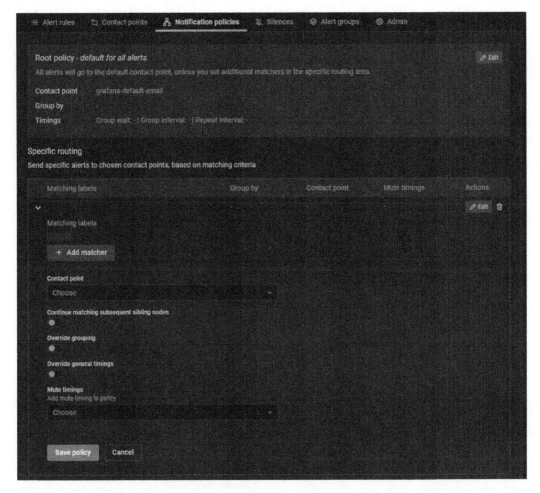

Figure 10.9 – Adding a new notification policy

After you have created a policy, you can add nested policies from there. The creation and configuration of child policies follow the same procedure discussed earlier.

Editing the root policy

You can edit the root policy in the following way:

1. Go to the **Notification policies** tab on the **Alerting** page, as you can see in *Figure 10.9*.

2. Click on **Edit** (next to the pen icon).

3. You can specify a contact point in **Default contact point**. This contact point will be used when the alert rule doesn't match any specific policy.

4. In the **Group by** option, you can specify the labels for grouping alerts.

5. In **Timing options**, you have three options:

    *   **Group wait**: This is the time to wait for alerts of the same group before sending an initial notification. The default value is 30 seconds.

    *   **Group interval**: This is the minimum time interval between two notifications in the same group. The default value is 5 minutes.

    *   **Repeat interval**: This is the minimum time interval for resending notifications if no new alerts were received for the same group. The default value is 4 hours.

6. Click on **Save** to apply the changes.

Now, let's see what mute timings are and how you can use them.

Mute timings

You can use mute timings when you want to silence notifications for a specific notification policy for some recurring periods. For example, you may want to avoid notifications during maintenance periods.

Take into account that mute timings don't disable alert rules evaluations, and the alerts are still shown in the user interface.

Creating and applying a mute timing

To create a mute timing, follow these steps:

1. Go to the **Alerting** page.

2. Click on **Notification policies**.

3. Click on the **Add mute timing** button.

4. Give a name to the mute.

5. Specify the periods in the **Time intervals** section. You can add more time intervals if you need to.

6. Click on the **Submit** button to apply the changes.

7. Go to the notification policy where you want to apply this mute and select the corresponding mute from the drop-down list.

To sum up, mute timing is a recurring period for muting notifications from specific notification policies.

Now, you will learn a slightly different concept from muting: silencing.

Silences

You can use silences to stop notifications from one or more alerting rules. Like muting, silences don't stop the evaluation of alerting rules, and the alert statuses are still shown on the user interface. Silences have a limited duration that you can configure.

Creating a silence

To create a silence, follow these steps:

1. Go to the **Alerting** page.
2. Click on the **Silences** tab.
3. Click on the **New Silence** button to open the **Create silence** page.
4. In the **Silence start and end** field, select the start and end times.
5. You can optionally specify how long the silence must be kept on by using the **Duration** option. This option updates the **Silence start and end** field.
6. In the **Name** and **Value** fields, you have to enter one or more matching labels.
7. In the **Comment** field, add some information about the silence.
8. In the **Creator** field, specify the name of the owner of the silence.
9. Finally, click on **Create**.

Differences between mute timings and silences

Although mute timings and silences have some common aspects, they differ in their uses. You can see the differences in the following table:

Mute Timing	Silence
It uses recurring interval definitions.	It has a fixed start and end time.
You have to create it and then add it to the notification policy.	It uses labels to match alerts and decide whether or not to apply the silence.

Table 10.5 – Differences between mute and silence

Take into account these differences to decide whether you need to apply one type or another.

Summary

In this chapter, you have learned about the alerting and notification systems included in Grafana.

First, you learned how to create and manage alerts using the Alertmanager embedded in Grafana.

Then, you learned about notifications, contact points, and contact point types.

Finally, you learned how to connect alerts and contact points using notification policies. Also, you have seen how to silence and mute notifications.

The next chapter starts a new part of this book: *Integrating Grafana with other Platforms*. In *Chapter 11, Using Grafana with Prometheus,* you will learn how to use Grafana in combination with Prometheus.

Part 5:
Integrating Grafana with Other Platforms

In this part, you will learn how to connect and use Grafana with other platforms.

You will see how to process, analyze, and show different types of data. You will take advantage of the structured data that is offered by these platforms.

This part contains the following chapters:

11
Using Grafana with Prometheus

You can integrate many applications with Grafana. In this chapter, you will learn how to get data from a **Prometheus** instance.

In the previous chapter, you learned how to use **Alertmanager**, which is embedded in **Grafana**. This piece of software is the same one that's used in the Prometheus system.

In this chapter, we will cover the following topics:

- What is Prometheus?
- Installing Prometheus
- Feeding Prometheus with data
- Integrating Prometheus and Grafana

Prometheus is a great partner for Grafana, and in this chapter, you will learn how to use both in IoT projects.

Technical requirements

To take advantage of this chapter, you will need the following:

- A running instance of Grafana
- A running instance of Prometheus
- Data to feed to Prometheus

Let's start by learning the basics about Prometheus.

What is Prometheus?

Prometheus is an open source monitoring and alerting system. It was developed by **SoundCloud** in 2012, but at the time of writing, it is a standalone project. So, it is entirely maintained by the community, independently of any company.

The main features of Prometheus are as follows:

- It has a multidimensional data model, with **metrics** pairs in key/value form.
- It uses a flexible query language called **PromQL**.
- It collects metrics using pulls over HTTP. You can also push metrics using a **push gateway**.
- You can build dashboards using the tools provided by Prometheus. However, in this book, you will learn how to use Grafana for that purpose.

The metric definition in Prometheus is the same one that we have been using throughout this book. It consists of pairs of keys and values that are delivered in a time sequence. These metrics are stored in a time-series database.

Architecture

Prometheus's ecosystem has many components:

- The core component is Prometheus itself, which gets the data and stores it.
- A push gateway for sending data from short-lived jobs.
- Client libraries.
- Alertmanager for managing alerts.
- Exporters for feeding data to Prometheus from systems and applications (**InfluxDB**, **MQTT**, **Graphite**, **SNMP**, and so on).

The architecture of Prometheus can be seen in the following diagram:

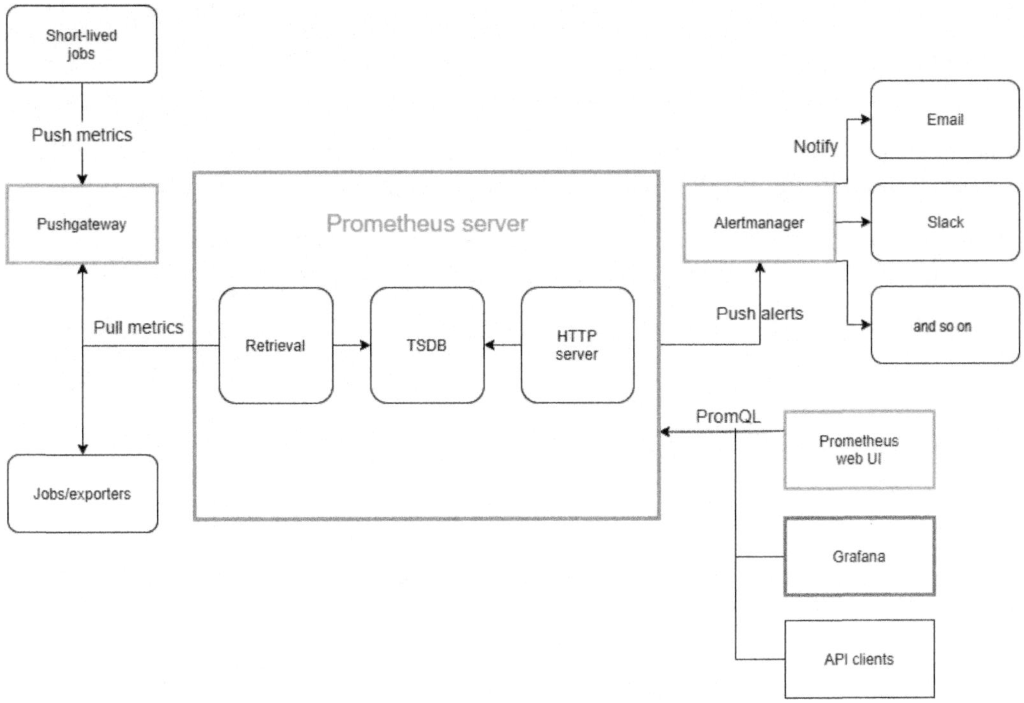

Figure 11.1 – The architecture of Prometheus and its external systems

As you can see, Prometheus scraps data, regardless of whether it's from exporters or the push gateway. Then, it stores those metrics in a **time-series database**. It also runs rules to generate alerts if necessary.

Prometheus also sends alerts to Alertmanager, which triggers notifications using one or more notification services.

Finally, the **Prometheus web UI** or Grafana requests data using PromQL to visualize it on dashboards.

Although Prometheus was originally built for monitoring IT systems, you can use it to process any numerical data coming from IoT devices. Prometheus is very efficient in doing so.

Data model

As we saw earlier, metrics in Prometheus consist of time-series key/value pairs.

Every metric has a `metric name` to identify it and can have one or many key/value pairs called `labels`. Let's see this through an example.

Imagine that you are monitoring the vibration of several machines. In this case, you can choose vibration for `metric name` and set the machine identification to `label`.

Each time-series value is a sample. A sample consists of a `float64` value and a `millisecond-precision` timestamp.

To identify a time series, you must specify the metric's name and the labels, as follows:

```
<metric name>{<label name>=<label value>, ...}
```

Taking the previous example of machines, a query can look as follows:

```
vibration_db{machine='001'}
```

As you can see, a metric can be as complex as you want. You can use as many labels as you need to identify a metric properly.

Metric names

There is a standardization for building metric names. This simplifies reading and interpreting metrics.

The following are the requirements:

- It must comply with the data model using valid characters – that is, `[a-zA-Z_:]` `[a-zA-Z0-9_:]*`.
- The prefix of the metric must be a relevant single word related to the field of use of the metric. For example, in `temperature_compressor_celsius`, the `temperature` part is the prefix.
- It must have a single unit. You must avoid mixing units in the same metric (such as minutes with seconds).
- It should use just base units, such as meters, bytes, seconds, and so on, not milliseconds, kilometers, or gigabytes.
- It should have a suffix specifying the unit of the metric. In the previous example, the suffix was `celsius`, which is the base unit that's used for temperature metrics.
- The metric must represent the same thing, regardless of what labels are you using.

You can verify the correctness of the metric definition by applying a simple rule: summing all the values of a metric across all the labels must return a valid value (although it wasn't useful in this case).

Metric types

There are four types of metrics you can use in client libraries. Take into account that these metric types are only used in the clients and the wire protocol to provide a differentiated API for each type. Internally, Prometheus doesn't use metric types and stores untyped metrics.

Let's start with the counter type.

Counter

You should use a counter when you have a quantity that can only increase – for example, the times a motor starts or a door is opened. Don't use counters if your metric can decrease, such as the number of goods in storage.

Counters can also be reset to zero to start the counting process again.

Gauge

You can use this metric type when you have a quantity that can take any arbitrary value and can go up and down, such as temperature, voltage, power, and so on. You can also use it for discrete quantities that can increase or decrease, such as the number of items in storage.

Histogram

You can use a histogram to count the samples that fit into specified buckets. Histograms also show the total number of observations.

When you scrape a metric with a name containing `<basename>`, the histogram will show the following time series:

- The count for the specified buckets:

```
<basename>_bucket{le="<upper inclusive bound>"}
```

- The total sum of all the values that have been observed:

```
<basename>_sum
```

- The count of all the samples that have been observed:

```
<basename>_count
```

Now, let's look at the last type of metric.

Summary

The summary metric type shows the total count and observations and the sum of them. With summary types, you can calculate configurable quantiles using a sliding time window.

When you scrape a metric with a name containing `<basename>`, the summary will show you the following metrics:

- Streaming quantiles of the observed events:

```
<basename>{quantile="<φ>"}
```

- The total sum of the observed values:

```
<basename>_sum
```

- The count of all the observed values:

```
<basename>_count
```

To see a detailed discussion about histograms and summaries, go to `https://prometheus.io/docs/practices/histograms/`.

Now that you have learned about the main concepts involved in Prometheus, let's learn how to install it.

Installing Prometheus

You can follow three different methods to install Prometheus. Let's look at each.

Installing from binaries

You can install Prometheus using precompiled binaries. All you have to do is download the binaries, copy them to some directory, and perform some configurations.

You can find the necessary pre-compiled binaries at `https://prometheus.io/download/`.

There, you will find also binaries for Alertmanager, pushgateway, and the official **exporters** – we will learn about exporters later.

You can install Prometheus for **Windows 64 bits**, **Linux 64 bits**, **Darwin 64 bits**, and even **ARM7** systems, such as **Raspberry Pi**.

The following steps apply to installing Prometheus on an Ubuntu server:

1. First, you must download the necessary binaries. You can find them at `https://prometheus.io/download/`.

2. Extract the binaries, go to the directory where you extracted them, and move the binaries to the `/usr/local/bin` directory:

```
$ tar xvf prometheus*.tar.gz
$ cd prometheus*/
$ sudo mv prometheus promtool /usr/local/bin/
```

3. Create data and configuration directories:

```
//Create a directory for the data
$ sudo mkdir /var/lib/prometheus
//Create directories for configuration under /etc/
prometheus
$ for i in rules rules.d files_sd; do sudo mkdir -p /etc/
prometheus/${i}; done
```

4. Create a user and a user group for running Prometheus:

```
//Create the system usergroup
$ sudo groupadd --system prometheus
//Create the user and assign it to the new usergroup
$ sudo useradd -s /sbin/nologin --system -g prometheus
prometheus
```

5. Move the configuration files from the download directory to the `/etc/prometheus` directory:

```
//Move the configuration template
$ sudo mv prometheus.yml /etc/prometheus/prometheus.yml
//Move the console libraries. This is optional, as we
will not use Prometheus dashboards.
$ sudo mv consoles/ console_libraries/ /etc/prometheus/
```

6. Configure Prometheus according to your needs by editing the
   `prometheus.yml` file:

```
$ sudo nano /etc/prometheus.yml
```

You can find all the configuration options at `https://prometheus.io/docs/prometheus/latest/configuration/configuration/`.

7. Create a system file, configure it, and start using the service:

```
$ sudo tee /etc/systemd/system/prometheus.service<<EOF
[Unit]
Description=Prometheus
Wants=network-online.target
After=network-online.target

[Service]
Type=simple
User=prometheus
Group=prometheus
ExecReload=/bin/kill -HUP \$MAINPID
ExecStart=/usr/local/bin/prometheus \
  --config.file=/etc/prometheus/prometheus.yml \
  --storage.tsdb.path=/var/lib/prometheus \
  --web.console.templates=/etc/prometheus/consoles \
  --web.console.libraries=/etc/prometheus/console_
libraries \
  --web.listen-address=0.0.0.0:9090 \
  --web.external-url=

SyslogIdentifier=prometheus
Restart=always

[Install]
WantedBy=multi-user.target
EOF
```

8. Now, change the directory's permissions so that it can use the Prometheus user:

```
for i in rules rules.d files_sd; do sudo chown -R
prometheus:prometheus /etc/prometheus/${i}; done
for i in rules rules.d files_sd; do sudo chmod -R 775 /
etc/prometheus/${i}; done
$ sudo chown -R prometheus:prometheus /var/lib/
prometheus/
```

9. Finally, reload the configuration, start the service, and enable it:

```
$ sudo systemctl daemon-reload
$ sudo systemctl start prometheus
$ sudo systemctl enable prometheus
```

After completing these steps, you will be able to access Prometheus by going to `http://your-prometheus-ip:9090`.

Installing from source

If you prefer, you can use source files and compile them in your system. You can download these files from this book's GitHub repository.

To compile, follow the instructions at `https://github.com/prometheus/prometheus#building-from-source`.

Finally, you can use Docker.

Installing Prometheus using Docker

One easy way of installing Prometheus is by using Docker. You can get an image from Docker Hub at `https://hub.docker.com/r/prom/prometheus/`.

If you just want to give it a try, simply run the following command:

```
$ sudo docker run -p 9090:9090 prom/prometheus
```

However, if your intentions are more serious, you will have to define some parameters. The following is an example of this:

```
docker run -d -p 9090:9090 --user userid:userid \
-v /path/to/prometheus.yml:/etc/prometheus/prometheus.yml \
  -v /path/to/data:/prometheus \
prom/prometheus
```

To have persistent configuration and data stores, you must specify some volumes and their corresponding container locations. The first volume copies the configuration file, while the second copies the data store.

Remember to take the files and directories permissions in the host into account. You should create a user for accessing these directories and use the same ID – see `userid` in the command line – when you deploy your container.

Now that you have learned the different ways of installing Prometheus, let's learn how to feed data into it.

Feeding Prometheus with data

In this section, you will learn how to ingest data into Prometheus. Let's look at all the different options that you have.

Prometheus clients

You can use client libraries to expose metrics on an endpoint that can be scraped by Prometheus using HTTP requests.

There are several language options you can select. You can find a complete list at `https://prometheus.io/docs/instrumenting/clientlibs/`.

You should choose the language that you used to implement your IoT application in your gateway or IoT device.

The idea behind the client libraries is to implement an endpoint that gets all the metrics that you need from the host and exposes them using HTTP. Then, Prometheus can scrap them by connecting to the endpoint through HTTP requests.

The client will serve the metrics using the metric types that we looked at in the previous section.

Exporters

You can expose metrics from endpoints using exporters. These are pieces of software that have been developed either by the external community or the Prometheus GitHub organization – these are called official exporters.

You can find lists of all the available exporters at `https://prometheus.io/docs/instrumenting/exporters/` and `https://github.com/prometheus/prometheus/wiki/Default-port-allocations`.

Some exporters are directly related to IoT. Let's look at some of them.

Exporters for messaging systems

You can export messages from MQTT brokers using either `https://github.com/inovex/mqtt_blackbox_exporter` or `https://github.com/hikhvar/mqtt2prometheus`.

These exporters will let you subscribe to MQTT topics and expose them so that they can be scraped by Prometheus. There are some limitations to their implementation, so you should read the documentation on GitHub.

If you use **RabbitMQ**, you can find the official exporter at `https://www.rabbitmq.com/prometheus.html`. Take into account that this exporter doesn't expose messages from devices. Instead, it provides the state of the RabbitMQ service by showing metrics such as queues, consumers, connections, and so on.

Exporters for hardware

Other interesting exporters for IoT systems are hardware-related. Let's look at some examples.

The **APCUPSD** exporter lets you expose metrics from **American Power Conversion (APC) Uninterrupted Power Systems (UPS)**. You can find the exporter at `https://github.com/mdlayher/apcupsd_exporter`.

With the **Bosch Sensortech BMP/BME exporter**, you can export temperature in Celsius, percent humidity, pressure in mmHg and Pascal, and altitude in meters above sea level. This exporter is available at `https://github.com/David-Igou/bsbmp-exporter`.

The **Modbus exporter** lets you expose metrics from a device using the Modbus protocol. You can get this exporter from `https://github.com/RichiH/modbus_exporter`.

There are many other hardware-related exporters that you can use, but only a few have been covered here.

Pushgateway

In some cases, scraping metrics from an endpoint may not be possible. This can occur due to the limitations of the network or the remote devices, security configurations, or some other reason. In any case, using a pushgateway should be a last resort as it has some negative implications.

A pushgateway serves as an intermediary between jobs and Prometheus. The pushgateway gets metrics from these jobs and pushes them to the Prometheus server.

If Pushgateway is a good option for your system, take a look at the following article: `https://prometheus.io/docs/practices/pushing/`.

Scraping configuration

Once you have configured one or more endpoints, you must scrap them from the Prometheus server.

To do this, you must add the edit the configuration file of Prometheus in the following way:

```
scrape_configs:
  - job_name: prometheus
    static_configs:
      - targets: ['endpoint-host-or-ip:9090']
```

There are many configuration options, all of which can be found at `https://prometheus.io/docs/prometheus/latest/configuration/configuration/`.

Now that you know how to feed data into Prometheus, let's learn how to use Prometheus as a data source in Grafana.

Integrating Prometheus and Grafana

So far, you have learned about the concepts surrounding Prometheus and the ways to get metrics into it. Now, let's learn how to add the Prometheus data source and perform queries from Grafana.

Once you have a running instance of Prometheus, you can add the data source in Grafana, as shown in the following screenshot:

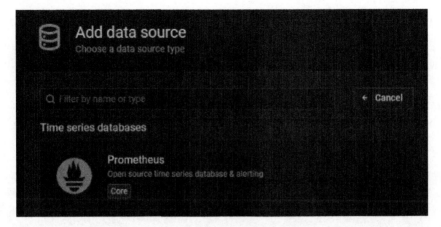

Figure 11.2 – Adding a Prometheus data source

Once you've added the data source, you will have to configure it so that it can access your Prometheus instance.

Let's look at each of the configuration settings:

- **Name**: Enter the name that you want to use to reference this data source.

- **Default**: Select it if you want to set this data source as the default.

- **URL**: The URL to access Prometheus.

- **Access**: Here, you must select the server option (default) to be able to access the Prometheus server.

- **Basic Auth**: Select this if you want to use basic authentication (user and password).

- **User and Password Fields**: Here, you must enter a username and password for the basic authentication method.

- **Scrape Interval**: Here, you can specify the scraping interval. The default value is 15 seconds.

- **HTTP Method**: Here, you can choose between POST and GET methods. POST is the recommended method because it allows you to perform bigger queries than GET.

- **Disable Metrics Lookup**: If you check this option, it will disable metrics from being autocompleted in the query field.

- **Custom Query Parameters**: With this option, you can send custom parameters in the URL query. For example, you can specify `timeout`, `partial_response`, `dedup`, or `max_source_resolution`. You can concatenate multiple parameters using the & symbol.

Once you have added and configured the Prometheus data source, you can start to query and build dashboards using Prometheus metrics.

Editing Prometheus queries in Grafana

Grafana offers a metric query editor that you can use to write your queries. There is also a metric browser that you can use to explore all the available metrics.

The following screenshot shows the Prometheus query editor:

Figure 11.3 – Query editor for Prometheus metrics in Grafana

Now, let's learn how to use Prometheus metrics in Grafana.

Using Prometheus and Grafana to show data from a DS18B20 sensor

In this case, Prometheus and Grafana have been installed on a Raspberry Pi. The Raspberry Pi has a DS18B20 temperature sensor connected. This sensor uses the 1-Wire protocol to transmit the temperature and other parameters, such as the sensor's address.

All the hardware connections and configurations have been previously made for the sensor to work.

As you saw earlier in this chapter, there are many ways to get and expose metrics for Prometheus. In this case, the Prometheus exporter has been used.

You can get this exporter from `https://github.com/hikhvar/w1_prometheus_exporter`.

To install this exporter, follow the instructions shown on the GitHub page.

Once the exporter is working, you must configure Prometheus to scrape it. You must add the job to the scrape config section, as shown here:

```
- job_name: temperature_sensor
  static_configs:
    - targets: ['endpoint-host-or-ip:8001']
```

You will have to restart the Prometheus service for the changes to take effect.

After that, you will be able to see the exporter in your Prometheus instance. To check this, go to http://your-ip-or-hostname:9090/targets. It will show you something similar to the following:

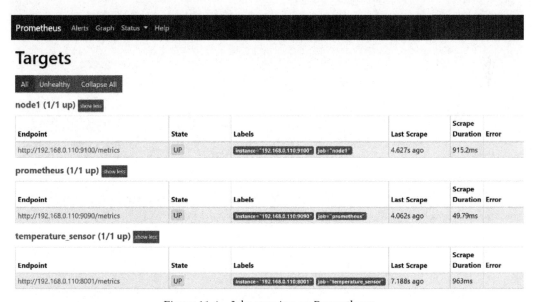

Figure 11.4 – Jobs running on Prometheus

Once you have verified that the job is running and Prometheus is getting metrics from it, you can go to Grafana and perform the query:

Figure 11.5 – Getting metrics from the Prometheus data source

The preceding screenshot shows the query for getting the temperature value from a specific sensor by using its address. This query looks as follows:

```
sensor_temperature_in_celsius{instance="192.168.0.110",
job="temperature_sensor", sensor="28-021312ddd5aa"}
```

By executing this query, you will obtain the temperature values for the specified time range in your visualization panel. For this example, you will see the following output:

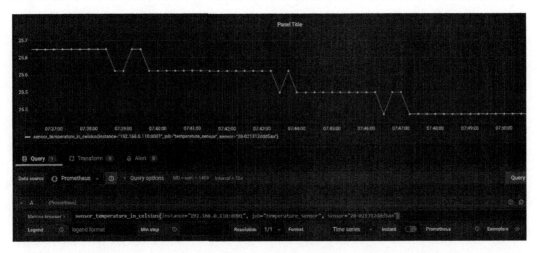

Figure 11.6 – Graphing values in Grafana from Prometheus metrics

As you can see, it's pretty easy to implement endpoints, get their metrics from Prometheus, and query them using Grafana.

Summary

In this chapter, you learned about the fundamentals of Prometheus, as well as how to install and configure it.

First, you looked at different options for exposing metrics from IoT devices before learning how to use a Prometheus data source in Grafana. Finally, we went through a practical example, which consisted of using a DS18B20 sensor and a Raspberry Pi.

Without a doubt, Prometheus is a good option to consider when you want to implement an IoT system. And in combination with Grafana, you can obtain great flexibility.

In the next chapter, we will look at another integration option for Grafana: OpenSearch.

12
Using Grafana with OpenSearch

In this chapter, you will learn about a powerful analytic platform – OpenSearch – and how to integrate it with Grafana.

With OpenSearch and Grafana, you can bring to your IoT project advanced analytics and impressive visualizations.

Across this chapter, you will learn the following:

- What OpenSearch is and what it is used for
- How to install and configure OpenSearch
- How to ingest data into OpenSearch
- How to integrate OpenSearch and Grafana
- How to visualize metrics and alerts coming from OpenSearch in Grafana

Without a doubt, you can use OpenSearch and Grafana together to build a powerful analytic platform.

Technical requirements

To take advantage of this chapter, you will need the following:

- A Grafana instance running
- An OpenSearch instance running – we will see how to install it
- Data coming from sensors or systems
- Data-ingesting software

The best option for trying these platforms is deploying them using Docker, which completes the work in minutes.

Let's see what OpenSearch is and what it is used for.

What OpenSearch is and what it is used for

OpenSearch is a fork from the Elasticsearch project. It happened after Elasticsearch became a non-open source project, early in 2021. The first version of OpenSearch appeared in the middle of the year 2021.

The major difference between the two projects is the advanced analytics capabilities, which are available for free in the OpenSearch version, whereas you have to pay for their use in ElasticSearch.

The OpenSearch system allows searching and analyzing data from several sources. You can build visualizations, run alarms, and create analytics. With OpenSearch, you can also implement anomaly detection and data classification.

In other words, OpenSearch offers very powerful tools for analyzing data. In this chapter, you will learn how to ingest data into OpenSearch, perform analytics on it, and show it in Grafana dashboards.

You can use OpenSearch for many things, such as the following:

- Data store and search engine
- Log analytics
- Application monitoring
- IoT monitor and analytics
- Data classifier
- Data visualization

In this chapter, you will learn how to use it to build IoT applications, run analytics, and show visualizations.

OpenSearch components

The OpenSearch system includes several components. Let's see each of them:

- **OpenSearch**: This is the core component. It includes the search engine and store.
- **OpenSearch Dashboards**: Implements visualizations and the search user interface.
- **Security**: Performs access control and authentication.
- **Alerting**: As the name implies, this component manages condition-based alerts and notifications.
- **SQL**: Lets you use SQL queries to search data.
- **Index State Management**: Automates index operations.
- **KNN**: Implements the **K-nearest neighbors** (**KNN**), an algorithm of supervised classification.
- **Performance Analyzer**: Monitors and optimizes your cluster.
- **Anomaly detection**: Detects anomalies in the data streaming.
- **ML Commons plugin**: Lets you train and run machine learning models.
- **Asynchronous search**: Runs search requests in the background.
- **Cross-cluster replication**: With this tool, you can replicate your data across several clusters.

As you can see, OpenSearch includes very powerful tools for processing, analyzing, and showing data, and the best part is that you can use it free of charge.

Now that you have had a first look at OpenSearch, let's see how you can install it easily.

Installing OpenSearch

At the time of writing, there are three methods for installing OpenSearch – Docker, tarball, and an Ansible recipe. Here, you will learn how to install it using Docker because that is the easiest and fastest way to deploy an OpenSearch instance, or even a cluster.

You can reach the Docker images in the Docker hub through the following link: `https://hub.docker.com/u/opensearchproject`.

To get the latest images of OpenSearch and OpenSearch Dashboards, you can run the following commands:

```
docker pull opensearchproject/opensearch:latest
docker pull opensearchproject/opensearch-dashboards:latest
```

To deploy a single instance of OpenSearch, run the following command:

```
docker run -p 9200:9200 -p 9600:9600 -e "discovery.type=single-node" opensearchproject/opensearch:latest
```

To check that it's working, go to your web browser and point it to this address: https://localhost:9200.

Accept the security risk warning of your browser, and you will get a response like this:

```
{
  "name" : "cb7ba4ddfc0b",
  "cluster_name" : "docker-cluster",
  "cluster_uuid" : "nY2P49bcQ1mwIN8S1N_Smg",
  "version" : {
    "distribution" : "opensearch",
    "number" : "1.3.0",
    "build_type" : "tar",
    "build_hash" : "e45991597c86ba1bbcc36ee1dfdc165197a913af",
    "build_date" : "2022-03-15T19:07:30.455415Z",
    "build_snapshot" : false,
    "lucene_version" : "8.10.1",
    "minimum_wire_compatibility_version" : "6.8.0",
    "minimum_index_compatibility_version" : "6.0.0-beta1"
  },
  "tagline" : "The OpenSearch Project: https://opensearch.org/"
}
```

As you can see, OpenSearch responds with a JSON object, including all the information about the instance. On the other hand, if you want to see the running nodes of OpenSearch, use https://localhost:9200/_cat/nodes?v, and you will see data similar to this:

ip	heap.percent	ram.percent	cpu	load_1m	load_5m	load_15m	node.role	master	name
172.17.0.2	25	49	3	0.24	0.12	0.04	dimr	*	cb7ba4ddfc0b

Table 12.1 – A response from OpenSearch

To see the installed plugins, go to `https://localhost:9200/_cat/plugins?v`:

```
name          component                          version
cb7ba4ddfc0b  opensearch-alerting                1.3.0.0
cb7ba4ddfc0b  opensearch-anomaly-detection       1.3.0.0
cb7ba4ddfc0b  opensearch-asynchronous-search     1.3.0.0
cb7ba4ddfc0b  opensearch-cross-cluster-replication 1.3.0.0
cb7ba4ddfc0b  opensearch-index-management        1.3.0.0
cb7ba4ddfc0b  opensearch-job-scheduler           1.3.0.0
cb7ba4ddfc0b  opensearch-knn                     1.3.0.0
cb7ba4ddfc0b  opensearch-ml                      1.3.0.0
cb7ba4ddfc0b  opensearch-observability           1.3.0.0
cb7ba4ddfc0b  opensearch-performance-analyzer    1.3.0.0
cb7ba4ddfc0b  opensearch-reports-scheduler       1.3.0.0
cb7ba4ddfc0b  opensearch-security                1.3.0.0
cb7ba4ddfc0b  opensearch-sql                     1.3.0.0
```

Disabling security for testing

Configuring **Secure Sockets Layer** (**SSL**) can be a bit exhausting for implementing a testing environment. So, disabling OpenSearch plugin security can help run tests faster.

To do this, you have to run the Docker command, as follows:

```
$ sudo docker run -p 9200:9200 -p 9600:9600 -e "discovery.
type=single-node" -e "plugins.security.disabled=true"
opensearchproject/opensearch
```

This will disable the SSL configurations in all OpenSearch plugins and let you use the ingestion systems without having to configure **Transport Layer Security/Secure Sockets Layers** (**TLS/SSL**) on them.

Now that you have OpenSearch running, you need to ingest data into it. Let's see how to do it.

Ingesting data in OpenSearch

In this section, we will work around the system described in *Figure 12.1*. There, you can see data-ingesting components on the left of OpenSearch. On the other side, OpenSearch feeds Grafana dashboards:

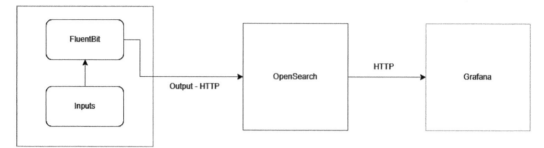

Figure 12.1 – System architecture

You can ingest data in OpenSearch by sending PUT or POST HTTP requests. So, you can send data to OpenSearch from a script, using curl or some similar command.

In this section, you will learn how to implement a data ingestion pipeline for use in IoT systems. In this case, we will use Fluent Bit. Let's see how to do it.

Fluent Bit

Fluent Bit is an open source log processor. It lets you gather data, process it, and send it to other systems, such as OpenSearch.

You can reach this project on Github at the following link: https://github.com/ fluent/fluent-bit.

You can install Fluent Bit on several Linux distributions, several versions of Windows, and macOS. To see detailed instructions, please visit the following link: https://docs. fluentbit.io/manual/installation/getting-started-with-fluent- bit.

Figure 12.2 shows the data pipeline of Fluent Bit:

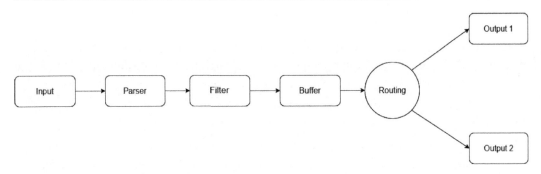

Figure 12.2 – The data pipeline of Fluent Bit

Let's look at each of the components.

Input

You can use different input plugins for gathering data from different sources, such as log files, system metrics, MQTT, HTTP, and many others. You can see the full list at the following link: `https://docs.fluentbit.io/manual/pipeline/inputs`.

Parsers

The parsers allow you to give structure to unstructured data. This is typically used with log entries, where each application can use a different approach for building its logs. You can configure different parsers for each input, and you can see the full list of parsers at the following link: `https://docs.fluentbit.io/manual/pipeline/parsers`.

Filters

You can use filters to restrict or add information to data obtained by the input plugins. You can see the full list of filters at the following link: `https://docs.fluentbit.io/manual/pipeline/filters`.

Buffer

The buffer component keeps data received at the previous stage unaltered. It provides a mechanism for storing and managing the data either in memory or the filesystem. The data in the buffer is immutable, so it can't be modified or filtered.

Routing

Routing is a core process that routes the data to one or several outputs, according to tags and matching rules. Tags are added in the input plugins. Matching rules are defined in the output configuration. The routing process looks for matching input tags and matching rules.

Output

The output plugins allow you to send data to multiple destinations, such as files, remote services, standard output, and so on. This part establishes the connection with OpenSearch, which you are going to see next.

Now that you know the components of Fluent Bit and have a general overview of it, let's see how you can use it with IoT devices.

Configuring Fluent Bit for receiving MQTT messages

MQTT is one of the main protocols used in IoT. You learned about it in *Chapter 3, Connecting IoT Devices*.

Now, you will learn how to capture MQTT messages using Fluent Bit and send data to an OpenSearch instance.

The Fluent Bit MQTT plugin acts as an MQTT broker itself. It can receive MQTT messages from clients, which must be formatted as JSON objects.

To configure the plugin, you must set just a couple of parameters. You can see them in the following table:

Key	Description
Listen	Network interface. Default – 0.0.0.0.
Port	TCP port for listening. Default – 1883.

Table 12.2 – The Fluent Bit MQTT input plugin configuration

To configure this plugin, go to the configuration file of Fluent Bit and add the following parameters:

```
[INPUT]
    Name    mqtt
    Tag     data
    Listen  0.0.0.0
    Port    1883
```

```
[OUTPUT]
    Name    stdout
    Match   data
```

With this configuration, Fluent Bit will listen to all MQTT connections on port 1883 on all interfaces. Then, it will output the data to the standard output.

As with all plugins, you can run this one from the command line or by using the configuration file. If you want to run a test, you can use the command line, as in the following example:

```
$ fluent-bit -i mqtt -t data -o stdout -m '*'
```

This command will listen to the MQTT connections with default configuration values and print them to the standard output.

To check it, you can use an MQTT client for sending messages. You can use, for example, the mosquitto_pub command, as follows:

```
$ mosquitto_pub  -m '{"yourkey1": 10, "yourkey2": 'test'}' -t
your/topic
```

Sending the data to OpenSearch

Before sending data from Fluent Bit to OpenSearch, let's see how OpenSearch organizes data in its database.

OpenSearch stores data in a document database. Each unit of data is a JSON document.

To search the data in OpenSearch, it must be organized. This is done using indexes. Indexing the data means giving it a unique identification that you can use to perform operations on. The process of indexing data produces a structure called an index.

Every time you create a new JSON document, it's stored within an index. Each index can include one or many documents. At the same time, each document is identified using an ID.

Summing up, we have two levels in the data structure. The first corresponds to the index, and the second to the document IDs.

For routing the messages to OpenSearch, you have to use the corresponding output plugin. You can see all of the configuration options of this plugin at the following link:

https://docs.fluentbit.io/manual/pipeline/outputs/opensearch.

With the OpenSearch output plugin, you can perform different write operations. The `write_operation` setting allows you to specify how writing on data in the database should be done.

The setting can take any of the following values:

- `create` (default): Adds new data. If data with the same ID already exists, the operation will not be performed.

- `index`: Adds new data. If the ID already exists, the data will be replaced and reindexed.

- `update`: Updates existing data based on its ID. If the ID doesn't exist, the operation will be omitted.

- `upsert`: Inserts data if it doesn't already exist according to its ID. If the data exists, it is updated.

Sending data using the command line

You can send data to OpenSearch using the command line in two different ways – using the `-p` argument, or the full URL.

If you choose the first option, the command will look as follows. Take into consideration the fact that before executing these commands, you need to configure the plugin, as you'll see next in *Configuring the output plugin*:

```
$ fluent-bit -i mqtt -t data -o opensearch -p Host=opensearch-
ip -p Port=9200 \
    -p Index=my_index -p Type=my_type -o stdout -m '*'
```

If you prefer using the URL, the command will be as follows:

```
$ fluent-bit -i mqtt -t data -o es://opensearch-ip:9200/my_
index/my_type \
    -o stdout -m '*'
```

Let's see how to use the configuration file.

Configuring the output plugin

To configure the OpenSearch output plugin in Fluent Bit, you can use a setting such as the following:

```
[INPUT]
    Name    mqtt
```

```
    Tag     data
    Listen  0.0.0.0
    Port    1883

[OUTPUT]
    Name    opensearch
    Match   data
    Host    your-opensearch-ip
    Port    9200
    Index   your_index
    Type    your_type
```

You can check your configurations visually using the online tool at `https://configurecalyptia.com/`.

Now that you have learned to get data from MQTT devices and send it to OpenSearch, let's see how to use the data in Grafana.

Integrating OpenSearch and Grafana

Grafana allows you to get OpenSearch data using a data source plugin. You can see the plugin at the following link: `https://grafana.com/grafana/plugins/grafana-opensearch-datasource/`.

To install this plugin, you can follow any of the procedures discussed in *Chapter 7, Managing Plugins*.

Adding the data source

Once you have installed the plugin, you can add a new data source from the data source configuration page.

> **Important Note**
> The OpenSearch plugin can't be installed on the build of Grafana made for Raspberry Pi.

To connect Grafana to the OpenSearch database, you'll have to configure the plugin. Let's see the configuration options.

First, you have to set the basic parameters:

- `Name`: Here, you can name the data source. This is the name that appears when you use this data source in the dashboard panels.

- `Default`: Select this if you want to set this data source as the default.

- `URL`: The full URL for accessing the OpenSearch instance. You have to specify the HTTP/HTTPS protocol, the IP or hostname, and the TCP port.

- `Access`: Here, you can choose between a server and a browser. The server is the recommended option, while the browser option will be deprecated soon. Take into consideration that when you use the server option, the URL specified in the previous option must be accessible to the server backend.

In the OpenSearch details section, you will see the following:

- `Index name` and `Pattern`: Here, you can specify the name of the index of the database. You can also use a time pattern, choosing between the following options – `Hourly`, `Daily`, `Weekly`, `Monthly`, and `Yearly`.

- `Time field name`: This field lets you specify the name of the timestamp field.

- `Version`: You have to set the version of OpenSearch that you are using. This is important because the queries vary across the different versions.

- `Min time interval`: Here, you can specify the minimum time interval. You should set it to a value equal to or greater than the writing period. You can also override this setting in the dashboard panels. The values supported must be followed by any of the following suffices – *y*, *m*, *w*, *d*, *h*, *m*, *s*, and *ms* (for example, "*5 minutes*" becomes "*5m*").

Let's see how you can build dashboards using the OpenSearch data source.

Building dashboards with the OpenSearch data source

As with other data sources, Grafana offers a graphical query interface.

In the case of OpenSearch, you can use two query languages – Lucene and PPL.

Lucene is a full-text library for searching indexed documents. Learning to use this language is far beyond the scope of this book. However, you can take advantage of the graphical user interface of Grafana for building the queries.

On the other hand, if you select **Piped Processing Language** (**PPL**), you will have to write queries by hand.

The data used in the following examples were generated from a Raspberry Pi running Fluent Bit with the following configuration:

```
[INPUT]
    Name cpu
    Tag cpu

[OUTPUT]
    Name opensearch
    Match *
    Host your_opensearch_address
    Port 9200
    Index my_index
    Type my_type
```

In *Figure 12.3*, you can see the result of two queries in Grafana using the data sent by the Raspberry Pi:

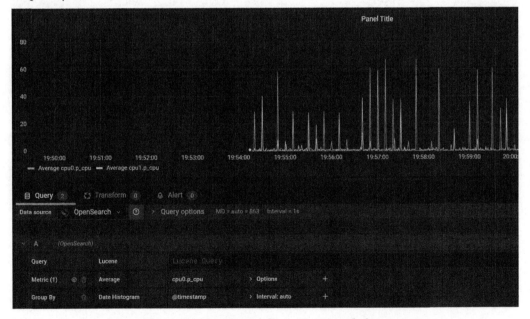

Figure 12.3 – Building queries for an OpenSearch data source

The query editor lets you select several metrics and group them by terms or filters. You can see all the options using the plus and minus icons.

You can assign an alias to the pattern using the `Alias` field in the query editor. This will let you easily get the metric from other places in Grafana.

You can apply some numerical and statistical calculations to the metrics using the query editor. These are pipeline aggregations.

The available aggregations are `Count`, `Average`, `Sum`, `Max`, `Min`, `Extended Stats`, `Percentiles`, `Unique Count`, `Moving Average`, `Moving Function`, `Derivative`, `Cumulative Sum`, `Bucket Script`, `Raw Document`, `Raw Data`, and `Logs`.

You can see an example of a moving average – the yellow line – in *Figure 12.4*.

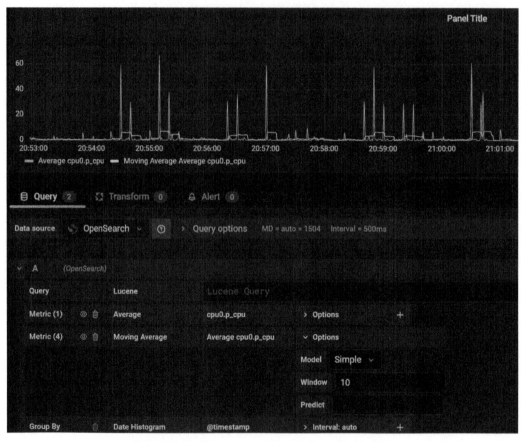

Figure 12.4 – Using aggregations in OpenSearch data

You can treat these metrics like any other, creating annotations, alerts, variables, and so on.

Now that you have learned how to show data coming from the OpenSearch data source, let's explore OpenSearch using its GUI, OpenSearch Dashboards.

Interacting with OpenSearch using OpenSearch Dashboards

The OpenSearch Dashboards application lets you explore, visualize, and analyze data from OpenSearch in many forms. In this section, you will learn to start using it.

First, you will have to install or run an OpenSearch Dashboards instance.

For a production environment, you must enable and configure all security options. Also, it's a good idea to run a cluster environment with at least two nodes of OpenSearch. For complete documentation, please visit the following links:

https://opensearch.org/docs/latest/opensearch/install/docker/

https://github.com/opensearch-project/opensearch-build/blob/main/docker/release/README.md

In a testing environment, however, you may not want to go through all the security configurations, which implies certificates, keys, and so on. Take into account that you will have to set SSL configurations not only on the OpenSearch instances but also on your ingesting software and Grafana.

So, if you want to try OpenSearch, just disable all the configuration settings. To do this, run the following commands in your Docker environment:

```
$ docker run -it -p 9200:9200 -p 9600:9600 -e "discovery.
type=single-node" -e "DISABLE_INSTALL_DEMO_CONFIG=true"
-e "DISABLE_SECURITY_PLUGIN=true" opensearchproject/
opensearch:1.1.0
$ docker run -it --network="host" -e "DISABLE_SECURITY_
DASHBOARDS_PLUGIN=true" opensearchproject/opensearch-
dashboards:1.1.0
```

> **Important Note**
> Take into consideration that this configuration is not stable or secure at all. You can use it solely for testing purposes.

Once you have the two instances running, you can access OpenSearch Dashboards using this URL: http://your-openserach-ip:5601.

You will see the page shown in *Figure 12.5*.

Figure 12.5 – Accessing OpenSearch Dashboards

To start using OpenSearch Dashboards, you have to have some data. You can either import some demo data or use your own. You can see this in *Figure 12.6*.

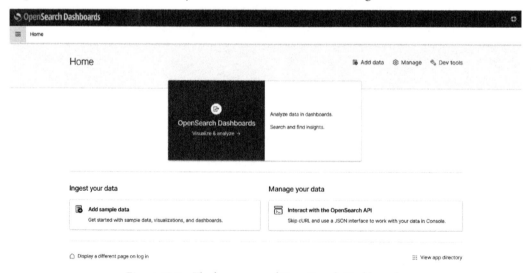

Figure 12.6 – The homepage of OpenSearch Dashboards

In our case, we will use the data forwarded from the Raspberry Pi.

To index the data, go through the following steps:

1. In the menu panel, go to **OpenSearch Dashboards | Discover**. This will lead you to the **Index Patterns** page, where you can explore and index the data ingested in OpenSearch.

2. Click on the **Create index pattern** button. Then, you will see the available indexes.

3. Ingress the name of the index you want to index and click on **Next step**. You can see it in *Figure 12.7*.

4. Select the field corresponding to the timestamp and click on **Create index pattern** (see *Figure 12.8*).

Figure 12.7 – Creating a new index pattern

Now you have indexed data that you can use to build dashboards.

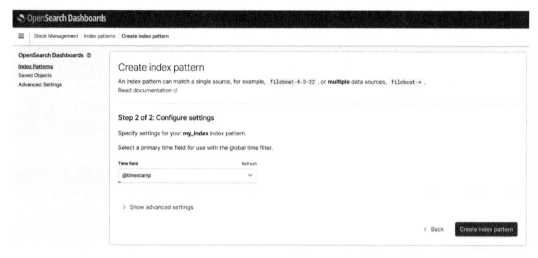

Figure 12.8 – Selecting the time field

Once you have the indexed pattern, you can explore the data on the **Index Patterns** page. You will see something similar to *Figure 12.9*:

my_index

Time field: '@timestamp'

This page lists every field in the **my_index** index and the field's associated core type as recorded by OpenSearch. To change OpenSearch Mapping API

Fields (21)   Scripted fields (0)   Source filters (0)

Q   Search

Name	Type	Format	Searchable	Aggregatable
@timestamp	date		●	●
_id	string		●	●
_index	string		●	●
_score	number			
_source	_source			
_type	string		●	●
cpu0.p_cpu	number		●	●
cpu0.p_system	number		●	●

Figure 12.9 – Exploring indexing data

Now, you can create a visualization following these steps:

1. Go to **OpenSearch Dashboards | Visualize**.

2. Click on **New Visualization** and select the type of visualization that you want to build (see *Figure 12.10*).

3. In the visualization configuration panel, select the metric for the *Y* axis, and then specify the aggregation for the *X* axis. You can see these options in *Figure 12.11* and *Figure 12.12*:

4. Now you will be able to see a visualization similar to *Figure 12.13*.

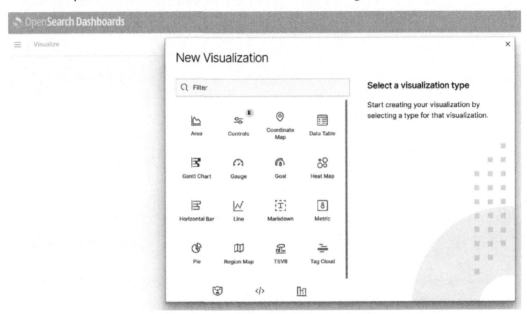

Figure 12.10 – Creating an OpenSearch visualization

The next screenshot shows the metric selection for the *Y* axis.

Figure 12.11– Adding a metric for the Y axis

You can see the aggregation and the field selection for the *X* axis.

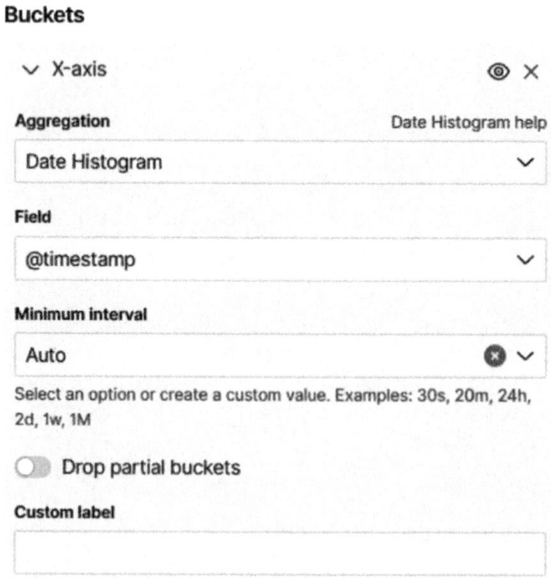

Buckets

˅ X-axis   ◉ ✕

Aggregation   Date Histogram help

Date Histogram   ˅

Field

@timestamp   ˅

Minimum interval

Auto   ⊗ ˅

Select an option or create a custom value. Examples: 30s, 20m, 24h,
2d, 1w, 1M

◯ Drop partial buckets

Custom label

Figure 12.12 – Selecting the aggregation and the field for the X axis

Finally, you can see the visualization obtained for the selected metric.

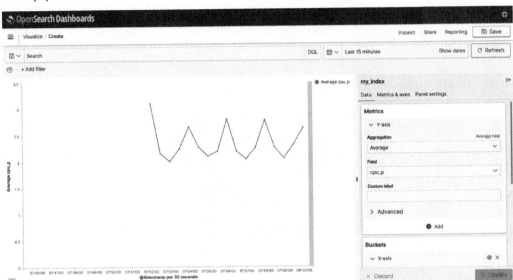

Figure 12.13 – Showing the visualization

Now that you have built your first OpenSearch visualization, you can explore other functionalities of OpenSearch, including anomaly detection, reporting, and notebooks.

Summary

In this chapter, you have learned how to use several tools for ingesting, storing, and analyzing data. These tools are Fluent Bit, OpenSearch, and OpenSearch Dashboards.

You also saw how to integrate Grafana with OpenSearch using the data source plugin.

You additionally learned how to build dashboards in Grafana using the OpenSearch data source and the query interface.

OpenSearch offers a lot of functionalities and advanced analytics. You may want to explore these options in more detail.

In the next chapter, you will learn how to integrate a useful network management system – LibreNMS – with Grafana.

Invitation to join us on Discord

Read this book alongside other Grafana users and the author Rodrigo Juan Hernández.

Ask questions, provide solutions to other readers, chat with the author via Ask Me Anything sessions and much more.

SCAN the QR code or visit the link to join the community.

https://packt.link/iotgrafana

13
Showing Data from LibreNMS in Grafana

LibreNMS is an open source platform for network monitoring, a **Network Management System** (**NMS**). It provides metrics that can be accessed through an InfluxDB database from Grafana.

In this chapter, you will learn how to use the data from LibreNMS and show it with Grafana.

This chapter covers the following topics:

- What LibreNMS is and how you can use it
- Configuring LibreNMS to use InfluxDB
- Showing LibreNMS data in Grafana dashboards
- Showing network topology diagrams with quasi-live data

Using LibreNMS data, you can build customized and enhanced Grafana dashboards, which LibreNMS itself doesn't have. In this chapter, you will learn how to extract more value from LibreNMS data using Grafana.

Technical requirements

To take advantage of this chapter, you should have the following:

- A running instance of LibreNMS – we will not cover the installation of LibreNMS in this book.

- Some devices that can be parsed using **Simple Network Management Protocol** (**SNMP**).

- An InfluxDB instance running.

- A running Grafana instance.

Now, let´s see what LibreNMS is and what it is used for.

What LibreNMS is and how you can use it

As discussed earlier, LibreNMS is an NMS. The purpose of these systems is to manage network devices, servers, appliances, and any device that can be parsed using SNMP.

You can find the website of the project at the following link:

`https://www.librenms.org/`

The main features of LibreNMS are the following:

- **Automatic discovery of devices**: LibreNMS uses SNMP, CDP, LLDP, OSPF, BGP, FDP, and ARP to find devices in a network.

- **API access**: You can interact with LibreNMS using its API to manage, graph, and get data.

- **Alerting**: LibreNMS has a very customizable alerting system. You can build your alerts or use the templates provided by default.

- **Automatic updates**: LibreNMS has a script to check on updates and run upgrades at midnight.

- **Distributed polling**: You can build a large system with distributed small nodes that send data to a central server.

- **Billing system**: You can generate bills based on the utilization of specific interfaces.

- **Apps**: You can access LibreNMS using native apps on iOS and Android.

LibreNMS is a mature open source project that offers great functionalities and works well in production environments.

Let's learn a little more about SNMP.

SNMP

SNMP is the main protocol that LibreNMS uses for discovering and managing network devices. LibreNMS allows using the SNMP protocol in any of its three available versions: SNMPv1, SNMPv2c, and SNMPv3. The selection of the right version depends mainly on the capabilities of the device to be monitored.

Most systems use SNMPv2c because it is easy to implement and offers minimum security.

Each device running an SNMP agent needs to be configured with at least the following parameters:

- **A community string**: This is a string that is used by the device to accept or deny the SNMP requests coming from the NMS. You will have to configure the community string both in the NMS and the devices.
- The version of SNMP used.
- In the case of SNMPv3, you will have to configure encryption parameters too.

Although SNMPv3 offers authentication and encryption, it is not generally implemented on many devices because of its complexity.

SNMP operations

The NMS can send SNMP requests to devices to gather data from them. Both the NMS and the devices use UDP port 161.

The NMS can request data using the following three options:

- `Get`: By using this operation, the NMS can request one or more variables.
- `GetNext`: With this operation, the NMS can request one or more consecutive variables.
- `GetBulk`: This operation allows the processing of several consecutive `GetNext` operations.

Anyway, you don't need to worry about SNMP operations because they are all implemented in the NMS. The only configuration parameters that you need to set up are the UDP port and the community word with reading permissions. If you want to use SNMPv3, you will have to configure the security options too.

Additionally, the devices can send SNMP messages without a request from the NMS. These types of messages are called **traps** and they are used by the device to send notifications to the NMS when some alarm condition is met. Trap messages use UDP port 162.

You can see the communication flow between the agent and the NMS in *Figure 13.1*.

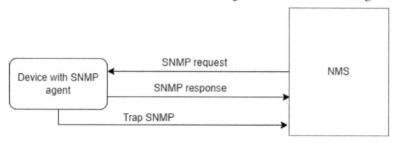

Figure 13.1 – SNMP communication

SNMP also supports SET operations. These operations need write access in the devices and can be used – rarely – to configure certain parameters. To use SET operations, you need to specify a community word with read/write permissions.

An SNMP community word is a kind of password used to authorize the scraping of data. Each SNMP agent has a community word configured. So, whenever it receives an SNMP request, it checks whether the community word sent by the NMS matches the one configured in the agent. If it matches, the SNMP agent allows the access; if it doesn't match, then it denies it.

MIB and OID

Each device has internal definitions – entities – for accessing the parameters to be monitored. These parameters, for example, can be CPU utilization, temperature, interface input traffic rate, and so on.

These entities are organized in a tree-structured database called a **Management Information Base** (**MIB**). You can see the main definitions of this tree in *Figure 13.2*.

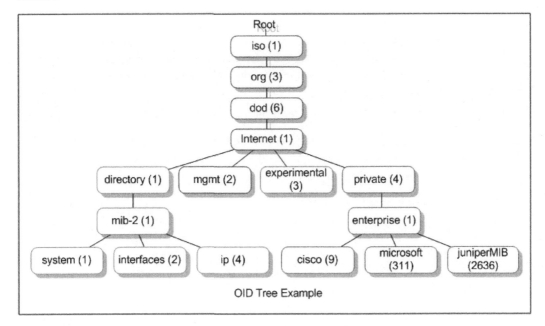

Figure 13.2 – OID tree example

Each element in the tree has an **Object Identifier (OID)** that is used in every SNMP request to parse the corresponding data.

An MIB object looks like 1.3.6.1.4.1.9 – in this case, it belongs to a Cisco device.

The top level of MIB OIDs corresponds to standard organizations, whereas the lower OIDs are used by manufacturers and associated organizations. You can even define your OID for your device.

Now that you have a basic idea about NMSs and SNMP, let's see how you can configure LibreNMS to use an InfluxDB database.

Configuring LibreNMS to use InfluxDB

By default, LibreNMS stores its metrics in RRD files. However, you can send the data to other databases, such as Graphite, InfluxDB, OpenTSDB, or Prometheus.

In this chapter, we are going to use InfluxDB. This integration allows you to save the metrics in a time-series database that can be accessed by other systems, such as Grafana.

> **Important Note**
>
> LibreNMS and InfluxDB are completely separate and independent projects. The LibreNMS website says that it doesn't guarantee that InfluxDB integration will always work. However, at the time of writing this book, all is going well.

Let´s see how to configure LibreNMS to send metrics to InfluxDB.

Before configuring LibreNMS, you have to create a database in the InfluxDB instance. Also, it's good practice to create a username and a password for accessing the database. For security reasons, avoid using the admin user.

The main configuration file of LibreNMS – `conFigurephp` – is located by default in the `/opt/librenms` directory. You have to open it and add or modify the following lines:

```
$config['influxdb']['enable'] = true;
$config['influxdb']['transport'] = 'http'; # Default, other
options: https, udp
$config['influxdb']['host'] = '127.0.0.1'; #the ip or hostname
of your influxdb instance
$config['influxdb']['port'] = '8086'; #TCP port for InfluxDB
instance
$config['influxdb']['db'] = 'librenms'; #name of the database
$config['influxdb']['username'] = 'user'; #the username for
accesing the database
$config['influxdb']['password'] = 'pass'; #the password
$config['influxdb']['timeout'] = 0; # Optional
$config['influxdb']['verifySSL'] = false; # Optional
```

The preceding configuration text is self-explanatory.

After you configure LibreNMS and restart the service, the metric data will be stored in the InfluxDB database. The writing period will depend on the configuration of the poller of LibreNMS. By default, LibreNMS polls the devices every five minutes. You can change this parameter, although five minutes is a good value.

In this section, you have learned the following:

- LibreNMS can use InfluxDB to store time-series metrics.
- How to configure LibreNMS to use an InfluxDB database for storing LibreNMS metrics.

In the next section, you will learn how to show LibreNMS metrics on Grafana dashboards.

Showing LibreNMS data on Grafana dashboards

Now that you have an InfluxDB database with the metrics from LibreNMS, you can access the data from Grafana by adding the InfluxDB database as a data source. You have learned how to do this in *Chapter 4, Data Sources for Grafana*. All you need to do is to enter the access parameters on the data source configuration page, as you can see in *Figure 13.3* and *Figure 13.4*.

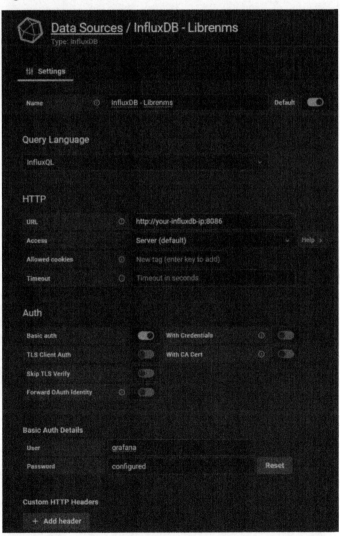

Figure 13.3 – Configuring the InfluxDB data source

After you have added the data source to Grafana, you can perform queries as with any other InfluxDB data source.

Figure 13.4 – Configuring InfluxDB database access

Let's look at some important measurements and tags in the LibreNMS InfluxDB database.

Depending on the type of device monitored by LibreNMS, you will have different measurements available, as you can see in *Figure 13.5*.

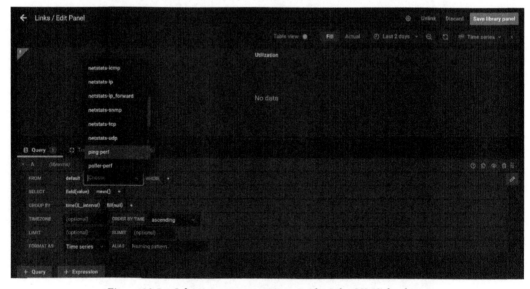

Figure 13.5 – Selecting measurements on the LibreNMS database

One measurement that is common for all types of devices is `ping-perf`. This metric represents the response from the device to the ICMP packets – the `ping` command – sent from the LibreNMS server.

Once you have selected this measurement, you must select the `hostname` tag and specify a value for it. Then, you can select the corresponding field, which in this case is `ping`. After you do this, you will see a result similar to *Figure 13.6*.

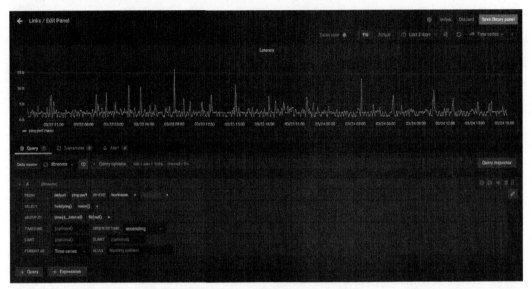

Figure 13.6 – Query of ping response for a host

Other typical measurements are `availability`, `processors`, `ports`, `sensor`, `storage`, `uptime`, and so on. `availability` and `uptime` don't depend on the type of device, whereas the other measurements can be available or not, depending on the OIDs of the devices.

You will have to see the datasheet of the device to check what OIDs are available. If the device is included in the LibreNMS, you will have automatic access to the metrics of the device.

At the following link, you can find the list of supported vendors:

`https://docs.librenms.org/Support/Features/#supported-vendors`

In this section, you have learned the following:

- How to connect Grafana to the InfluxDB database used by LibreNMS
- How to query metrics using the measurements and tags provided by LibreNMS in the InfluxDB database
- How to build dashboards using these queries

Now, let's see how you can build topology diagrams in Grafana.

Showing network topology diagrams with quasi-live data

Network topology diagrams are very useful when you need to monitor your communication infrastructure. All IoT systems depend on IP networks, so having a clear picture of physical connections is crucial to addressing communication problems.

The interruption of data transmission from an IoT device can be related to problems in the network, for example, the loss of power in a network device, or the unplugging of a cable on an interface.

To build topology diagrams, we will use two software tools:

- The software draw.io for drawing the diagrams
- The Grafana FlowCharting plugin for showing dynamic diagrams

Let's start with the draw.io software.

Building diagrams with draw.io

draw.io is a diagram software that you can use for free either online or locally. draw.io allows you to draw different types of diagrams, from basic forms to network topologies and mind maps.

This software offers a very broad palette of blocks, including specific shapes of many manufacturers.

You can reach the online version at `https://draw.io` or `https://app.diagram.net`.

The GitHub project is at `https://github.com/jgraph/drawio` and you can download a desktop version at `https://get.diagrams.net`.

Using the software is very easy and intuitive. If you have already used diagram software, this one will offer pretty much the same experience. You can see a capture of the main screen in *Figure 13.7*.

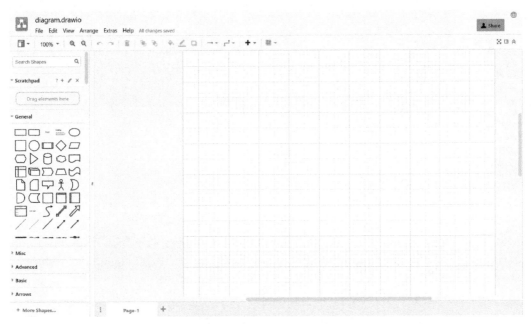

Figure 13.7 – Main screen of draw.io

draw.io works with open source standards, such as XML, SVG, HTML, and so on. So, you can completely customize the elements in the scheme. With this tool, you can forget about using paid software for building diagrams.

Creating a diagram is as easy as dragging and dropping elements into the diagram section. Then, you connect them using some of the link types available. You can change shapes, colors, texts, styling, and so on. In *Figure 13.8*, you can see an example of a basic IoT infrastructure.

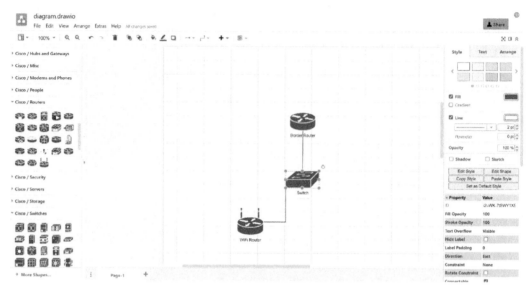

Figure 13.8 – Building diagrams in draw.io

As you can see in *Figure 13.8*, there are plenty of options that you can use. If you don't find the correct shape for your diagram, you can add more shapes by clicking on the + **More Shapes** button. Then, you will get a dialog box like the one shown in *Figure 13.9*.

Figure 13.9 – Adding more shapes to the library

Once you have finished your diagram, you can export it using the **File | Export as | XML…** menu option.

You can choose whether to compress the XML data or not. Then, you have to select the destination of the XML file.

Now that you have generated the XML data, let's see how to use it in the FlowCharting panel.

Using the FlowCharting panel

To install the FlowCharting panel plugin, you can use any of the methods described in *Chapter 7, Managing Plugins*.

The steps for building the diagram in Grafana are the following:

1. Open the XML file previously generated with any plain text editor. Then, you have to select all the text and copy it.

2. After that, go to Grafana, create a new dashboard, and add a new panel. In the panel menu, select the **FlowCharting** panel.

3. Go to the FlowChart configuration section and paste the text into the **Source Content** field, as shown in *Figure 13.10*.

4. After you ingress the XML code, you will see the diagram in the graph panel.

5. The next step is relating the XML objects to the metrics. To do this, you have to identify the objects, whether by their ID or by their label.

6. To relate metrics and objects and control their behavior, you have to build rules. You can create these rules in the **Mapping** section of the FlowCharting plugin. See *Figure 13.11*.

Set all of the configuration options. You can configure the behavior of the XML objects. These options include `Thresholds`, `Tooltips`, `Color/Tooltip Mappings`, `Label/Text Mappings`, `Link Mappings`, and `Event/Animation Mappings`.

You can play with all the available options to adapt the visualization and behavior of the diagram to your needs.

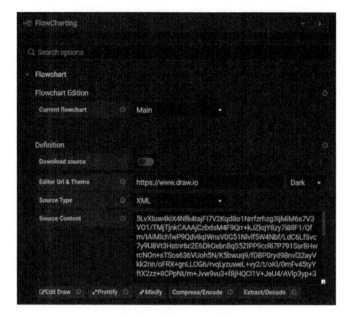

Figure 13.10 – Ingressing XML code

You can control the aspect of devices, links, and texts using the options in the **Mapping** section.

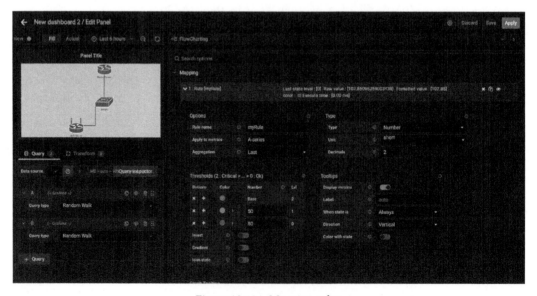

Figure 13.11 – Mapping rules

Some possible uses of the FlowCharting panel are the following:

- Showing state of devices – online or offline
- Showing link utilization metrics – bandwidth
- Showing data exchanged between objects
- Showing response times of requests
- The visualization of any metric where a topological diagram view can be useful

Although this chapter is focused on the integration of LibreNMS and Grafana, take into account that the FlowCharting panel can be used with any type of data source. So, you can relate XML objects with metrics coming from InfluxDB databases, Prometheus instances, and so on.

In this section, you have learned the following:

- How to draw diagrams using the open source tool draw.io, which you can use online or locally
- How to export these diagrams in XML format
- How to embed the XML code in a Grafana dashboard
- How to relate elements in the XML diagram with queries from a data source
- How to change the aspect of elements in the dashboard according to the values of metrics

Thus far, you have learned how to integrate LibreNMS with Grafana and how to use the FlowCharting plugin to show topological views.

Summary

In this chapter, you have learned how to integrate the open source project of LibreNMS with Grafana.

You have explored the basics of the main protocol used by LibreNMS – SNMP – and you have learned how to send the metrics to an InfluxDB database.

You have also learned how to get LibreNMS metrics from an InfluxDB data source.

Finally, you were introduced to the FlowCharting plugin and learned to build topology diagrams for showing quasi-live data.

The integration of LibreNMS and Grafana offers great flexibility and can be used for monitoring a very broad range of devices and systems.

In the next chapter, you will learn how to integrate Grafana Cloud with many systems.

14
Integrations for Grafana Cloud

In this chapter, you will learn how to use the Grafana integrations in the **Grafana Cloud service**.

The integrations allow you to gather metrics from hosts and systems and build dashboards rapidly and easily. You just have to enable them in the Grafana Cloud service and deploy a Grafana agent in the host where you have the system you want to monitor.

In this chapter, you will learn the following:

- What is the Grafana Agent?
- Using the Linux Node integration.
- Using the Home Assistant integration.
- Using the RabbitMQ integration.

When you finish this chapter, you will be able to install, configure, and use these integrations. Also, you will have the ability to use any other integration.

Technical requirements

To get the most out of this chapter, you should have the following:

- A Grafana Cloud service account – it's free.

- A Linux node – here, we use a Raspberry Pi 3.

- A Home Assistant instance running on a Linux machine.

First, let's see what the Grafana Agent is.

What is the Grafana Agent?

The Grafana Agent is a piece of software – based on `remote_write` from **Prometheus** – that you can run in the host where you have your application. This software gathers metrics from your host and its services and sends them to the Grafana Cloud service.

> **Important Note**
>
> To learn more about the `remote_write` functionality in Prometheus, please go to `https://prometheus.io/docs/practices/remote_write/`.

Unlike Prometheus, the Grafana Agent just implements `remote_write`, leaving all other Prometheus features aside. In particular, the Grafana Agent delivers `remote_write`, services discovery, and relabeling rules. This approach saves a lot of memory. Typically, you can expect a saving of 40 percent compared with the Prometheus alternative.

On the other hand, the Grafana Cloud service brings you ready-to-use dashboards, where you can view all the metrics exported by the Grafana Agent.

So, the Grafana Agent makes it easy to collect and display metrics associated with many applications.

You can run several instances of Grafana Agent, each of which has different `scrape_configs` sections and `remote_write` rules.

You can deploy the Grafana Agent in three different modes:

- **Prometheus remote_write drop-in**: This is the default deployment mode of the Grafana Agent, where it acts as a Prometheus `remote_write` process. This mode does service discovery, scraping, and remote writing.

- **Host Filtering mode**: In this mode, you can set a `host_filter` flag in an instance of the Grafana Agent. When you do this, the instance will only scrape the metrics from targets that belong to the same machine as the instance itself.

- **Scraping Service mode**: In this mode, you can use a cluster of agents with shared configurations. The scrape jobs will be distributed automatically between the cluster of agents.

In this chapter, however, we will be using the Prometheus `remote_write` mode for getting the metrics from several systems and services.

Grafana Agent is open source software, and you can get the code and documentation at `https://github.com/grafana/agent`.

You can install and configure the Grafana Agent according to your needs by following the instructions at `https://grafana.com/docs/grafana-cloud/agent/#installing-the-grafana-agent`. However, you can also use the ready-to-go integrations that the Grafana Cloud service offers.

Grafana Agent configuration

The Grafana Agent uses a configuration file for setting the scraping and forwarding parameters. This configuration is located at `/etc/grafana-agent.yaml`.

You can edit it with any text editor. This is a **Yet Another Markup Language** (**YAML**) file, so you have to take into consideration the tabulation of each sentence. You can see an example here:

```yaml
integrations:
  node_exporter:
    enabled: true
    relabel_configs:
    - replacement: hostname
      source_labels:
      - __address__
      target_label: instance
  prometheus_remote_write:
  - basic_auth:
      password: your-GCLOUD_API_KEY
      username: your-cloud-user-number
    url: https://prometheus-blocks-prod-us-central1.grafana.
net/api/prom/push
```

```
metrics:
  configs:
  - name: integrations
    remote_write:
    - basic_auth:
        password: your-GCLOUD_API_KEY
        username: your-cloud-user-number
      url: https://prometheus-blocks-prod-us-central1.grafana.
net/api/prom/push
    scrape_configs:
    - job_name: integrations/rabbitmq
      static_configs:
      - targets:
        - rabbitmq:15692
    - bearer_token: <your-long-live-token>
      job_name: integrations/hass
      metrics_path: /api/prometheus
      scheme: http
      static_configs:
      - targets:
        - your-ip-here:8123
  global:
    scrape_interval: 15s
  wal_directory: /tmp/grafana-agent-wal
server:
  http_listen_port: 12345
```

When you use an integration, GCLOUD_API_KEY is provided automatically. This key is configured by the command provided by the integration configuration page – as you will see later in each of the sections of the integrations.

However, if you have problems with the feeding of the data in the dashboards, you should check that this value in the configuration file matches the one shown in the Grafana Cloud.

Also, if you don't use Loki, you can remove the corresponding section. Loki is a system for managing, correlating, and debugging logs.

Grafana Cloud service integrations

You can easily implement the Grafana Agent using the Grafana Cloud service integrations.

These integrations give you the following:

- A pre-configured Grafana agent to export metrics related to specific services or applications
- A group of dashboards already built to show the metrics in the Grafana Cloud service

You can explore all the available integrations at the following link: `https://grafana.com/docs/grafana-cloud/integrations/integrations/`.

You should keep the Grafana Agent updated to include integrations added by the Grafana development team. Also, you can edit the configuration of the Grafana Agent to choose the metrics that you want to send.

Each integration in the Grafana Cloud service comes with an installation script that you can use to install the agent in your nodes.

Let's see some examples of integrations.

Using the Linux Node integration

The **Linux Node integration** offers the typical system metrics that you may use to monitor any Linux host. This can include **Internet of Things (IoT)** end devices, IoT gateways, and servers.

To use this integration, you need the following:

- A Grafana Cloud service account
- A Linux node
- Access to the Linux console

To install the integration in the cloud and your host, follow these steps:

1. Log in to your Grafana Cloud account.

2. Click on **Integrations and Connections** on the left menu bar. This will lead you to the integration page, where you can search for and select **Linux node integration**. You can see the page in *Figure 14.1*:

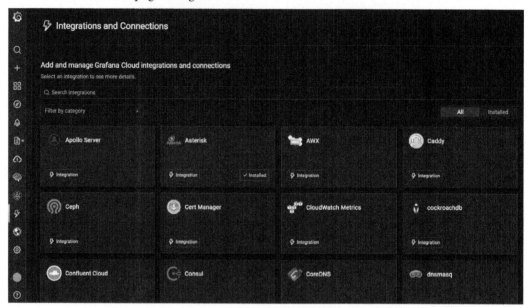

Figure 14.1 – The Integrations and Connections page

3. To install this integration in your instance of Grafana Cloud, just click on the corresponding box. This will install the integration automatically.

4. Then, click again on the box to open the **Configuration Details** page. This page brings you all the information that you need to install the agent in your node.

5. The first part of the configuration page lets you select the architecture of the host, as you can see in *Figure 14.2*:

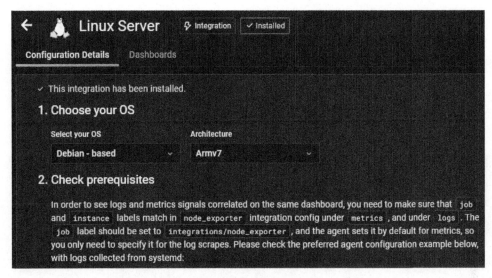

Figure 14.2 – Selecting the OS and the architecture

6. In step **2**, you can check the configuration of the agent, although in general you don't need to modify it.

7. In step **3**, you can see the command line that you have to execute in the console of your Linux node to install the preconfigured the Grafana Agent. This will install the Grafana Agent and connect it to the Grafana Cloud service. You can see this in *Figure 14.3*:

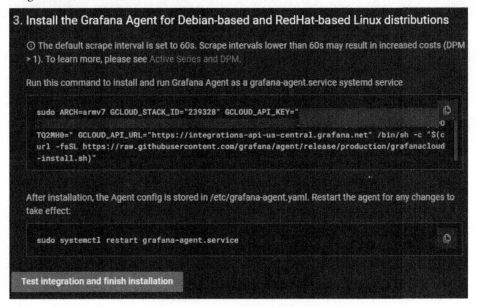

Figure 14.3 – Installing the agent in the Linux node

8. After you have installed the agent in your Linux node, you should start seeing the metrics in the dashboard. To access the dashboard, click on the **View Dashboards** button. This will lead you to the dashboard directory, where you can select the dashboard.

9. Once in the dashboard, you have to select the `grafanacloud-your_ instance-prom` data source. This will show you the metrics captured by the Grafana Agent, as you can see in *Figure 14.4*:

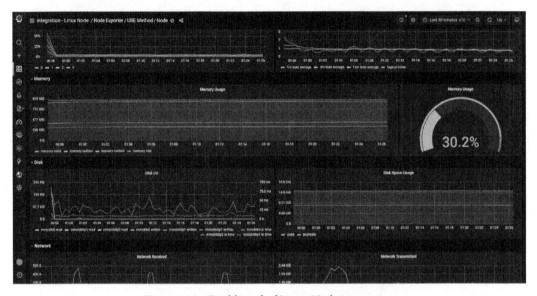

Figure 14.4 – Dashboard of Linux Node integration

Now that you have learned how to use the Linux Node integration, let's continue with the Home Assistant integration.

Using the Home Assistant integration

Home Assistant is an open source home automation system. You can run it locally on your server or even on a Raspberry Pi. It's a very mature project, which integrates more than 1,900 devices and services.

You can find all the documentation and the project files on its website at `https://www.home-assistant.io/`.

Although Home Assistant was born as a home automation system, you can also use it as part of an IoT system. You can, for example, integrate it with Grafana, InfluxDB, MQTT, and many other services and applications.

The Grafana Cloud service integration lets you monitor your Home Assistant instance, getting metrics from its services.

> **Important Note**
> To be able to scrap the Home Assistant instance from the Grafana Agent, you have to use the Home Assistant Core version. You can see how to install it at `https://www.home-assistant.io/installation/linux#install-home-assistant-core`.

Let's see how to install and configure this integration:

1. Log in to your Grafana Cloud account.

2. Go to **Integrations and Connections** and search for `Home Assistant integration`.

3. Click on the box of **Home Assistant**. This will install the integration in your Grafana Cloud instance.

4. Now click again on the box. This will lead you to the configuration page of the integration.

5. Follow the instructions on the page to install the Grafana Agent in your Home Assistant host. You can see this page in *Figure 14.5*.

6. Select the operating system and the architecture.

7. Enable the embedded Prometheus in Home Assistant by adding the `prometheus:` directive in the configuration file of **Home Assistant**.

8. Copy the command line shown in the third step in this section and paste it into the console of your Home Assistant host. This will install the Grafana Agent with preconfigured metrics.

9. Although the Grafana Agent configuration file is created automatically, you may have to modify some parameters:

    - You have to generate a long-lived token in Home Assistant so the scrape job can access its metrics. To generate this token, go to your user profile and click on the **CREATE TOKEN** button, as you can see in *Figure 14.6*.

    - If you are using HTTP instead of HTTPS in your Home Assistant instance, you will have to change the scheme parameter accordingly.

    - Also, you may need to change the default value of localhost to your hostname or IP address. See the following example:

```
scrape_configs:
    - bearer_token: <your-long-live-token>
      job_name: integrations/hass
      metrics_path: /api/prometheus
      scheme: http
      static_configs:
      - targets:
        - your-ip-here:8123
```

10. After installing the Grafana Agent, you can click on the blue **Test integration and finish installation** button.

11. If everything is okay, you can click on **View Dashboards** to see the metrics collected by the Grafana Agent.

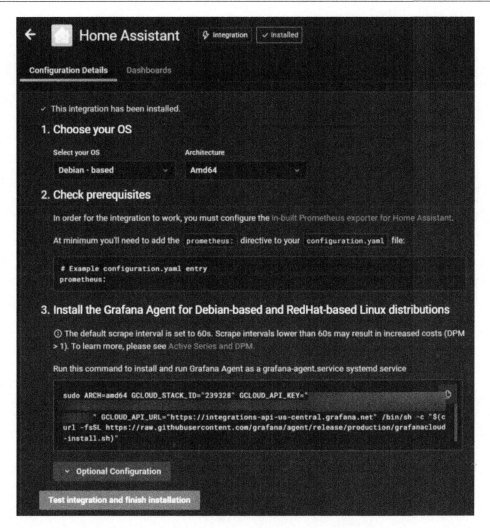

Figure 14.5 – Configuration page of the Home Assistant integration

Take into account that you can add more metrics, including data from sensors connected to Home Assistant. To do that, you need to include the scraping configuration in the Prometheus section of the configuration file of Home Assistant. You can see an example of this in the following code:

```
# Advanced configuration.yaml entry
prometheus:
  namespace: hass
  component_config_glob:
    sensor.*_hum:
```

```
      override_metric: humidity_percent
  sensor.*_temp:
      override_metric: temperature_c
  sensor.*_bat:
      override_metric: battery_percent
filter:
  include_domains:
    - sensor
  exclude_entity_globs:
    - sensor.weather_*
```

The next screenshot shows the user configuration page, where you can generate a long-lived token:

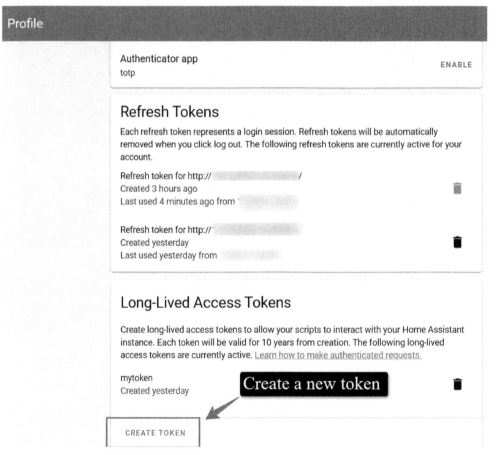

Figure 14.6 – Generating a long-lived token

You can see a dashboard example of the Home Assistant integration in *Figure 14.7*. Some of the dashboard panels show no data because it's a fresh install of Home Assistant:

Figure 14.7 – Dashboard of the Home Assistant integration

Now that you have learned how to integrate metrics from Home Assistant in Grafana Cloud, let's see how to integrate the RabbitMQ message broker.

Using the RabbitMQ integration

RabittMQ is an open source message broker. You can deploy it on a single server or in a cluster, either in the cloud or locally.

You can visit the project website at `https://www.rabbitmq.com/`.

It supports a wide range of operating systems, such as Linux, **Berkeley Software Distribution (BSD)**, UNIX, Windows, and macOS. You can find installation documentation at the following link: `https://www.rabbitmq.com/download.html`.

There are a lot of libraries in different languages that you can use for connecting to RabbitMQ. You can take a look at them at `https://www.rabbitmq.com/devtools.html`.

RabbitMQ supports a wide variety of protocols. It implements natively **Advanced Message Queuing Protocol (AMQP)** 0-9-1 and supports STOMP, MQTT, AMQP 1.0, HTTP, and WebSockets by using plugins.

As you can see, RabbitMQ is a versatile message broker and is very useful for any IoT system architecture.

Now that you have met RabbitMQ, let's see how you can monitor it using the Grafana Cloud integration.

To use the Grafana Cloud integration, follow these steps:

1. Sign in to your Grafana Cloud account.
2. Go to **Integrations and Connections** and search for RabbitMQ integration.
3. Click on the RabbitMQ box. This will install the RabbitMQ integration in your Grafana Cloud instance.
4. Click again on the box to go to the configuration page of the integration.
5. Follow the instructions on the page to install the Grafana Agent in your host. You can see this page in *Figure 14.8*.
6. Select the operating system and the architecture.
7. Then, you have to execute the Prometheus plugin, which has been included in the RabbitMQ server since version *3.8.0*. This plugin collects metrics from health parameters and memory allocations. To run the plugin, execute the following command:

```
$ rabbitmq-plugins enable rabbitmq_prometheus
```

8. After enabling the Prometheus plugin, copy and paste the command shown in the third step of the integration page. This will install the preconfigured Grafana Agent in your RabbitMQ host. After that, the agent will start sending data to your Grafana instance.
9. Then, click on the **Finish installation and test integration** button.

10. Finally, you will be able to see the dashboards by clicking on the **View Dashboards** button. You can see an example of a **RabbitMQ** integration dashboard in *Figure 14.8*:

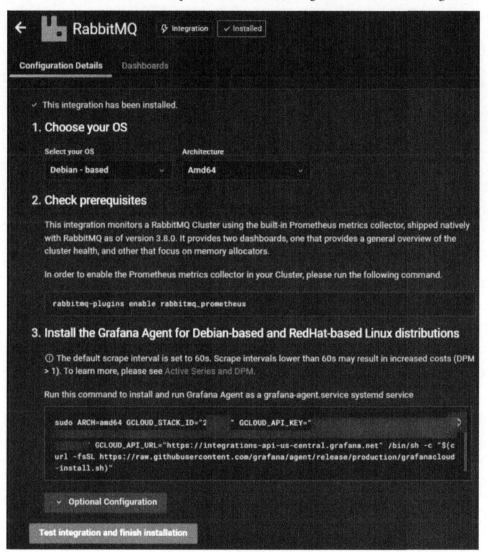

Figure 14.8 – Configuration page of RabbitMQ integration

The next screenshot shows the Grafana dashboard, where you can see the RabbitMQ metrics:

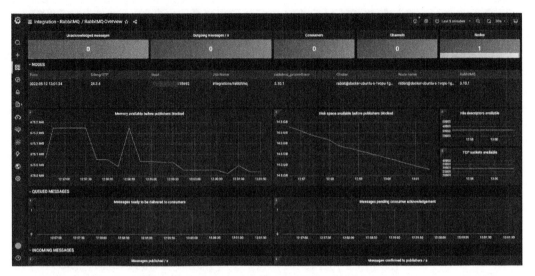

Figure 14.9 – Dashboard of the RabbitMQ integration

So far, you have learned about Grafana Cloud integrations. Also, you have seen three specific examples: Linux Node, Home Assistant, and RabbitMQ.

Summary

In this chapter, you have learned how to use Grafana Cloud integrations. These integrations let you build complex Grafana dashboards in a matter of minutes.

The metric data is sent from the hosts using the Grafana Agent software. This software is built on the Prometheus `remote_write` functionality. The Grafana Agent comes with preconfigured parameters for scraping relevant data from the host.

On the other side, the integration deploys ready-to-use Grafana dashboards, showing all the data collected by the Grafana Agent.

As you have seen, it's pretty easy to build specific application dashboards using the Grafana Cloud integrations.

In this chapter, you have seen how to implement the integrations for Linux Node, Home Assistant, and RabbitMQ. You can apply similar procedures to use any other integration.

You have reached the last chapter of this book. I hope you have enjoyed it and thank you very much for reading it.

Index

D

Packt>

Packt.com

Subscribe to our online digital library for full access to over 7,000 books and videos, as well as industry leading tools to help you plan your personal development and advance your career. For more information, please visit our website.

Why subscribe?

- Spend less time learning and more time coding with practical eBooks and Videos from over 4,000 industry professionals

- Improve your learning with Skill Plans built especially for you

- Get a free eBook or video every month

- Fully searchable for easy access to vital information

- Copy and paste, print, and bookmark content

Did you know that Packt offers eBook versions of every book published, with PDF and ePub files available? You can upgrade to the eBook version at packt.com and as a print book customer, you are entitled to a discount on the eBook copy. Get in touch with us at customercare@packtpub.com for more details.

At www.packt.com, you can also read a collection of free technical articles, sign up for a range of free newsletters, and receive exclusive discounts and offers on Packt books and eBooks.

Other Books You May Enjoy

If you enjoyed this book, you may be interested in these other books by Packt:

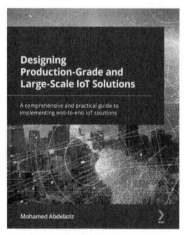

Designing Production-Grade and Large-Scale IoT Solutions

Mohamed Abdelaziz

ISBN: 9781838829254

- Understand the detailed anatomy of IoT solutions and explore their building blocks
- Explore IoT connectivity options and protocols used in designing IoT solutions
- Understand the value of IoT platforms in building IoT solutions
- Explore real-time operating systems used in microcontrollers
- Automate device administration tasks with IoT device management

- Master different architecture paradigms and decisions in IoT solutions
- Build and gain insights from IoT analytics solutions
- Get an overview of IoT solution operational excellence pillars

Intelligent Workloads at the Edge

Indraneel Mitra, Ryan Burke

ISBN: 9781801811781

- Build an end-to-end IoT solution from the edge to the cloud
- Design and deploy multi-faceted intelligent solutions on the edge
- Process data at the edge through analytics and ML
- Package and optimize models for the edge using Amazon SageMaker
- Implement MLOps and DevOps for operating an edge-based solution
- Onboard and manage fleets of edge devices at scale
- Review edge-based workloads against industry best practices

Packt is searching for authors like you

If you're interested in becoming an author for Packt, please visit `authors.packtpub.com` and apply today. We have worked with thousands of developers and tech professionals, just like you, to help them share their insight with the global tech community. You can make a general application, apply for a specific hot topic that we are recruiting an author for, or submit your own idea.

Share Your Thoughts

Now you've finished *Building IoT Visualizations using Grafana*, we'd love to hear your thoughts! Scan the QR code below to go straight to the Amazon review page for this book and share your feedback or leave a review on the site that you purchased it from.

https://packt.link/r/1-803-23612-4

Your review is important to us and the tech community and will help us make sure we're delivering excellent quality content.

Printed in Great Britain
by Amazon

84585838R00208